Cases in
Management Accounting

We work with leading authors to develop the strongest educational materials
in accounting and finance, bringing cutting-edge thinking and best learning
practice to a global market.

Under a range of well-known imprints, including *Financial Times Prentice Hall*, we
craft high-quality print and electronic publications which help readers to
understand and apply their content, whether studying or at work.

To find out about the complete range of our publishing please visit us on the
World Wide Web at:

www.pearsoneduc.com

Cases in Management Accounting

Accounting

Current Practices in European Companies

EDITED BY
TOM GROOT AND KARI LUKKA

An imprint of **Pearson Education**

Harlow, England · London · New York · Reading, Massachusetts · San Francisco · Toronto · Don Mills, Ontario · Sydney
Tokyo · Singapore · Hong Kong · Seoul · Taipei · Cape Town · Madrid · Mexico City · Amsterdam · Munich · Paris · Milan

Pearson Education Limited
Edinburgh Gate
Harlow
Essex CM20 2JE
England

and Associated Companies throughout the world

Visit us on the World Wide Web at:
http://www.pearsoneduc.com

First published 2000

© Pearson Education Limited 2000

ISBN 0-273-64616-8   PPR

British Library Cataloguing-in-Publication Data

A catalogue record for this book can be obtained from the British Library.

Library of Congress Cataloguing-in-Publication Data

Cases in management accounting : practices in European companies / edited by Kari
Lukka and Tom Groot.
      p. cm.
   Includes bibliographical references and index.
   ISBN 0-273-64616-8
   1. Managerial accounting--Europe--Case studies. I. Lukka, Kari. II. Groot, Tom.

HF5657.4 .C373 2000
658.15′11--dc21   00-044273

Set in Melior 9.5 point
Typeset by 63
Printed and bound in Great Britain by Henry Ling Ltd.,
at the Dorset Press, Dorchester, Dorset

Contents

List of tables and figures

Tables

Figures

Preface

The majority of accounting textbooks provide material which mainly focus on management accounting practices in the United States and Japan. Though some material about individual European firms is available as well, most of it is only available on a national basis. The original idea behind this book is to make management accounting practices in European companies available to a wider international audience. The cases in this volume are detailed descriptions of existing companies, most of which are fully disclosed by their company names. The book as a whole gives the reader a feeling for the wide variety in corporate cultures, management accounting practices and institutional differences within the European region. The cases it includes are prepared in order to provide profound insights into the multitude of current European management accounting practices for teaching in universities, and other corresponding institutions.

For this purpose we approached major European accounting researchers, representing twelve European countries, who had proven their ability in doing case study research in management accounting. They were invited to prepare teaching cases, based on their recent or current research, for publication in a casebook. The response to our invitations was magnificent, as almost everybody we approached agreed to participate. As a consequence, we are proud to present this set of teaching cases, based on thorough analyses of management accounting practices in the European region.

This joint effort means that we have a lot of people and institutions to thank for the realization of this casebook. First of all, we thank our casebook project partners who spent a lot of time and effort analyzing management accounting practices and preparing teaching cases which fitted the format of this casebook. Secondly, we thank the companies and institutions that figure in the cases. The co-operation of their management, the access to their internal data, their willingness to discuss the case subjects, and their checks of early versions of the texts, make the cases of this volume represent the actual management accounting practices of European companies. Thirdly, we thank all the people who made the production and international publication of the book possible through their supporting activities, such as the casebook secretariat at the Vrije Universiteit (Amsterdam, The Netherlands) of which Peter Smidt deserves special mention for his enthusiastic support of this project. Finally, we thank the European Union for supporting the project through its Socrates European Modules program. This program supports the development of European teaching material that is used across the borders of member states.

In order to enhance the cases' accessibility and ease of use the cases will also be available on the Internet (please see www.booksites.net/groot_lukka). We hope and expect that this casebook will serve to satisfy part of the international need for real-world teaching case material in management accounting.

TOM GROOT, *Amsterdam, The Netherlands*
KARI LUKKA, *Turku, Finland*

Introduction

Tom Groot
Kari Lukka

Contemporary organizations are confronted with increasing demands from shareholders, customers, employees and the public at large. Markets are becoming increasingly competitive and technology changes at an increasing pace. These factors make the current business environment less stable and predictable. Management needs to develop new practices and systems to meet these high demands and higher risks. One important area is management accounting: this business function aims at providing information to assist managers in their planning and control activities. Management accounting activities include collecting, classifying, processing, reporting, analyzing and interpreting information. Management accounting systems provide information about past activities (*ex post* information) and assist in making projections into the future (*ex ante* information). The scope of management accounting therefore extends beyond the traditional transactions-based financial information provided by the bookkeeping system to include also non-financial and prospective information about current and future capacities and performance. Much of this extension has been introduced in the last ten years, leading to a different function of accounting information in many organizations and to a different position of the management accountant. Management accounting information is increasingly being used in combination with other information, such as measures of market position, customer satisfaction, internal efficiency and employee motivation. Consequently, management accountants seem to be more and more involved in other business areas like marketing, product development and human resource management. Traditional accounting methods alone do not seem to suffice any more; the management accountant's role is developing from providing periodic financial statements to securing the provision of relevant financial and non-financial information for decision making in a wide range of professional areas, such as marketing, finance, organization, product development, strategic planning and control.

These recent practical developments have implications for teaching and research in management accounting. The broader scope of management accounting information to assist management in making planning and control decisions, and the increased interrelations between accounting and other business areas make it necessary to study management accounting also in its relation with business problems and with other disciplines. Case studies either for research or teaching purposes are particularly well suited to analysing management accounting in its wider context. They provide the opportunity to gain an in-depth understanding of the interrelationships, dynamics and roles management accounting plays in real-life situations. This casebook contains 15 realistic case descriptions of companies in 12 European countries, with a view to using them as teaching cases (for an overview see Table 1). Each description aims at giving the reader a realistic and in-depth view of current management accounting practices in European companies. The names of all the companies with the exception of two (Case 4 and 5 in Table 1) are fully disclosed as well as much of their internal practices and information. We are grateful to these companies for permitting access, for their support, and for their permission to publish their experiences.

Many of the current developments in management accounting practice are not confined to a specific country or region, but belong to a global evolution (Granlund and Lukka, 1998). This makes it not very problematic for European teachers to use case material which is developed elsewhere. While developing the teaching cases for this volume, however, we came to the conclusion that cultural and institutional environments in European countries sometimes differ considerably. These differences gain in importance when the management accounting function becomes more and more interrelated with managerial and organizational issues. At the same time we expect these cases to add to the existing non-European cases. First, they provide European students a better opportunity to identify with the organizations and the problems described in this casebook. Second, the rich descriptions in these cases may also give non-European students more insight into the different institutional, organizational and managerial arrangements in European companies, and their (combined) influence on the management accounting function. And third, the cases as a whole cover a wide range of institutional, strategic and organizational situations, leading to a deeper understanding of the different roles management accounting plays under these circumstances.

Despite the many diversities among the cases, some similarities can also be found. Cultural and institutional aspects appear to be important in almost all cases. Cultural aspects relate, for instance, to the position of managers and the way conflicts are resolved. Institutional aspects are found in the relationship between companies and the government (some are recently privatized institutions) and in the educational background of managers and management accountants (a good example is German cost accounting). Despite the large variety in management accounting problems presented, all cases have one theme in common and that is *change*. In some cases change is imposed upon the organization, in other cases local management strives for change in order to proactively secure the company's future position. In these change processes, relatively new topics emerge, like management of intellectual capital, accounting for product design and development, and the changing role of management accountants in strategy development and implementation. While describing these dynamic processes, we came to the conclusion that only few accounting publications address the dynamics of

Table I Overview of cases by sector, country and author(s)

Title[a]	Author(s)	Country
Manufacturing activities:		
1. Cost control in product design and development: the **Volvo** Car Corporation experience	Urban Ask	Sweden
2. **Wisapaper**: the role of management accounting in managing customer relationships	Vesa Partanen Marko Järvenpää Tero-Seppo Tuomela	Finland
3. Introducing the commercial manager: management accounting support for the sales function of **Bass Brewers**, UK	Thomas Ahrens	United Kingdom
4. **Diamed problem**	Thomas M. Fischer	Germany
5. **Ondina**, S.A.	Salvador Carmona Luis Fernández	Spain
Service activities:		
1. ABC-ABM at **Hewlett-Packard** Europe for customer support	Isabelle Lacombe Pierre-Laurent Bescos	France
2. The **Royal Hotel**	Peter Clarke	Ireland
3. Intellectual capital at Den norske Bank Group (**DnB**): the customer account manager's support system (CASS)	Hanno Roberts	Norway
4. **KCI** Konecranes: developing non-financial measures in a global crane company	Kari Lukka Markus Granlund	Finland
Recently privatized companies:		
1. Management control in the **Credito Italiano** Bank during passage from a protected to a competitive market	Angelo Riccaboni Antonio Barretta	Italy
2. **CSC** Scandinavia: controlling and accounting for time	Per Nikolaj Bukh Poul Israelsen	Denmark
3. **PTT Post**	Tom Groot Peter Smidt	Netherlands
Governmental and non-profit organizations:		
1. ABC in Norwegian State Railway's passenger transport (**NSR**)	Trond Bjørnenak	Norway
2. **Scandlines** Ltd – Privatization and accounting stability in a political environment	Preben Melander Peter Skærbæk	Denmark
3. Scottish National Blood Transfusion Service: issues in the development of a costing system (**SNBTS**)	Falconer Mitchell Shao Huajing	Scotland

[a] The bold printed parts of the titles contain the abbreviated title used in the text and in the following case overviews.

organizational and accounting change. We will use part of this introduction to build a theoretical framework that may be helpful in analyzing change processes in general and also the teaching cases in this book. This introduction will be concluded by presenting the teaching cases of the book and giving some suggestions of how to use these cases in teaching programmes.

Models of organizational change

Organizational change can be studied from at least three different perspectives: population ecology, rational adaptation theory and random transformation theory (Hannan and Freeman, 1984). The first approach differs from the other two mainly in the level of analysis: *population ecology* views the dynamics of organizational change at the level of the population of organizations as a whole. The variability in organizational structures is caused by the creation of new organizations and organizational forms and the replacement of old ones. The remaining two theories analyse organizational change at the level of individual organizational entities. The *rational adaptation theory* claims that organizational change comes about through deliberately designed changes in strategy and structure in response to environmental changes, threats and opportunities. Several theoretical variants can be distinguished in this category, depending on the variables considered and the proposed relations among them. *Contingency theories*, for example, view organizational change as an attempt to match organizational properties and arrangements with internal and external circumstances (Fisher, 1995; Waterhouse and Tiessen, 1978). *Institutional theory* explains the change and stability of institutions by the way their formal organizational structure reflects internally the institutionalized rules of the wider state and society (Meyer and Rowan, 1977; Meyer *et al.*, 1978). The last category, the *random transformation theory*, relaxes the presupposition of deliberate change and views organizational change as only loosely coupled with the desires of organizational leaders and with the demands of the environment (Laughlin *et al.*, 1994). Theories of *organized anarchy* (Cooper *et al.*, 1981) and *garbage can models* of organizational decision making (Cohen *et al.*, 1972; Padgett, 1980) belong to this category.

Based on a review of a large number of publications across disciplines, Van de Ven and Poole (1995) introduce four basic types of process theories explaining how and why change unfolds in social or biological entities. These four types are based on two dimensions: the *unit of change* and the *mode of change*. The unit of change variable is equivalent to the level of analysis we used before and refers to single entity or multiple entities analyses. The mode of change depicts why and how changes unfold. Van de Ven and Poole only make a distinction between 'prescribed' and 'constructive' modes of change. This excludes the possibility to capture random transformation modes of change. We therefore expand the original model from four to six basic models of organizational change[1] (refer to Figure 1 for an overview).

The three multiple-entities settings belong to the population ecology category mentioned earlier. In a multiple-entities setting, change may unfold as a repetitive sequence of variation, selection and retention events among entities in a population

	Prescribed	Constructive	Random
Multiple Entities	**Evolution** Selection by competition	**Dialectic** Confrontation and conflict	**Chaotic** Disturbance and discontinuity
Single Entities	**Life cycle** Regulation by immanent program	**Teleology** Purposeful enactment	**Uncoupled** Development by chance

Unit of Change

Figure I   Six basic models of organizational development and change
Source: Based on Van de Ven and Poole (1995)

competing for scarce resources. This process contains a prescribed mode of change and is labelled 'evolution.' When the process of change is guided by purposeful action of multiple entities, the resulting model of change can be described as 'dialectic': conflicts emerge between entities holding opposing thesis and antithesis that collide to produce a synthesis, which itself becomes the thesis for the next stage of dialectical development. Our third category is dominated by sudden positive and negative disturbances and discontinuities, which present themselves randomly to the entities. Chaos theory models help to interpret and predict the dynamics and results of organizational change.

When the analysis is restricted to single entities, three basic models are identified. The 'life cycle' model represents change as a process consisting of a necessary sequence of development stages. This sequence may be built into the system by natural, institutional or logical programmes. Products on the market-place, for instance, mostly undergo a natural sequence of start-up, grow, harvest and termination stages. Content and sequence of stages may be decided upon by decision makers within the entity, which leads to the 'teleological development model'. In this model, development and change are guided by purposeful social action, leading to a cycle of goal formulation, implementation, evaluation and modification. The rational adaptation theories belong to the teleological category. In this category most organizational turnaround processes take place. When organizational change is not guided by prescribed or constructive modes of change, the dynamics of organizational development are not fuelled by a specific 'motor' of change, but are a product of 'spontaneous', independent flows of participants, problems, solutions and decision opportunities (Cohen *et al.*, 1972; March and Olsen, 1982). The independence of these flows leads to an 'uncoupled' development of the organizational entity. This category relates to the random transformation theories.

In practice, development and change processes are more complicated than these six basic models because each development may simultaneously be influenced by more than one model. Change processes extend over space and time, providing internal and external participants to the firm the opportunity to exert their influence in different time periods and in different parts of the organization. Each influence may originate from different levels and apply different modes of change (Van de Ven and Poole, 1995). This may lead to hybrid change processes taking place on several organizational levels, applying multiple modes of change and developing along different time dimensions.

Referring to the framework of Figure 1, the teaching cases in this book are single entity descriptions of organizational change processes. Most of the cases in this volume describe change processes on several levels within and outside the organizational boundaries. All cases relate to more than one model of organizational change. In most cases the organization has partially prevented a future situation (according to the *life cycle* of products, services or markets) to which it purposefully enacts by a well-developed change programme (a *teleologic* action). In most cases however, sudden unexpected developments in the market, in competitors' reactions or in employees' behaviours lead to disturbances in the change process (*uncoupling* of change elements). Each case contains elements of each of these three models. Looking at the change processes in more detail may convey more about how these models interact and lead to change outcomes.

Processes of change

As depicted by the taxonomy of basic change models, development and change can take place in different ways and in different forms. In order to provide a meaningful description of change, it seems necessary to provide a full description of the change processes as they have developed. This leads to a process view of change and development, consisting of three main stages: drivers of change, change processes and outcomes of change.

Drivers of change are actions, developments, actors and (changes in) circumstances that cause, provoke or facilitate change processes to take place. According to Innes and Mitchell (1990), drivers of change can be distinguished into three categories: facilitators, motivators and catalysts. *Facilitators* comprise a set of factors conducive to change: they are necessary but in themselves not sufficient for change to occur. *Motivators* are factors that influence change processes in a general manner: they provide decision makers the reasons and grounds to initiate and permit change. *Catalysts* contain factors directly related to the timing of change: they are occurrences which lead directly to the initiation of change. They provide the opportunity for change to take place. Facilitators, motivators and catalysts need not be related to each other as they occur. However, change drivers become related to each other by the role each of these drivers plays in the change process, as is depicted in Figure 2.

The resulting *change actions* generally take two consecutive pathways, which we will label *business reorientation* and *business systems development*. Change actions which take place in business reorientation involve shifts in the

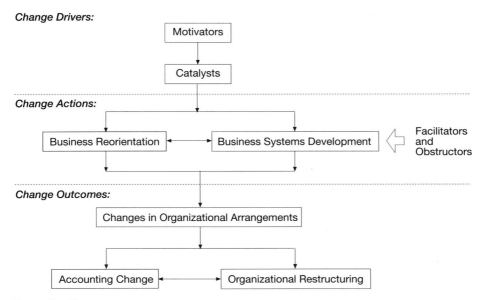

Change Drivers:

Change Actions:

Facilitators and Obstructors

Change Outcomes:

Figure 2 Change process

organizational value systems, often also known as 'interpretive schemes' (Broadbent, 1992). These change processes are also called 'second-order change', since they may have lasting effects on the future nature and functioning of the organization (Laughlin *et al.*, 1994). Change actions regarding business systems relate to directly observable alterations and innovations in organizational structure and processes. Examples include the implementation of new accounting principles, new information system designs and organizational restructuring. They lead to changes in organizational arrangements, which are also referred to as 'first-order changes'. In our view, first-order changes may or may not take place based on changes in business orientations.[2] The process by which motivators and catalysts lead to business reorientation, business systems development and changes in organizational arrangements is influenced by facilitators and obstructors. *Facilitators* comprise a set of conditions conducive to change which are in themselves necessary but not sufficient for the change to occur (Innes and Mitchell, 1990). Examples of facilitators are support from top management and the availability of adequate information systems. *Obstructors* work in a sense contrary to facilitators: they contain a set of conditions blocking, hindering or delaying change processes. Examples are complex decision processes and forces of structural inertia[3] (Hannan and Freeman, 1984).

We distinguish the eventual *change outcomes* into two broad categories: accounting changes and organizational restructuring changes. Accounting changes relate to innovations in and alterations of accounting principles, systems and processes. Organizational restructuring changes comprise alterations in organization structure, processes of decision making and production systems. In most cases, accounting change and organizational change are interrelated: they influence one another, strengthening and sometimes weakening the effectiveness of new organizational arrangements (see also Hopwood, 1988). Based on the change processes which became visible in the cases of this volume, we developed the sequences of change activities outlined in Figure 2.

In the following section an overview will be given from the cases included in this book. The conceptual framework given in Figure 2 is used to structure the following section and to analyze the dynamics of change in our cases.

Accounting for change in European companies

Successful organizations tend to be able to proactively change the circumstances under which they have to operate, and continuously adapt to changes in their environment. The accounting function plays multiple roles in change processes. On the one hand, the accounting function may provide timely information about threats and opportunities that should proactively be avoided or exploited (see also Atkinson *et al.*, 1997). Accounting information signals potential future problems and opportunities, and at the same time provides assistance in the consecutive decision-making processes. The accounting function plays an important role in *improving* the organization's capacities for adaptation and change. On the other hand however, the accounting function by its very nature also *inhibits* change. Accounting information for performance measurement and control, for instance, is meant to motivate predictable and reliable organizational behaviour. Stability and continuity in production processes and in accounting procedures enhances organizational control and eases accountability to internal and external parties. Frequent disruptions of measurement systems and frequent changes in control arrangements increase the probability of unreliable future organizational performance. In change processes, accounting plays the double role of facilitator and obstructor. It balances between two virtues, namely between *flexibility* and *stability*: between the capacity to adapt quickly to changing circumstances and the ability to reach high levels of reliability and predictability.

The cases in this casebook are developed with a special emphasis on the multiple roles the accounting function plays in enabling and inhibiting change processes. In the remainder of this section we will describe briefly the sample firms' change drivers, change actions and change outcomes.

Change drivers

The change processes we encountered appear to be driven by four categories of motivators. We have listed these categories according to the frequency in which they were mentioned in the teaching cases.

1. *Dynamics of (international) competition*
This factor clearly is most frequently reported in our cases. It relates to actions of competitors on the market-place and to general developments in market circumstances. The internationalization of markets (Volvo), new competitors entering existing markets (Diamed, Ondina, DnB, CSC), a shift in the power balance within supply chains (Bass Brewers, CSC), lower customer loyalty (Ondina), changing patterns of business line growth rates (KCI) and declining markets (Bass Brewers) motivate management to initiate change actions. In some cases (PTT Post, DnB) companies also contribute to the dynamics of competition by entering new markets and introducing new products.

2. *State regulation and deregulation*
Many companies experience some change in government policy. They range from the issuing of new (Bass Brewers) or tightened regulations (KCI) and the liberalization of markets (Credito Italiano) to independency (NSR, Scandlines) and privatization of governmental organizations (CSC, Credito Italiano and PTT Post). For all organizations involved, state legislation has led to higher dynamism in the corporate environment.

3. *Increase in customer demands*
Technological developments, shifts in customer values and changes in societal values may lead to higher customer demands, leading to higher product quality and the addition of new products and services. The motives for these improvements do not, as in the first motivator, stem from the necessity to cope with the actions of competitors, but from customers' new demands. Not responding to these indications may lead to the opening of possibilities for competitors to successfully enter the market. Advanced information technology leads to the demand for more and more integrated financial services (CSC) and intensified, on-line IT-support (Hewlett-Packard). Customers require better service (Wisapaper, Royal Hotel, PTT Post). Societal values stress the importance of safety, leading to extra service by manufacturing companies (KCI) and additional safety measures by non-profit organizations working in the health care sector (danger of aids and human BSE in SNBTS).

4. *Restrictions in the availability of scarce resources*
Changes in organizational arrangements are sometimes made in order to (re)gain access to resources which have become scarce. Mergers with larger companies give access to strategic know-how (CSC, Volvo), attractive subcontracting arrangements invite specialists to participate (Scandlines) and improvements in working conditions attract scarce human resources (CSC).

In most cases, momentum was needed to kick off a change process. Momentum was created by a *catalyst event*, which can be virtually anything. We found in our cases as catalyst for organizational change the breakdown of an alliance plan (Volvo), the use of a new larger plant with idle capacity (Ondina), a sudden drop in profits (CSC), sickness of a key decision maker (Royal Hotel), privatization (Credito

Italiano, PTT Post), a take-over (CSC), independency from direct State control (NSR), the arrival of new management (Scandlines) and sudden threats of disasters (SNBTS). Catalysts did not directly relate to the change motive in all cases.

Change actions

There is always management discretion regarding what actions are factually implemented, based on external and internal pressures and managerial preferences. One of the most important drivers of change is thus the adoption of a new strategy, often having fundamental accounting-related implications. Change drivers often lead to reconsideration of the existing business orientation. It appears that for change in organizational arrangements to take place, it is not a prerequisite that business orientations change as well. Sometimes, change drivers reinforce the existing business orientation and induce more rigorous change programmes. In most of our cases however, change drivers also led to changes in business orientation. We detected the following changes in business orientation as responses to each of the four change drivers.

Dynamics of (international) competition seemed to lead to the following new business orientations:
- *Redefining the company's competitive position.* Volvo shifted its strategy from 'car production' to 'transportation business'. Bass Brewers introduced commercial advice and coaching as a new service to customers. PTT Post expanded its operations from mail delivery to logistical services and inventory handling. CSC aimed at integrating different services to the customer. At KCI attempts were made to change the company's 'mind set' so that the maintenance business would be considered at least equally important as the selling of new machines.
- *Placing the customer at the centre.* Some organizations strive to be better informed about customers' preferences (Bass Brewers, DnB, CSC) and about customer target groups or market segments (Wisapaper, Hewlett-Packard). Some companies try to relate customer information to product development (Diamed, CSC), assortment decisions (Ondina) and service quality (Hewlett-Packard, Royal Hotel, Scandlines).
- *Drastic improvement of financial performance.* Dynamic competition leads to the need for 'deep pockets' (see also D'Aveni, 1994; 1995). This can be realized by increasing efficiency drastically (Volvo, PTT Post), by reduction of overhead (Credito Italiano) and quick cost reductions (Bass Brewers).
- *Change to a more proactive management style.* Management accounting information will also be used to predict new opportunities and prepare the organization to face new challenges (Wisapaper, Credito Italiano, Volvo).

State regulation and deregulation changed companies' business orientations in several ways:
- *Development of new products and new markets.* Measures of market liberalization

induces companies to introduce new products and enter new markets (Credito Italiano, PTT Post, Scandlines).

- *Reduction or elimination of activities.* State regulation forbids (exclusive) selling of certain products (Scandlines, PTT Post, NSR) or the use of certain sales organizations (Bass Brewers).
- *Adoption of business-like management practices.* Almost all former state agencies which have become independent favour the use of more business-like management practices, like decentralization into responsible and accountable business units (Scandlines, PTT Post, Credito Italiano, CSC), the use of ABC-systems (SNBTS), market-oriented performance measurement systems (DnB, Credito Italiano) and financial reward systems (Credito Italiano, CSC).

Increase in customer demands motivated organizations to adapt the following 'high-quality/functionality' and 'low-cost' business orientations:

- *A more customer-oriented strategy.* This is seen as a successful way of expanding the market (Wisapaper, CSC, KCI).
- *Improve quality of product and service.* This strategy is meant to attract more customers (Wisapaper, Royal Hotel, KCI) and to prevent customers' claims (SNBTS, KCI).
- *Increasing efficiency of operations* by focusing on profitable sections and products (NSR), by redesigning operations (PTT Post, Hewlett-Packard) and by assessing/rewarding efficiency gains (CSC, Credito Italiano).
- *Reducing costs* by budget reductions (SNBTS, Bass Brewers) and benchmarking financial performance (Hewlett-Packard, Diamed).

Restrictions on the availability of scarce resources lead to actions like:

- *Enlarging the investment base.* This is done by merger (Wisapaper) or acquisition (CSC) or by considerable reductions in expenditures (Bass Brewers).
- *Engaging in co-operative agreements with other companies.* Examples are increased co-operation with retailers (Bass Brewers), joint product development activities (Volvo) and alliances with similar organizations (CSC).
- *Dissolution of co-operative arrangements.* A joint sales organization was liquidated because the contract partners wanted to become better informed about and more responsive to customers' demands through wholly owned, dedicated sales forces (Wisapaper).

The above mentioned changes in business orientation are 'second-order changes': changes in value systems and strategy. In order to make these changes work, organizations need to operate differently ('first-order changes'). In most cases, new business systems have been introduced to facilitate organizational change.

In developing new business systems, organizations appear to follow two approaches (see also Mintzberg *et al.*, 1976). The first approach is *search*: companies seem to look for 'ready-made' standard solutions. Most organizations respond to a new business orientation by looking for systems and methods that may be conducive in developing and implementing the new challenge. Here we encounter well-known instruments like activity-based costing (HP, SNBTS, Wisapaper, Ondina), non-financial measurement system (KCI), balanced scorecard (NSR), the EFQM-model for quality improvement (PTT Post), transfer pricing (CSC) and target costing (Diamed, Volvo).

In some instances, no standard solution can be found and 'tailor-made' solutions need to be developed. Organizations then use the second approach of *design* by engaging in creative activities developing novel instruments. Notable examples are the 'project gate system' for controlling developing activities (Volvo), a novel system of internal business reporting (Bass Brewers), a newly designed sales support system (DnB), and special reward systems (Credito Italiano, CSC).

In most cases however, new business systems are a result of a combination of search and design activities. Most organizations scan their environment for instruments 'suitable' to the new business orientation. When these instruments are found useful they still need considerable design activities to accommodate the standard solutions to the specific demands of the particular environment in which they will be applied.

The ease of running the change actions is dependent on how the potential facilitators and obstructors work in the situation at hand. The cases of the book give a number of examples of these factors, which intervene in the process. Examples of obstructors becoming visible in the cases of the book are the following:

1. Factors obstructing the conveyance of change necessity.
   - Poor data, preventing participants from gaining a good understanding of the necessity of change (Volvo).
   - Slack resources, diminishing the need for change (Ondina).
2. Factors obstructing participants' motivation to co-operate.
   - Resistance to change by individuals or groups (Volvo, Ondina).
   - Inadequate human resources to carry out change process (Volvo).
   - Limited communication with parties concerned in the change process or opportunity to participate (DnB, KCI, Scandlines).
3. Factors obstructing change outcomes from becoming an enduring part of future business practice.
   - Change is not supported by appropriate standard planning, performance evaluation or reward systems (KCI, DnB, Credito Italiano).
   - Lack of training in new business processes when change process is completed (DnB).
   - Key participants do not perceive change outcomes as being helpful in managing the business (KCI, Credito Italiano).

All factors lead to a decrease in participants' propensity to co-operate in the change process. Each factor however relates to a different set of reasons: the first factor relates to perceptions of the need to *initiate* change (a 'sense of urgency'); the second is the incapacity to motivate participants *during* the change process to give preference to (some) change activities, and the last factor includes *expectancies* participants hold of the new permanent situation to which the current change process would lead.

The so-called facilitators are basically situations, decisions and actions increasing the ability and motivation of participants to contribute to the change process. The facilitators identified by the teaching cases can be placed in similar categories to the obstructors, but stated with opposite meaning. Examples of facilitators in the change processes include:

1. Perceptions of the need to change.
   - Data availability to convince participants of the change's added value (Wisapaper).
   - Clear malfunctioning of old systems (PTT Post).
2. Motivation to participate.
   - Senior executives protagonizing the change process (Wisapaper, Hewlett-Packard, KCI).
   - Availability of sufficient resources for the change project (Hewlett-Packard).
   - Information technology's capacity to support the change process (Bass Brewers, Diamed, CSC).
3. Expectancies of the new situation.
   - Enhanced flexibility to adapt to different, local needs (Hewlett-Packard).
   - Increased capabilities to face competition and satisfy customers' demands (Credito Italiano, Wisapaper).

Change outcomes

The change processes described in the 15 teaching cases culminate in two, mostly interrelated, classes of innovations which we have labelled 'accounting change' and 'organizational restructuring'. Accounting changes relate to changes in accounting information systems or in the use of accounting information. Organizational restructuring includes changes in organizational structure, in decision-making processes or in the allocation of managerial responsibilities. In most cases, both are used in combination, they work together. In all cases, accounting changes are accompanied by the adaptation of organizational structures and a reallocation of responsibilities. The reverse appears not to be true: in one case (Ondina) a redesign of production processes has taken place without any change in accounting practices.

Most of the cases do not provide information about the extent to which the change outcome has actually improved company performance. In some cases, financial information is given about company performance after the change process while in other cases *ex post* reflections of company management on the change outcome are provided. We find that it is difficult to assess the value of change outcomes for the company, because in many cases it turns out to be too early to evaluate the effects on company performance, and in most cases the value of change outcomes appear to be multidimensional. Most cases are more explicit about

Table 2 Overview of cases by themes, business problems and use in classroom

Case	Title (abbreviated)	Themes	Business problems	Organization	Case type
Part 1: Decision making					
1	Hewlett-Packard Europe	ABC ABM	ABC in international organization	Service sector	Calculation & Discussion
2	Norwegian State Railway (NSR)	ABC for product costing Cost allocation	Product costing for state funding of loss-making products	State-owned service organization	Discussion
3	Scottish National Blood Transfusion Services (SNBTS)	ABC system design Joint costs	Design of ABC system Behavioural and pragmatic aspects	Non-profit organization	Discussion
4	Diamed	Target costing Value engineering	Microeconomic analysis of demand and cost functions in product development	Manufacturing	Calculation & Discussion
5	Royal Hotel	Decision making Benchmarking Critical success factors	Accounting for decision making and strategic planning	Service sector	Calculation & Discussion
Part 2: Customer orientation					
6	Volvo	Accounting in product development Barriers to change	The co-operation of product development and management accounting	Manufacturing	Discussion
7	Wisapaper	ABC design Accounting and customer orientation	Accounting in support of customer-oriented management	Manufacturing	Design & Discussion
8	Bass Brewers	Organization of management accounting function The roles of management accountants	How to organize the co-operation of sales and management accounting	Manufacturing	Discussion

'success' of the change processes in terms of the degree to which change programmes are successfully (in the meaning of 'as intended') executed.

Successful implementation of change processes appears to be dependent on the
degree to which management is able to convince parties involved of the necessity
of change, on the level of motivation of participants to devote enough time and
effort to the change processes while it evolves and on the grade of assurance that
can be given to participants that the after-change permanent situation will be
significantly better than the current situation.

The contents of this book

The book is structured along the main topics addressed in the cases (see Table 2).
Some of the cases are of a technical nature, explaining the design and use of management accounting techniques for supporting managerial decision making. They
are concentrated in Part 1, Decision making.

In practice, management accounting is entering other areas like marketing and
product development. The combination of management accounting and other
disciplines is explained by the necessity to provide customers with well-designed,
functional, high-quality, and yet low-cost products. This can only be done with a
concerted effort, in which accountants, product designers, production people and
marketing professionals work together. The cases in Part 2, Customer orientation,
provide examples of the way in which accounting and other professionals co-
operate in a concerted effort to enhance customer value.

Part 3, Performance management, focuses on the consequences for performance
measurement and reward systems for controlling strategic activities and key
results. In practice there is an increasing awareness that accounting and financial
numbers alone do not suffice. Implementing and controlling strategy implies measuring and rewarding not only financial but also non-financial performance. Several
instruments have been suggested in the literature, like the balanced scorecard, the
performance pyramid and the EFQM model. In Part 3, real-life examples will be
presented of the use of complex measurement and reward systems by European
companies, in which each company is looking for a well-balanced set of performance measures.

In the final Part 4, Accounting and organizational change, we focus specifically
on the role accounting plays in the development of organizations. Sometimes
accounting plays a role fostering change, sometimes accounting hinders effective
organizational change. In this part, examples of both roles are included. These
cases try to follow the development of organizations for a longer period of time and
try to illustrate the interrelationships between accounting, organization, strategy
and control in the development and growth of these organizations.

The division into four parts is only a very crude way of classifying the cases.
Most cases discuss more topics than the one that relates to the book part in which
they are located. Table 2 provides a more comprehensive overview, indicating to

readers and teachers what the content of each case is. This may facilitate in select-ing the most interesting cases for teaching purposes.

Concluding remarks

We think this book provides some novel approaches to teaching cases in several ways. The cases of this volume are developed in culturally diverse business situ-ations in Europe. This gives each case a specific cultural flavour, which makes them particularly suitable for international business courses. Each of the cases por-trays management accounting in a broader organizational context, providing the reader the opportunity to discover the interrelationship between accounting and other business functions and specializations. Each case contains, furthermore, a description of organizational change, emphasizing the potential of management accounting and control systems to bring about and also to hinder organizational change. Quite a few cases describe, for instance, privatization processes of former state-owned companies. These cases can rarely be found in the US, because large privatization processes do not play such a dominant role in the US as they do in some European countries. And finally, this casebook discusses the design and use of novel management accounting and management control methods, like ABC/ABM, the balanced scorecard, target costing, non-financial performance measures and quality management systems. The teaching cases developed for the book permitted us to demonstrate practical design issues as well as the inter-relationships between these management accounting and control instruments and other business functions in European companies.

   We hope that the European focus in the teaching cases, the novel topics and the dynamic descriptions of organizational change make this book attractive for an international audience of students, academics and practitioners.

Acknowledgements

We gratefully acknowledge the financial support given by the European Commission's Directorat-General XXII (Education, Training and Youth) under the 'Complementary Measures' provision of the Socrates Programme.

Endnotes

1 Van de Ven and Poole appear to have difficulties locating garbage can theories of organiza-tional change: these models do not have any of the two basic dimensions' properties. Our approach tries to meet this difficulty by adding a third mode of change to the basic model.
2 Here we divert from Laughlin *et al.* (1994) who state that first-order change involves shifts in the managerial arrangements but in such a way that the interpretative schemes remain

undisturbed. In our view, this leads to an analytical scheme that excludes first-order changes purposefully driven by shifts in interpretative schemes. In the cases described, this sequence of changes appeared to occur frequently.

[3] Structural inertia relates to the resistance to change organizational structure, strategy and business processes. Structural inertia mostly has a negative connotation, but it also produces positive effects. Inertia strenghthens two important organizational competencies, namely *reliability of performance* (repeated production of goods and services of a given quality) and *accountability for decisions and actions* (documentation and reconstruction of organizational decisions, rules and actions) (Hannan and Freeman, 1984).

References

Atkinson, A., Balakrishnan, R., Booth, P., Cote, J., Groot, T., Malmi, T., Roberts, H., Uliana, E., and Wu, A. (1997). New directions in management accounting research. *Journal of Management Accounting Research*, **9**, 79–108.

Broadbent, J. (1992). Change in organizations: a case study of the use of accounting information in the NHS. *British Accounting Review*, **24**, 343–367.

Cohen, M.D., March, J.G., and Olsen, J.P. (1972). A garbage can model of organizational choice. *Administrative Science Quarterly*, **17**, 1–25.

Cooper, D.J., Hayes, D., and Wolf, F. (1981). Accounting in organized anarchies: understanding and designing accounting systems in ambiguous situations. *Accounting, Organizations and Society*, **6**(3), 175–191.

D'Aveni, R.A. (1994). *Hypercompetition, Managing the Dynamics of Strategic Maneuvering*. New York: The Free Press.

D'Aveni, R.A. (1995). *Hypercompetitive Rivalries, Competing in Highly Dynamic Environments*. New York: The Free Press.

Fisher, J. (1995). Contingency-based research on managment control systems: categorization by level of complexity. *Journal of Accounting Literature*, **14**, 24–53.

Granlund, M., and Lukka, K. (1998). It's a small world of management accounting practices. *Journal of Management Accounting Research*, **10**, 153–179.

Hannan, M.T., and Freeman, J. (1984). Structural inertia and organizational change. *American Sociological Review*, **49**, 149–164.

Hopwood, A.G. (1988). Accounting and organisation change. *Accounting, Auditing and Accountability Journal*, **3**(1), 7–17.

Innes, J., and Mitchell, F. (1990). The process of change in management accounting: some field study evidence. *Management Accounting Research*, **1**(1), 3–19.

Laughlin, R., Broadbent, J., Shearn, D., and Willig-Atherton, H. (1994). Absorbing LMS: the coping mechanism of a small group. *Accounting, Auditing and Accountability Journal*, **7**(1), 59–85.

March, J.G., and Olsen, J.P. (1982). *Ambiguity and Choice in Organizations*. Bergen, Norway: Universitetsforlaget.

Meyer, J.W., and Rowan, B. (1977). Institutional organizations: formal structure as myth and ceremony. *American Journal of Sociology*, **83**(2), 340–363.

Meyer, J.W., Scott, W.R., Cole, S., and Intili, J.K. (1978). Instructional dissensus and institutional consensus in Schools. In M. W. M. *et al.* (eds), *Environments and Organizations*. San Francisco: Jossy-Bass, pp. 233–263.

Mintzberg, H., Raisinghani, D., and Theoret, A. (1976). The structure of 'unstructured' decision processes. *Administrative Science Quarterly*, **21**, 246–275.

Padgett, J.F. (1980). Managing garbage can hierarchies. *Administrative Science Quarterly*, **25**, 583–604.

Ven, A.H.v.d., and Poole, M.S. (1995). Explaining development and change in organizations. *Academy of Management Review*, **20**(3), 510–540.

Waterhouse, J.H., and Tiessen, P. (1978). A contingency framework for management accounting systems research. *Accounting, Organizations and Society*, **3**(1), 65–76.

—

ABC-ABM at Hewlett-Packard Europe for customer support

Isabelle Lacombe
Pierre-Laurent Bescos

Introduction

Hewlett-Packard (HP) is an American group created in 1939 in Palo Alto (California) by two engineers, Bill Hewlett and Dave Packard.[1] Its first product was an audio-oscillator. HP worked in the Test and Measurement sector. During the Second World War, HP expanded greatly because it supplied the army. In 1942, it employed sixty people and bought its first building. In 1943, its turnover was one million dollars with one hundred employees.

During the 1950s, HP grew fast. Manufacturers needed test and measurement instruments to develop electronic circuits and HP launched several products such as a high-speed frequency counter and a functions generator. In 1958, Hewlett-Packard took over Moseley, the specialist in electronic recorders. Then it launched the first oscilloscope that worked using sampling. By the end of the 1950s, Hewlett-Packard was quoted on the New York Stock Exchange.

During the 1960s, HP diversified its activities all over the world. In 1961, Hewlett-Packard bought Sanborn, thus entering the medical instrumentation market. In 1965, Hewlett-Packard bought F&M Scientific, a chemical analysis specialist. Technology changed from analogue to digital calculators, and counters with needles incorporated in the measurement products were replaced by electroluminescent diodes. Counters were perfected and needed the integration of calculators, so in 1966 and 1968 Hewlett-Packard changed its business.

In the 1970s, HP launched pocket calculators.

During the 1980s, HP went into the computing sector. In 1988 Hewlett-Packard offered a complete range of products from workstations to netservers. HP sold printers and scanners too. And finally in the 1990s, HP went into the communications market.

Organization and activities

Now, Hewlett-Packard is organized by product into several Business Units. Figure 1.1 shows the current product groups.[2]

Imaging and printing systems: 44%

Computing systems: 43%

I.T. services: 13%

Figure 1.1 Product groupings as a percentage of FY99 net revenue

Worldwide Hewlett-Packard had 85,400 employees in 1999, with revenues of 45.5 billion Euros, and 3.3 billion Euros net profit (see Figure 1.2). The Company Headquarters are in Palo Alto (California). It is the leading firm in the test and measurement market and the second largest American computer maker (and the third largest in the world).

• Net sales	€ 45.5 billion
• Net profits	€ 3.3 billion
• Headquarters	Palo Alto
• Company	1939
• Fortune 500	#13
• Fortune Global	#41
• Employees	85,400

Figure 1.2 HP company overview FY99

The French subsidiary has existed for more than 30 years and in 1999 had net revenues of 5,213 billion Euros with net profit of 153,36 million Euros. It employs 5,310 people and is the forty-sixth largest manufacturing company in France. Just before 1970, the Eybens plant (near Grenoble) was created. There are manufacturing activities for personal computers, for which HP France has a Worldwide manufacturing capacity, and networks and telecommunication production.

In 1985, the Isle d'Abeau plant south of Lyon was opened. It produces the Vectra computer for all of Europe, and a very powerful RISC computer called Emerald. The European centre for tele-teaching and videoconferencing is in Lyon. Hewlett-Packard France was the leading French exporter of microcomputers and the third largest exporter of computer products in 1999.

The traditional cost accounting system

In Hewlett-Packard, the traditional reporting system has been appreciated and accepted by all managers and controllers in all countries. Its main advantage is that the worldwide results are available by the fifth working day of the following month. It uses a software application built by Hewlett-Packard. The application is the same everywhere in the world and it uses the same structure.

Each country has to follow the rules established by the headquarters and central financial services. Each country, however, can decide the list of cost centres because each country has a different size, organization, market and customers.

Costs are recorded using a codification as shown in Figure 1.3. The codification contains details about each operation or bill recorded:

- country code;
- area: region of a country;
- department: e.g. marketing, sales, production, etc.;
- workforce: group of people working on repair types (e.g. software problems, hardware breakdowns, etc.);
- product line: group of products repaired (e.g. printers, PC, netservers, etc.);
- account: type of cost (e.g. salaries, occupancy, etc.).

Figure 1.3 Accounting codification at Hewlett-Packard

The traditional accounting system gave information on costs per department. Each manager knew what his costs were, and had details of costs by type. For example, costs for salaries, occupancy, information technology, and external costs for each department.

Although all countries had to follow the structure and rules of the worldwide cost accounting system, they were still able to create other systems to obtain different information.

Developing a new ABC system

The declared strategy of Hewlett-Packard is to continuously innovate. For example, more than half of net revenues are derived from products launched less than 2 years ago. The Research and Development budget represented about 10% of net revenues at the beginning of the 1990s. HP needs to be profitable to finance these investments.

Because the computer sector is very competitive, Hewlett-Packard must also reduce its costs to keep its margins up. In the past, competition was based on technological innovation, the quality of the products and the efficiency of the resellers. Now, it is important to control and reduce costs and for this purpose to improve the traditional cost accounting system. The new management accounting system would provide information to help in the conceptualization of new products (target costing), to produce at low costs and to make decisions about localization of factories.

The strategy of Hewlett-Packard was to advise all subsidiaries and business units to adopt activity-based costing (ABC) systems. All business units were able to choose the rules and to define their own ABC model. The result was that a lot of business units launched their own ABC projects.

Several ABC models were implemented before launching the project in France. Hewlett-Packard started to use ABC in 1984 at the Roseville Network Division (RND) in the United States.

In France, HP started with ABC at the Grenoble factory in 1987 following the example of the RND project. The ABC project in Grenoble was the first project for the manufacturing activities of Hewlett-Packard in France. After the project, the financial controller of Grenoble took a new job in Evry (France). He became the controller for the sales of products and service activities (mainly WCSO – Worldwide Customer Support Organisation – including after-sales services). Because he was satisfied with the results of the ABC project at Grenoble, he decided to launch a new ABC project for the service activities. So in 1993, Hewlett-Packard France adopted ABC for the service activities of computer maintenance.

Figure 1.4 shows the dates of the different main ABC projects that existed before the computer maintenance project. All projects shown in Figure 1.4 had an impact on the ABC project of 1993. Computer maintenance benefited from experiences gained with all previous projects.

Hewlett-Packard hasn't really created a methodology concerning ABC. Controllers involved in these projects have learned mainly from informal contacts with project managers of previous ABC systems. This is due to the culture of Hewlett-Packard: project managers usually communicate on the results, on difficulties encountered and on tools used on previous projects. Controllers have also exchanged documents on ABC projects.

The Worldwide Customer Support Organisation (WCSO) and its ABC project

WCSO is one of Hewlett-Packard's business units. WCSO delivers several services:

- system maintenance;
- preparation of sites, cabling, networks maintenance and supervision;
- hardware and software maintenance;
- study and installation of test platforms;
- facilities management for customers' information systems.

In France, WCSO employs about 1,000 people.

Dates of the ABC projects	Industrial area	Services
1984	Rosevile Network Division (USA)	
1985		
1986		
1987	Grenoble factory: project 'cost driver' applied to all businesses and integrated with the management information system	
1988		
1989		
1990		
1991		
1992	Grenoble factory: the 'cost driver' project is deconnected from the management information system	
1993		Maintenance (HardWare + SoftWare) – France
1994	Grenoble factory: several new independent ABC projects deconnected from the management information system	Hardware Maintenance – Europe (France, Germany, UK and Italy)
1995		Hardware Maintenance – Worldwide (Europe + Australia, Japan and USA)
1996		Software Maintenance – USA (pilot at the Mayfield site)
1997		Software Maintenance – Europe (pilot in France + Extension to other countries)

Figure 1.4 Main ABC projects at Hewlett-Packard between 1984 and 1997

Computer maintenance is the most important function of WCSO by net revenues and represents about 80% of WCSO's employees. The role of this organization is to repair computers, netservers, printers or other products (hardware maintenance) or to solve software problems (software maintenance). Repairs can be done within the scope of warranty, or maintenance contracts. These activities are also used by HP people for their own needs (internal support).

The Customer Support Organisation is a profit centre. It uses three different schedules to analyze costs and results:

- a cost schedule;
- a profit schedule;
- a statistical schedule.

The traditional accounting system was not adapted to calculate the costs of delivering a service to customers. Departments didn't know how they contributed to deliver a service to customers. They just knew generally on which product line they worked, but not on which activity. The traditional accounting system was adapted to a hierarchical form based on departments. It allowed managers to manage their budgets.

Table 1.1   Evolution of the ABC project for computer maintenance

	French model (from November '93 to beginning of '95)	European model (from the beginning of '94 to end '96)	Worldwide model (from mid-'96 to now)
Scope for the analysis	All costs for the hardware (HW) and software (SW) maintenance (including sales and administrative costs)	Only core activities (= delivery) of the HW maintenance (excluding sales and administrative costs)	Same scope as the European project
Countries included	France	France, Germany, UK, Italy = the four most important countries for Hewlett-Packard in Europe	The four European countries + USA, Japan and Australia, then Switzerland in 97, and Nordic countries in 98
Number of activities in the model	45	17	25 + more activities per country
Dimensions studied in the model	▪ 45 activities ▪ 2 segments of products (desktop and systems)	▪ 17 activities ▪ 6 processes ▪ 2 segments of products (desktop and systems) ▪ 2 segments of work forces (low qualifications and high qualifications)	▪ 25 activities ▪ 7 processes ▪ 17 product lines ▪ 2 segments of work-forces (low qualifications and high qualifications) ▪ 3 types of contracts
Main uses of the results	▪ Analysis of the cost per activity in order to reorganize or subcontract them ▪ Pricing	▪ Benchmarks between countries	▪ No analysis per activity. Activities are just used to allocate costs on processes and on product lines. Analysis per activity are done by each country for the local management ▪ Calculation of costs per product line and per types of contract
Software tool used	Multidimensional spreadsheet (= IMPROV)	Spreadsheet (Lotus 123) + database manager (TM1)	Specialized software tool (Hyper ABC)
Frequency for the results calculations	Quarter	Quarter	Quarter in 1996, then month since 1997

Table 1.1 Continued

	French model (from November '93 to beginning of '95)	European model (from the beginning of '94 to end '96)	Worldwide model (from mid-'96 to now)
Composition of the project team	• Financial controller of the customer support division • a trainee • an external person (consultant role) • an employee from the administrative service	• 1 manager from European financial departments for computer maintenance • 1 co-ordinator at the European level (consolidation of the results and training of the controllers and operational people in the countries) • 2 contacts in each country (financial controller and an operational person)	• European team + • 1 co-ordinator at the Worldwide level (consolidation of the results and training) • 1 person to parameter the software tool • 2 contacts in each country (financial controller and an operational person)
Sponsor of the project	Manager of the customer support division in France	Manager of HW maintenance in Europe	Manager of worldwide HW maintenance

The objectives of the ABC project at WCSO

In 1993, managers at Hewlett-Packard considered that the context had changed significantly. Competition had increased and prices were greatly reduced. Complexity became more and more important: the number of services delivered and the number of products supported increased. Financial reporting by workforce and by department was still not adapted to understand the new business. Managers needed to understand the cost of delivering a service to a customer by type of repair and by product supported. So, the customer support division decided to launch an ABC project. The objectives were:

- to measure the efficiency of the activities;
- to find the link between departments and activities;
- to measure profit per repair (at client, contract or product level).

The different steps of the ABC project

Within computer maintenance, the ABC project changed considerably. In Table 1.1, all evolutions are described from the French model to the European and worldwide models.[3]

The project had three steps:

- *the project began in France (1993–1995)* for the entire customer support area (hardware and software maintenance);
- *then it was extended to Europe (1994–1996)* with France using the European model and giving up the French model created in 1993. Countries integrated in this model were France, Germany, Italy and UK. The project was limited to hardware maintenance and to delivery activities (excluding sales and administrative costs);
- *finally, the project became a worldwide project in 1996.* In this way, Europe was integrated into the worldwide model. At the beginning the project integrated France, Germany, Italy, UK, USA, Japan and Australia. Switzerland in 1997 and Nordic countries in 1998 were later integrated into the project.

The sponsors of the project

The project had a strong sponsorship in order to define the operational objectives of the implementation:

(a) At the beginning the sponsor was the manager for computer maintenance in France, based in Evry, the French headquarters. He was interested in the results. He had attended a two-day training seminar in a business school on ABC and thought it was a method well-suited to managing HP activities. When the financial controller spoke about ABC, the maintenance manager agreed to implement it.

(b) The European manager of hardware maintenance was the second sponsor. He was based at Geneva in Switzerland. The European financial controller heard about the French project during a European meeting for financial controllers. He was interested and decided to convince the maintenance manager. The manager had heard about ABC because before being an operational manager, he had worked in financial services at Hewlett-Packard. He decided to sponsor the ABC project for Europe, following the example of France.

(c) The worldwide manager of hardware maintenance was the third sponsor of the ABC project. He was based at Palo Alto in California. He had asked the American financial team to give answers concerning the profitability per product, per customer and per contract type. The American financial controller saw the results of the European project. He thought it was a method capable of adaptation to calculate the costs to determine the profitability per product, per customer and per contract type. He came to a European ABC meeting to see the results of the project. He found this project interesting and wanted to implement it for worldwide maintenance. Instead of creating a new model, he decided to use the existing European model and to extend it to the USA, Japan and Australia. He convinced the worldwide manager of hardware maintenance to implement ABC, and to provide money and objectives for the project.

The project team

The project had successively three different sponsorships (French level, then European level, and then worldwide level). The project teams changed at each level, but they kept some members from the beginning. The French trainee stayed in the project from the beginning to the end. The European team stayed when the USA arrived on the project. The team had two different types of people:

1. Permanent members working full time on the project. They had an internal consultant role. They were from the financial area and their role was to promote ABC at Hewlett-Packard, to train people on the concepts and on the project, to calculate and to consolidate the results, to choose software tools and to improve the model (with new activities for example).
2. Non-permanent members who didn't work full time on the project. They provided information and data and were interested in using the results. They were two people per country: the financial controller for the financial data and an operational manager for operational data. At the beginning of the project, only the financial controllers belonged to the ABC team, but after 3 months, team members asked the operational people to get involved because they had problems defining the process and knowing which operational data were available to feed the ABC model.

Presentation of the ABC model

Not all the steps of the ABC model will be presented (the French one, the European one and the Worldwide one). Only the worldwide one will be detailed because it was built following the example of the French and European versions. In fact, it was basically the same model that was developed and improved each time. The worldwide model is more detailed and it uses a specific software tool, called HyperABC. In Figure 1.5, the dimensions of measurement of the worldwide ABC model are presented. It integrates three types of dimensions concerning cost objects:

1. delivery processes to solve problems (on-site, sending a courier with the parts to the customer site, etc.);
2. product lines for the products repaired and supported (printers, PC, netservers, etc.);
3. types of contract (because customers can choose different levels of service depending on the importance of their problems – if the customer is under warranty or has a repair contract, if repairs are needed quickly or if the customer can wait, preferring to pay less).

Each cost of cost object can be broken down into activity costs. The activities are performed during the repair (e.g. call receipt, dispatching (people and parts), logistics, on-site HP CE repair, etc.).

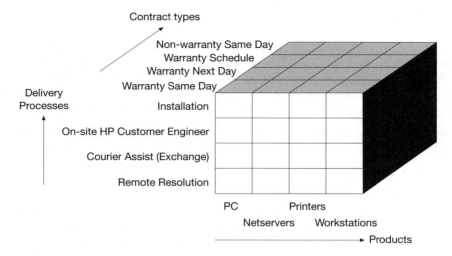

Figure 1.5 The ABC model for worldwide hardware maintenance (cost objects)

Tables 1.2 and 1.3 provide definitions of all activities and cost objects of the ABC model. Tables 1.4–1.11 show some examples of ABC results by cost centre, by delivery process and by product.

Process of calculating the results and ABC closure

At the beginning of the project, in April 1994, HP wondered if it would be more interesting to integrate or to not integrate ABC results into the cost accounting information system. HP decided not to integrate for several reasons:

- The traditional cost accounting information system is a worldwide one used by all business units. It is a complex system and is very difficult to change. Since this ABC project concerns only one business unit, it was considered unwise to change the whole system for just one business unit.
- With an integrated system, it is necessary to reorganize the codification of all operations in the cost accounting system. For example, it is necessary to add an activity code for all operations as shown below:

Accounting codification without ABC

Country
Code   Product
Line

XX XX XXXX XX XX XXXX

Area   Workforce   Account

Accounting codification with ABC integrated into the information system

Country Code	Department	Product Line	Activity
XX XX	XXXX	XX XX	XXXX XX
Area	Workforce	Account	

HP consider that integrating ABC would add too much complexity and that it would take too long to change the codification structure in a company of 112,000 people. Many operational managers and accounting people would have to be trained to this new codification system. It is very difficult to change the model because the cost accounting information system must be modified and it is very complex. It was the beginning of the ABC project and HP chose not to integrate ABC with the accounting information system, but HP considers it possible that one day this decision will change.

ABC results were calculated for each country using the same list of activities and cost objects (processes, product lines and contract types). Costs were calculated:

- in dollars in order to compare countries on the same basis;
- in local currency to allow countries to compare results with their local markets and to understand results using their own currency.

Each country has a more detailed list of activities specific to its situation, so the activity list had two levels:

- aggregated: the same list for all countries at the worldwide level;
- detailed: under each worldwide activity, countries show more details.

For example, it was interesting for German managers to have the activity *Call Receipt* detailed at three levels of detail. The German HW maintenance manager explained: 'in the beginning, the ABC model contained just the activity *Call Receipt*. It was not adapted to manage my business. I had no tool to understand if it was less expensive to subcontract the *Call Receipt*, to use HP employees, or to use a new software tool. So I asked to subdivide the activity *Call Receipt* into three subactivities. The Worldwide ABC manager disagreed because the ABC model would have got more complicated. But I told him that if he didn't want to do it, I would not use the results and I would not give data to calculate the results. So, he accepted and he created new activities for me!'.

The solution adopted by the worldwide ABC manager was to create specific activities only shown at the country level. In this example, all countries perform the activity *Call Receipt*, so in the aggregated list of activities, the activity *Call Receipt* exists for every country.

At the detailed level, Germany has three activities to show more detail of the activity *Call Receipt*:

1. *Call Receipt by Hewlett-Packard* using employees paid by HP and working at the HP office.

Table 1.2 Definition of activities[a]

Activities	Definition	Drivers
Call receipt	Call receipt for fix HW is defined as the reception, logging and validation of calls. The call receipt function stops calls that are not repair related (e.g. wrong number). It identifies needs for parts and needs for capacities. The cost pool includes the costs of the people that perform the call receipt activity as well as the cost of their direct management.	Number of hardware (HW) phone calls logged in call receipt.
Call qualification	Call qualification is defined as the identification of the problem behind the customer's call. The cost pool includes the costs of the people that perform the call qualification activity as well as the costs of their direct management.	Number of repairs qualified.
Dispatching (people and parts)	Dispatching is defined as the assignment of engineers to service customer equipment on-site as well as the assignment of parts. The cost pool includes the costs of people that perform dispatching as well as their direct management.	Number of dispatches.
Logistics (parts handling)	Logistics is defined as the set of the following subactivities: logistic people, material admin. specialist, inventory admin, parts co-ordinators, management (logistics, inventory systems, secretaries), and warehousing.	Number of repairs with parts moved.
Freight	Freight is defined as the freight costs, trading expenses, transport between HP sites.	Number of repairs with parts moved.
POP (customer assist (parts/unit sent))	The customer performs the repair with/without HP remote assistance. Replacement parts/units are dispatched to the customer. Examples: (1) customer replaces keyboards or mice using documentation sent with the parts; (2) Customer replaces LaserJet Fuser Assembly using instructions.	Number of customer assist repairs.
On-site HP CE	On-site HP Customer Engineer is defined as the activity of servicing the customer equipment through an HP engineer who does the service at the customer site. The cost pool includes the costs of customer engineers (CE) dedicated on customer sites and their direct management.	Number of hours for HP CE repair + travel.
On-site temps	Same function as above, but the work is performed by a temporary workforce.	Number of hours for Temps repair + travel.
On-site 3rd party CE	On-site 3rd party CE is defined as the activity of a non-HP engineer performing service on the customer's site.	Number of repairs where a 3rd party engineer went on-site.

Table 1.2 Continued

Activities	Definition	Drivers
Courier	A courier goes to the customer site to give new parts (and he can take the old ones). This activity is composed of: • transport of parts, • exchange of parts.	Number of repairs that go through courier.
CE Assist	The HP engineers that provide technical assistance to the on-site engineer while he is repairing the equipment at the customer site.	Number of repairs that require CE assist.
Escalation	It is the activity with increase in the level and type of resources required to address deviations and process breakdowns. It solves critical problems at client site and consists of the set-up of additional material and human means depending on the customer problem.	Number of repairs that require HW escalation.
Rops	Includes costs of repair order processing people (billing).	Total number of repairs in repair order processing.

[a] Note that HP chose to give the same or nearly the same names to some processes and some activities. It is the case when the activity is the main activity in the process, for example the activity 'On-site HP CE' in the process 'On-site HP CE'.

2. *Call Receipt subcontracted* because Germany subcontracted some calls. Costs are not the same for a subcontractor and for an HP employee with full equipment.

3. *Call Receipt using a new software tool.* Germany used a new software tool to record data about calls (name of the customer, problem type, needs, etc.) and to give an initial answer to the customer. Using this tool, HP employees were able to provide a lot of information in the first answer that they gave to the customer. This tool was like a database containing examples of common problems with possible solutions.

In order to manage several levels of detail in the same model, Hewlett-Packard bought the HyperABC software to automate data collection and calculation of the results. In Figure 1.6 we see the countries that have an HyperABC licence in order to calculate ABC results and to do 'what-if' analysis (simulations). In this process, the US unit centralizes information, does ABC reporting and extracts data from the Information Systems (operational databases and financial databases).

The United States unit takes information given directly by the various countries and which does not exist in the Information Systems, such as subcontractor costs, for example. This centralized way used to calculate the results allowed Hewlett-Packard to obtain results quickly and in the same way for all countries. Countries accepted centralization because they took advantage of it. The controller of the

Table 1.3 Definition of delivery processes (cost objects)[a]

Delivery processes	Definition
Remote resolution	Remote support provided by HP to the customer to resolve product performance problems without consuming replacement parts or further on-site work. Examples: correcting user errors, replacing consumables (toner cartridges), product adjustments/alignments, etc.
Courier assist (exchange)	The repair is done as a unit exchange, or the courier performs an easy repair.
POP (parts/unit sent)	The customer performs the repair with/without HP remote assistance. Replacement parts/units are dispatched to the customer. Examples: (1) Customer replaces keyboards or mice using documentation sent with the parts. (2) Customer replaces LaserJet Fuser Assembly using phone assistance.
On-site HP CE	An HP engineer performs the repair at the customer site.
On-site temps	A temporary workforce engineer performs the repair at the customer site.
On-site subcontract	A third party organization is dispatched to perform an on-site repair. Example: A PC power supply is dispatched to a third party repair organization. The third party repair organization performs the repair. HP provides the material.
Installation	HP installs material at customer site (mainly systems). Site preparations are included.

[a] Note that HP chose to give the same or nearly the same names to some processes and some activities. It is the case when the activity is the main activity in the process, for example the activity 'On-site HP CE' in the process 'On-site HP CE'.

Italian subsidiary said: 'The fact that the United States load the data for them is interesting, because we didn't need to dedicate somebody in Italy to do it. We save a lot of time we can spend analyzing the ABC results'. Moreover, countries kept some controls on the results. For example, countries let the United States calculate a first run of results and they were able to check the results, then they had possibilities to ask the United States to change the results after this calculation. In fact, if countries disagreed with the results calculated by the United States, they took the final decision and corrected them so that results were like countries wanted them to be. However, countries had to explain why they wanted corrections: they can ask for corrections if there were some bad allocations of costs. For example, if the costs of a cost centre do not have to be allocated to the activity *A* because the engineers worked on activity *B* during the last quarter (for a new job for example). The United States didn't have the data to see this need to modify the allocation because they were far from the operational people in the particular country. Countries considered it was a good solution for them that the United States calculated the results because they were not obliged to dedicate somebody to extract the data.

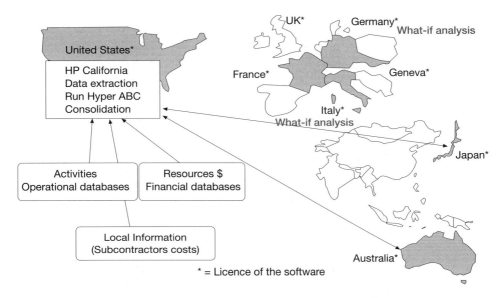

Figure 1.6 Calculation of the ABC results, extraction of data from existing systems[4]

Table 1.4 Calculation of the ABC results[a] for Q3 1998: cost per activity in € thousands

Activity	France	Germany	Italy	UK	Total
Call receipt		2,250	900	1,500	
Call qualification		3,000	800	2,000	
Dispatching (people and parts)		1,000	950	975	
Logistics (parts handling)		4,950	2,600	3,900	
Freight		3,150	1,200	3,000	
POP (Customer Assist (Parts/Unit sent))		1,350	800	2,100	
On-site HP CE		17,100	5,600	9,000	
On-site Temps		900	600	600	
On-site 3rd party CE		900	600	1,050	
Courier		1,350	500	300	
CE Assist		2,475	1,000	1,200	
Escalation		2,475	1,100	1,500	
Rops		4,050	1,800	2,100	
Total	30,500	44,950	18,450	29,225	123,125

[a] In this case, in order to respect the confidentiality, all data are fictional. But the structure of the model is real and conforms to the ABC project of Hewlett-Packard Europe for Customer Support.

Table 1.5 Allocation of cost centre costs to activities for France for Q3 1998

Activity	Call centre	Qualification centre	Engineers	Courier costs (transportation)	Administration	Logistics (warehousing)	Logistics (transportation)	Subcontracting costs
Call receipt	100%							15%
Call qualification		60%						15%
Dispatching (people and parts)		40%						15%
Logistics (parts handling)						100%		
Freight							100%	
POP (Customer Assist (Part/Unit sent))			10%					
On-site HP CE			65%					
On-site Temps			5%					
On-site 3rd party CE								55%
Courier				100%				
CE Assist			10%					
Escalation			10%					
Rops					100%			
Total	100%	100%	100%	100%	100%	100%	100%	100%

Percentages are determined according to resource drivers of each cost centre as shown in Table 1.6.

Table 1.6 Resource driver's name and costs by centre for France in Q3 1998

Cost centre	Cost of the centres for Q3 98 (€ thousands)	Resource driver
Call centre	1,000	Number of HW calls
Qualification centre	2,000	Number of qualifications
Engineers	15,500	Time spent
Courier costs (transportation)	600	100% on one activity. No need for a resource driver
Administration	2,400	100% on one activity. No need for a resource driver
Logistics (warehousing)	3,500	100% on one activity. No need for a resource driver
Logistics (transportation)	2,500	100% on one activity. No need for a resource driver
Subcontracting costs	3,000	Bills of the subcontractors allocated by activity
Total	30,500	

The solution adopted by Hewlett-Packard managed local and global interests: global interests with standardized and centralized calculation of the results and extraction of data, and local needs because countries could ask for corrections and had the final decision concerning the results.

The calculation model is presented below:

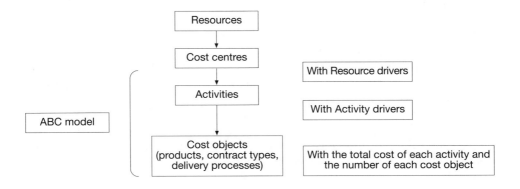

In fact, the ABC model has provided a lot of relevant information, obtained by centralization of the data treatments under control of the subsidiaries. These subsidiaries also have control of the level of detail of activities used. Therefore, it was possible to use the information for decision making at the central level and at the local level. For these reasons, the ABC model has been accepted and used by all the countries involved.

Table 1.7 Activity drivers per activity for France in Q3 1998

Activity	Driver	Volume
Call receipt	Number of phone calls	91,300
Call qualification	Number of call qualifications	61,875
Dispatching (people and parts)	Number of dispatchings	36,500
Logistics (parts handling)	Number of repairs with parts moved	40,000
Freight	Number of repairs with parts moved	40,000
POP (Customer Assist (Parts/Unit sent))	Number of customer assist repairs	3,000
On-site HP CE	Number of hours for HP CE repair + travel	40,000
On-site Temps	Number of hours for Temps repair + travel	10,000
On-site 3rd party CE	Number of repairs where a 3rd party engineer went on-site	12,000
Courier	Number of repairs that go through courier	5,000
CE Assist	Number of repairs which require CE Assist	10,000
Escalation	Number of repairs that require HW escalation	400
Rops	Total number of repairs in Repair Order Processing	83,000

Uses of the model and decisions taken

The ABC model is used for several types of decisions.

European and worldwide level

(1) Benchmarking, in order to compare countries per activity, per process and for some product lines. HP presents the ABC results each quarter for all countries. All the countries receive all the results so they can compare their results with those of other countries. They use these data to compare the different unit costs per activity (total cost of the activity/number of activity drivers). For example for the activity *Call Receipt*, they compare the unit cost per phone call received and per repair (total cost per process/number of repairs of the process). They can also compare the different unit costs per repair for one product line (for example, the cost of repair for printers). Results and benchmarking are used by two categories of people:

- marketing managers and sales people for the cost per repair and the cost per product line in order to determine the price for customers regarding the level of costs;
- operational managers for the cost per activity and the cost per process in order to decrease the costs if they see that they have higher costs than others. They can decrease costs by increasing volumes in order to absorb fixed costs or by re-organizing the way they perform the activities.

Table 1.8 Repartition of the number of activity drivers per activity and per delivery process (cost objects) for France in Q3 1998

Activity	Remote resolution	Courier Assist (Exchange)	POP (Parts/Unit Sent)	On-site HP CE	On-site Temps	On-site Subcontract	Installation	Total
Call receipt	26,400	5,500	3,300	24,200	9,900	13,200	8,800	91,300
Call qualification	19,800	4,125	2,475	18,150	7,425	9,900		61,875
Dispatching (people and parts)		5,000	3,000	20,000	8,500			36,500
Logistics (parts handling)		5,000	3,000	20,000	8,500	3,500		40,000
Freight		5,000	3,000	20,000	8,500	3,500		40,000
POP (Customer Assist (Part/Unit sent))			3,000					3,000
On-site HP CE				38,000			2,000	40,000
On-site Temps					10,000			10,000
On-site 3rd party CE						10,000	2,000	12,000
Courier		5,000						5,000
CE Assist				8,000	1,000	1,000		10,000
Escalation				350			50	400
Rops	24,000	5,000	3,000	22,000	9,000	12,000	8,000	83,000

Table 1.9 Unit cost of repair per delivery process for France, Q3 1998 (in €)

Activity	Remote resolution	Courier Assist (Exchange)	POP (Parts/Unit Sent)	On-site HP CE	On-site Temps	On-site Subcontract	Installation	Total
Total cost in € (a)							30,500	83,000
Number of repairs per process (b)								
Unit cost per repair in € = (a)/(b)*1000								367

Table 1.10   Number of repairs per delivery process (number of cost objects) for France (Q3 1998)

Remote resolution	24,000
Courier Assist (Exchange)	5,000
POP (Parts/Unit Sent)	3,000
On-site HP CE	22,000
On-site Temps	9,000
On-site Subcontract	12,000
Installation	8,000
Total	83,000

Table 1.11   Cost per repair and per activity (Q3 1998): cost by activities for the delivery process 'HP On-Site' (in €)

Activity	France	Germany	Italy	UK
Call Receipt		7.5	6.7	9.1
Call Qual		50.6	24.8	24.7
Dispatch		21.5	15.1	19.6
Parts Handling		21.5	22.7	57.1
Freight		51.2	8.0	37.9
POP		0.0	0.0	0.0
On-site HP CE		554.8	368.7	526.7
On-site Temps		0.0	0.0	0.0
On-site 3rd Party		0.0	0.0	0.0
Courier		0.0	0.0	0.0
CE Assist		20.1	22.6	35.0
Escalation		20.0	13.0	24.2
Rops		4.0	2.0	6.0
Total		751.2	483.6	740.4

(2) Re-engineering, in order to determine the best practices from some countries. Each quarter, operational managers and the manager of the re-engineering programme for Europe analysed the ABC results. When a country had lower unit costs on one process or one activity, an analysis was done to understand why. Then two cases were possible:

- Either the cost is lower because the practices in the country are better than those in the other countries. For example, repair is done within a shorter time or with less operations than in the other countries. In this case, the European re-engineering manager tries to see if it is possible to apply these working methods to the other countries.
- Or the cost is lower because the country has some specificities and differences compared to the other countries. For example, UK has a lower level of taxes on

salaries, or some countries have their offices close to customers' sites so the logistical costs concerning travel are low. In this case, it is impossible to have the same situation in the other countries. But sometimes it is possible to take advantage of these specificities at the worldwide level to localize some activities in the same centre in one country for all of the world. But it is only possible for activities when HP doesn't need to be near the customer (phoning for example).

(3) Pricing, in order to review some prices regarding the ABC costs. These possibilities are used by the marketing managers and sometimes by the operational managers for some big deals.

For this purpose, the marketing managers have a look at the unit ABC costs per contract, per repair and per product in order to compare them with the competitors' prices. Then they have more information with which to determine the prices for standard services sold by HP.

The operational managers use the ABC results to gain an idea of the cost of some specific large contracts. When a customer asks HP to undertake the maintenance of the 2000 PCs and printers in his/her company, HP has to make a quotation. HP evaluates the consumption of activities for this contract in order to calculate the costs of this contract. After that, it is possible to determine the price.

(4) To give objectives to the country managers. When the project was launched at the worldwide level, the manager for worldwide hardware maintenance, who was the sponsor, wanted to have a better insight into the costs per repair, per product repaired and per contract type. He wanted to have a good market position for almost all services delivered. To improve his performance, he must give objectives to country managers. They must reach some cost objectives per process and per product line and contract type according to their ABC costs. For example, they have to decrease the cost of repairing a printer under warranty at the customer's site. ABC allows HP to give objectives based on the realities of business described by the list of the activities.

Country level

The same model was used at the country level. At this level, it was possible to have more detailed activities. ABC was used in the following ways.

(1) To understand the business and the organization. All operational managers in a country can understand costs by seeing the costs of the activities per product, delivery process and contract type. ABC helps the country manager to understand his or her business. For example, he or she can choose to focus on product lines or on contract types.

(2) To do 'what-if' analysis (simulations) at the operational level. Operational managers use the ABC results to manage their activities, using what they call 'what-if analysis'. For example the French Hardware Maintenance Manager said in 1997:

'I am doing what-if analysis to see the impact some decisions will have on costs. For example, what is the impact if I decide to decrease the number of repairs for PC? It helps me to decide if I need to hire more people and where I need to allocate more or less resources'. To do that, they test several hypotheses using the ABC results. They can change the cost of one resource – for example, the cost of the engineer salaries – in order to determine the new cost of one repair.

Today, in 1998, ABC still exists at HP and is used. The project is not really a project now: each quarter results are calculated and used in this way. More countries are using the model. In 1998, HP is implementing ABC in the Nordic countries: Sweden, Denmark, Norway and Finland.

Endnotes

[1] Packard D., *The HP Way – How Bill Hewlett and I built our company*, Harper Business, New York, 1995.

[2] For more information concerning this firm, use these Web addresses:

www.hp.com/financials   www.fortune.com
www.hp.com/abouthp/company-facts   www.lexpansion.com
www.france.hp.com/main/france/chiffres

Note that 1 Euro = 6.5596 French francs

[3] At HP, the term 'ABC model' means the list of processes, activities, cost drivers and cost objects used to calculate the ABC results. These lists changed from the beginning in France to the extension to all worldwide countries included in the project.

[4] Note that in this map, HP only represented countries concerned with the ABC project (for example, Africa, South America and some European countries are not represented).

STUDENT ASSIGNMENTS

1. Using the data in Tables 1.4–1.11:
    (a) Calculate the cost of the activities for France (complete Table 1.4 with missing data).
    (b) Calculate the unit cost of the delivery processes for France (cost for one repair for each delivery process, complete Table 1.9) and the unit cost of the delivery process 'HP On-Site' by activities for France (cost for one repair for each activity, complete Table 1.11).
    (c) Compare and comment on the costs of the delivery process 'HP On-Site' for all European countries (Table 1.11).

2. Describe all possible uses of ABC for decision making and compare them with Hewlett-Packard needs and possibilities.

3. Explain the interests and disadvantages of the non-integration of ABC in the cost accounting Information System.

4. What kind of difficulties could HP have in implementing ABC in an international environment with a lot of subsidiaries?

CASE TWO

ABC in Norwegian State Railway's passenger transport[1]

Trond Bjørnenak

Introduction

The limited liability state-owned company Norwegian State Railway (NSR) is by Norwegian standards a big enterprise (Table 2.1). Until 1996, NSR was an enterprise within national government, i.e. an integral part of the state. This meant that the central government granted NSR financial resources in the Budget and that the use of resources was authorized by the Storting (Parliament). As for responsibility, NSR was considered to be a mixture of cost centre and profit centre. The external accounts were presented according to the principles of cash flow accounting. However, separate accounts, according to the accrual principle, were presented as a supplement, where the different areas of activity were emphasized. As a consequence, the profitability of goods and passenger transport was reported separately.

Table 2.1 Descriptive data for NSR

	1994	1995	1996	1997
Number of persons employed				
▪ Goods and passenger transport	9,217	9,138	7,382	7,273
▪ The rail network (now *Jernbaneverket*)	2,910	3,005	N/A	N/A
Passenger transport				
▪ Number of journeys (million)	37.9	39.6	40.7	44.7
▪ Passenger kilometres, total (million)	2,398	2,381	2,447	2,562
Goods transport				
▪ Tons carried, total (million)	20.0	20.9	14.6	6.6
▪ Ton-kilometres, total (million)	2,678	2,715	2,636	2,361

On 1 December 1996, NSR (the Norwegian State Railways) was divided into two independent units: the administrative body *Jernbaneverket* (the Norwegian

National Rail Administration) and the limited liability state-owned company NSR. From an accounting point of view, this division was made as early as 1990. *Jernbaneverket* is a continuation of the previous NSR Infrastructure division. The main task of this activity is to manage the national railway infrastructure and see to it that passenger and goods transport run smoothly. The fact that *Jernbaneverket* was separated from the operation of transport services can be viewed as an attempt to separate a natural monopoly from the operation of services that are exposed to competition. The natural monopoly consists primarily of the development and upkeep of the rail network. The building and change of the infrastructure is normally viewed as a public task where assessments concerning national economy are more prevalent than those which generally apply to business administration.

The separation of the infrastructure, and who is to make use of it, is also a consequence of how the railway system is operated in Europe. Therefore, we find similar divisions in many other countries. Principally, according to EU regulations, the infrastructure is to be made accessible on non-discriminative terms to different service operators. This implies that *Jernbaneverket* is not allowed to give the previous NSR special advantages compared to other potential operators. From a management point of view, *Jernbaneverket* is regarded as an expense centre and is managed through financial budgets, given by the Parliament. In addition, NSR pays compensation to *Jernbaneverket* for the transport of goods on the rail network. This compensation is to make sure that NSR Goods is not subsidized by *Jernbaneverket*. No such compensation is to be paid for passenger transport. However, compensation has been discussed to avoid discrimination against other forms of transport (buses).

In connection with the separation of *Jernbaneverket*, the passenger transport and goods transport were converted into a limited liability state-owned company NSR BA (BA = limited liability) subject to a special Companies' Act for state-owned companies. The main difference from an ordinary limited liability company is, however, that the employees keep their rights as these are laid down in the Civil Servants Act. Among other things, this implies stronger protection against lay-offs in connection with reorganizations and assurance of payment according to the salary scale of the state. From a company point of view this can lead to less flexibility than in an ordinary limited liability company. This form of company organization was established in connection with organizational changes in *Posten* ('the Post Office') and NSR.

NSR BA has two main separate forms of transport; passenger and goods. These are divided into separate business units. In addition, there are two support units. NSR Eiendom ('*NSR Property*') manages and lets the considerable buildings and land property of NSR. Technical support functions, like repairs and maintenance of materials, are carried out by NSR Engineering. Internal deliveries between the different divisions are in most cases effected at cost based prices. NSR Property uses market prices for internal rent of properties. An organizational chart of NSR BA is shown in Figure 2.1.

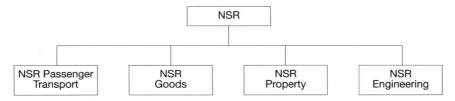

Figure 2.1 A simplified organizational chart of NSR BA

NSR passenger transport is the only company which offers rail passenger transport in Norway, and with one exception (one special route in northern Norway) also the only company providing goods transport by rail. However, this does not imply that there are no competitors. Alternative forms of transport (road, sea and air) exist in most cases. Airborne traffic and long-distance buses, have taken a greater share of the passenger market in recent years. As mentioned earlier, competitors also have access to the national railway infrastructure on equal terms with NSR.

The business unit's strategy, in a situation with steadily increasing competition, is to focus on areas where one has natural competitive advantages (e.g. local traffic and long-distance traffic between the large cities) focusing on products for the future, involving the operation of high-speed tilting trains. In addition, there is a strong wish to strengthen the economy through making the rail services run more efficiently. One means is to reduce the variety of equipment used (locomotives and couches). This may reduce structural costs as far as repairs and maintenance are concerned.

Management control system

The management control system of NSR Passenger Transport is based on the fact that the activity is supposed to function as a business unit with focus on the profitability of the different sections and departures. However, political interests may conflict with assumptions underlying management control. The reorganization of the railway network is one example of this. Therefore, pressure from local politicians, public economic interests, and other considerations plays a part. To avoid a mixture of managerial and political considerations, public buying agreements have been introduced. This implies that the state is looked upon as a customer who in a business-like way can buy services or parts of services. One example is when train departures cannot be maintained on a private business basis; instead, the state pays for the 'loss' so that the service may continue. 'The price' of each product in the public buying agreement is a function of costs and other product revenues. The agreement is set before the beginning of a fiscal year, and included in the budget for the next year. The main function of the agreement is to separate public choices from management considerations. Without public buying agreements, operation of rail services in Norway would not have been possible today. This is clear from the income statement of NSR Passenger Transport as shown in Table 2.2.

Table 2.2 Income statement of NSR Passenger Transport for 1997 (in NOK million[2])

Revenues from passenger transport	1,841
Other revenues	453
Public buying	984
Total revenues	3,278
Operational costs	2,942
Income from operations	337
Financial income and expenses	61
Net income	276

A central part of the management control system of NSR Passenger Transport is the control of costs and profitability. The main principle of the control system is built around two objectives; product development and areas of responsibility. The profitability control, and the basis of calculation for the public buying agreement, lies first and foremost in the product costing system (activity-based costing, see later). The responsibility accounting system is based on control of revenues and costs, and is monitored monthly. The main activities, Passenger Transport and Goods, are considered separate business units and are followed up and evaluated by net income (including public buying, but not general overhead). However, there is no bonus system related to net income. The support units charge costs for the activities they carry out, based on cost absorption. Furthermore, the Passenger Transport Division is divided into four regions (East, West, North and South). Each region is regarded as a separate business unity, which is further classified by products. The central building block of the income statement is therefore the calculation of revenues and cost per product.

In addition to the financial control, operations are monitored through a variety of non-financial performance measures such as punctuality and absence due to sickness etc. In order to emphasize the importance of a focus on certain performance measures, graphic representations are made of:

- income from operations;
- changes in income from passenger transport and goods (compared with budgeted amounts and actual data from last year);
- punctuality;
- the number of travellers;
- absence due to sickness.

These presentations are announced centrally in the administrative offices of the Passenger Transport Division, and used in the evaluation of the different regions (similar performance measures are also developed for the Goods Division). Separate customer accounts (customer satisfaction), employee accounts and environmental accounts are prepared for the different business units. These are included in the annual report and can also be read via the Internet (www.nsb.no).

The ABC accounting system

Two aspects underlie the development of an activity-based costing (ABC) system for NSR Passenger Transport:

- Increased emphasis on profitability in the organisation.
- The design of a strategy for concentration on and reconstruction of products.

Future route changes are therefore one of the principal aims of the ABC system. In addition, one needs costing systems in connection with agreements on public buying of services. In order to offer political authorities the desired choice situation, one has to calculate which products may require support buying, and how much financial backing each product actually requires. In this connection, the ABC costing system functions as a legitimization of the 'bill' to the Ministry of Transport.

The definition of products is critical and problematic for the preparation of a costing system for the operation of trains. NSR chose to define the product by train number. This represents a departure from certain sections of the rail network, and is very similar to the flight number used in air transport. A train number includes information on which section of the railway it covers (e.g. the Bergen line) and the specific time of departure. Through this system, aggregation in several directions is possible, for example the profitability of express trains or night trains on a certain section of the rail network. Note, however, that this is not identical with the product which the customer buys, that is to say a ticket valid between two stations. If travel distances had been taken as one's point of departure, the number of products would have become unmanageable. Another problem is that tickets can be valid for several different train numbers. Fare tickets and interrail tickets are part of this category. When a ticket is sold, one does not know what product will be used. One ticket may also cover several sections on the rail network; for example, a ticket on the section Gothenburg–Bergen will include a section abroad and two sections in Norway (The Østfold line and the Bergen line).

Since one cannot trace revenue directly to a product, it has to be based on allocations. The revenue per product is calculated on the basis of three factors: the number of travellers; average journey length; and average revenue per passenger kilometre. First, the number of passenger kilometres are calculated based on the actual number of travellers and estimated average journey length. The data material underlying average journey length is taken from surveys of the ticket structure based on calculations of what ticket category the passenger has, how much he has paid for it, and for what distance it is valid. For each product, one then estimates the average journey length. This measurement can stay constant for several years. In addition, an average revenue per passenger kilometre is calculated per product. This measurement is updated by price adjustments. One reaches the calculated revenue of the product in the following way:

Calculated revenue

= Number of travellers * Average journey distance * Average ticket price per passenger kilometre

= Number of travellers * Average calculated ticket revenue per traveller

The cost allocation is also problematic. The main principle of the ABC costing system is that all costs are traced to a product. To have a more correct picture of capital costs, the capital base has also been changed to replacement cost. In connection with the reorganization from an enterprise within national government to the NSR BA form (the limited liability state-owned company NSR), parts of the running gear were heavily written off. Depreciation based on replacement costs were therefore higher than depreciations used in the financial accounts. On the other hand a longer depreciation period is used in the internal estimate (e.g. 30 years on locomotives) than in the financial accounts (15 years on locomotives). The total effect was, however, that depreciation used in the activity-based costing system (1997) was higher than in the financial accounts.

In addition to depreciation, imputed interest is calculated on capital tied up in each product.[3] This is done through the allocation of capital to the products, which then are multiplied by an interest rate. The allocated imputed interest is considerably higher than financial expenses. In 1997, the total effect of the adjustment of capital costs was NOK 342 million. The activity-based accounting system therefore allocated NOK 342 million more than the costs that were included in the financial accounts. On the other hand, one defines in the ABC accounting system some facility-sustaining costs. These are not allocated to products. The total effect of these are NOK 93 million. In Table 2.3, the adjustment from product income to financial income is shown. The table also distinguishes between two different product groups (commercial and public buying of train products). Note, however, that this distinction is in a state of flux, as public buying agreements represent a partial financing of the product. A distinction between primary and secondary trains has also been made. Primary trains are those which are classified as strategically important, for

Table 2.3 Differences between product profit and financial income (in NOK million)

Commercial trains:	
Primary commercial trains	−27
Secondary commercial trains	−15
Public buying trains:	
Primary public buying of trains	74
Secondary public buying of trains	−5
Total product profit	27
Adjusted capital costs	342
Other adjustments (incl. facility sustaining costs)	−93
Financial income	276

example stretches of rail network where there are no alternative forms of transport, or where railway transport has natural competitive advantages. Local trains in the Oslo area and Inter City trains to and from Oslo are in the primary train group.

Some costs can be traced directly to a product. This applies, for example, to the daily cleaning of carriages which is performed by the support division, NSR Engineering. The costs of this activity can be traced directly to a product (departure) based on the transfer price from this division. The main part of the costs are, however, traced indirectly via allocations based on a two-step procedure. First, costs are allocated to cost pools. These cost pools are activity-oriented, and prepared for the different organizational units. The main activity can be divided into eight principal cost pools. These are shown in Table 2.4. Activities which are performed by units other than NSR Passenger Transport, and cannot be traced directly, will be further allocated based on a chosen cost allocation base. Control of locomotives, for example, is carried out by NSR Engineering. The cost allocation for this activity is based on the number of kilometres.

Table 2.4 Overview of main activities. The percentage column shows which part of total product costs is traced to the respective main activity

Main activity	Percentage of total	Examples of subordinate activity/costs that are included
Sales/marketing	16	Sale of tickets (telephone, barrier)
		Information
		Marketing
		Office rent
Conductor services	11	Conductor
Train services	2	(Direct traced to departure)
Cleaning	5	Cleaning including rent of premises
Clearing	7	Controller
		Inspections
Maintenance	11	Requisitions
		Storage costs
Train operation	32	Handling of materials
		Engine driver
Administration	16	Administration

The choice of allocation bases from activities to products is based on three guidelines. First, the allocation base should vary in proportion to the cost level. Second, the cost base should be able to relate the activity to the product. Last but not least, it should be possible to quantify the cost base objectively. These criteria resulted in four main types of bases for cost allocation which were used for further allocation:

- passenger dependent (costs caused by the number of travellers);
- kilometre dependent (costs caused by travel distance);
- departure dependent (costs caused by the number of departures);
- time dependent (costs caused by the time consumption of an activity).

The various pools of cost drivers were further specified for the different activities. For example, a distinction is made between the number of train kilometres with locomotive and the number of train kilometres with locomotive plus coaches, because of the difference in fuel consumption. The specification of activities in some cases has to be related to other aspects, for example region or type of running equipment. One example of this is the maintenance of running equipment. Various checks are carried out on different kinds of running equipment. To have a meaningful allocation, the maintenance activity is therefore combined with information on what running equipment (for example type of locomotive) the maintenance is carried out on. This is necessary to later be able to trace the maintenance costs to a product.

The final step of the calculation is to allocate costs from activity to product. This is done through a combination of the products' consumption of activities with the cost per unit of the allocation base for each activity. The structure of the calculation is shown in Table 2.5.

Table 2.5 The main principle of the calculation

Factors affecting the cost	Examples of activities involved
Type of equipment used	Clearing and maintenance
Distance and time	Conductor, train operation
Number of departures	Some types of cleaning and clearing of trains
Number of passengers	Sale and marketing

The final calculation can be presented per activity area or in total. A central key figure of the accounts is 'funds generated from operations', defined as follows:

$$\frac{\text{Revenues before public buying}}{\text{Total costs (including imputed interest)}}$$

This key figure draws the attention towards products with more or less need of public grants, and if necessary towards the reorganization of products. The concept 'funds generated from operations' for the different products is shown in Figure 2.2.

Capacity costs and capital costs

Although many are of the opinion that the present ABC costing system gives a good picture of the profitability of the different products, some problems remain. One of these is the allocation of capacity costs, predominantly capital costs for the running equipment. The variation in the tying up of capital between the various groups of running equipment is high. Even though replacement costs is used, some very old running equipment is fully written off, whereas newer running equipment has a book value of a considerable amount. This causes considerable differences in

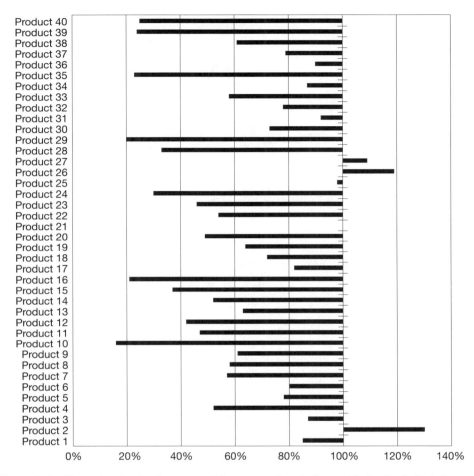

Figure 2.2 Chart showing funds generated from operations before public buying (calculations are based on replacement cost)

imputed interests. Newer equipment has considerably lower maintenance costs than older equipment.

> It is difficult to find rational allocations for capacity costs. The capacity utilisation of the different types of running equipment vary considerably on a daily, weekly and yearly basis. Re-adjustments and changes in running equipment also cause the capacity utilisation of for example railway workshops to vary.
>
> (Erik Brodal, controller NSR Passenger Traffic)

The capacity utilization of running equipment varies dramatically between day and night. This is shown in Figure 2.3, which shows the distribution of the number of passengers travelling during the day for three products. There are also

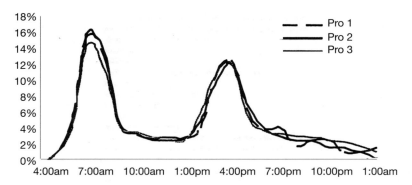

Figure 2.3   Chart showing the traffic pattern during day and night (local traffic in Oslo area)

considerable fluctuations during the week and between different seasons. In the ABC costing system, the actual capacity utilization is used as a basis for the calculations. Practical capacity might be higher for some activities and for some types of running equipment.

Endnotes

[1] The author would like to thank Erik Brodal from Norwegian State Railway's Passenger Transport for making the writing of this case possible.
[2] Exchange rate 1/1 1999: 1 EURO = 8,80 NOK
[3] Imputed interest is traditionally included as a full cost component in costing systems in Scandinavia.

STUDENT ASSIGNMENTS

1. NSR is divided into two independent units, an infrastructure unit and a traffic unit. What is the purpose of this separation? Is this type of separation found in other industries?

2. Describe the management control system in NSR. What is the focus of the control system?

3. Describe and discuss the functions of the ABC system in NSR. Does the ABC system correspond with NSR's strategy?

4. Describe and discuss the design of the ABC system. Do other industries have the same design problems? Include the following elements:
   - the definition of products;
   - the allocation of revenues to products;
   - the information value of the activity concept;
   - the criteria for choosing cost drivers; and
   - the difference between the income in the financial statement analysis and the product income in the ABC system (Table 2.3 in the case).

5. The cost of capital is treated differently in the financial statement and the ABC system. Design an example to describe the difference.

6. The variations in demand is described in Figure 2.3. What problems does the variation in demand cause for the allocation of capacity cost to products?

—

Scottish National Blood Transfusion Service: issues in the development of a costing system

Falconer Mitchell
Shao Huajing

Introduction

The Scottish National Blood Transfusion Service (SNBTS) is a public sector body whose remit is to safely collect and supply sufficient blood and related products to meet the needs of patients in Scotland (population approximately 5.5 million). Table 3.1 summarizes the main products and services provided by the SNBTS. It currently employs approximately 1,100 people (800 whole time equivalents) ranging from clinical staff (doctors and nurses) and research scientists through to engineers and administrative staff. Table 3.2 shows annual expenditure and employment level in the service during the last four years. All blood donations are given on a voluntary basis. While advertising and symbolic reward schemes (badges awarded to denote volume of donations) are used to enhance supply, the decision to donate remains a personal and largely altruistic one for each individual donor.

Structure and activities

The SNBTS comprises:

- a headquarters unit which co-ordinates the work of the SNBTS and provides a range of central administrative services (e.g. planning, finance, personnel);
- a small set of research and development support units;
- five regional transfusion centres, covering the whole of Scotland, with responsibilities for collecting, processing, storing and supplying blood within their geographical area;

Table 3.1   Components, products and services provided by the SNBTS

Product/Service	Type	Use	Shelf life (days)
Whole blood	Component[a]	Replacement of blood fluid	35
Red cells	Component	Increase level of blood oxygen	5
Cryoprecipitate	Component	Correction of specific blood disorders	365
Platelets	Component	Replacement of platelets	5
Fresh frozen plasma	Component	Replacement of coagulation factors	365
Factor VIII	Fractionated[b]	Haemophiliac treatment	730
Factor IX	Fractionated	Haemophiliac treatment	1,095
Immunoglobulins	Fractionated	Treatment of immunodeficiency (e.g. Tetanus)	730–2,191
Albumin	Fractionated	Replacement of blood fluids and severe burns	365–1,095
Stem cells	Therapeutic	Replacement of stem cells (e.g. after chemotherapy)	3,650
Bone marrow	Therapeutic	Replacement of bone marrow	3,650
Reagents (diagnostic products)	Manufactured[c]	Grouping of blood and antibody identification	various
Immunochemistry	Diagnostic testing[d]	Confirm allergies in blood sample	n/a
Blood bank	Diagnostic testing	Identify suitable blood products for patient transfusion	n/a
Tissue typing	Diagnostic testing	Pre-transplant compatability testing of tissues	n/a
Ante-natal serology	Diagnostic testing	Evaluate requirement to treat mother/baby for anti-D reaction	n/a
Bone banking	Clinical service	Collect, process, store and issue donated bone	+10 years
Tissue banking	Clinical service	Collect, process, store and issue donated tissues (e.g. ligaments, tendons)	+10 years

[a] 16 products
[b] 19 products
[c] 120 products
[d] 90 regular tests

Table 3.2   SNBTS expenditure and employment

	1994/95	1995/96	1996/97	1997/98
Total Expenditure (£ millions)	33.75	34.95	37.62	37.78
Number of Staff	1,208	1,192	1,154	1,110

Note on 1 January 1999 1 Euro = £0.7

- the Protein Fractionation Centre (PFC) which is essentially a manufacturing facility where blood plasma supplied by the regional transfusion centres is used as the raw material for the production of more than two dozen different blood products (e.g. Factors VIII and IX for haemophilia and immunoglobulins for immunodeficiencies).

The SNBTS is organized and managed as a divisionalized organization. Although each region has considerable autonomy over the way it operates, issues of general policy are discussed and ratified by a central board comprising the National Director, the National Scientific and Medical Director, the four central services Directors (Quality, Finance, Operations, Support Services), the five Regional Directors, the Director of the National Science Laboratory and the Director of the PFC. Most donations are obtained in a whole blood form although a small but growing number are in the form of plasma or platelets only (apheresis donations). However very little blood is used in its whole form. At each regional transfusion centre donations are tested, subjected to a range of quality control procedures and broken down into their main constituents of plasma, red cells and platelets. Most of the plasma is sent to the PFC for further processing into a variety of composite products. The other blood components are stored in local hospital blood banks ready for clinical use.

Some current operational issues in running the SNBTS

Considerable uncertainty surrounds the supply of blood which is based on the goodwill of the Scottish public. Donors' motives lie in helping others rather than in the gaining of any personal reward. Although, in the main, Scotland is self-sufficient in blood donations, supply is somewhat seasonal (normal supply falls in the Summer) and is extremely sensitive to issues such as HIV and hepatitis. An international market does exist in most of the products of the SNBTS but, given the organization's remit, recourse to the market is viewed as something of a failure. Managing the supply is further complicated by the need to ensure adequate availability of different blood groupings and the short shelf life of many blood products. For example, whole blood has a maximum shelf life of 35 days while for platelets and red cells it is only five days (see Table 3.1 for further details of product shelf lives). Moreover some products have a long manufacture lead-time. Many of the products manufactured by the PFC take three months to produce and it takes time to adjust supply levels. Consequently significant buffer stocks have to be held for several products as the effects of a stock-out can be critical for medical treatment. However, where a product's shelf life is short the accumulation of too large a stock can lead to significant waste. Attempts to manage blood supply to cope with these circumstances centre on the constant efforts made to recruit new donors, to retain existing donors and to maintain the good donor records and relationships which allow for selective call-up of those needed at any particular point in time. Demand for blood and blood products is derived from clinical activity in Scottish hospitals. It is primarily dependent on the levels of relevant surgery and other therapies. Surgical developments, particularly in the transplant area and other cancer treatments, have created a substantial increase in demand for blood products in recent years. Disasters may also cause temporary but major fluctuations in demand. All of these factors render the level of demand extremely difficult to predict. In recent years a number of additional factors have compounded the challenges facing the management of the SNBTS.

(1) **Cost containment.** The government treats the SNBTS as a cost centre with a budget allocation made to it each year. This has fallen markedly in real terms over the past decade and has made cost control and reduction one of the key managerial tasks during this period. Figure 3.1 highlights the efficiency savings already made. These have largely been attained by requiring across-the-board percentage savings from all parts of the service. The pressure to reduce costs remains and general cost reduction targets are now considered dangerous as they may compromise care activity. This has created an internal demand for better cost accounting information to

Efficiency savings

Efficiency savings are a means of coping with inflation and of generating funds to reinvest in clinical services, increased product supply and improved information technology support.

Total savings of over £5 million have been found in the last eight years (see efficiency graph, below).

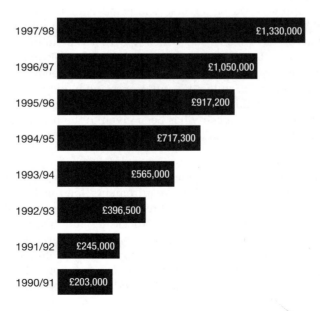

1997/98	£1,330,000
1996/97	£1,050,000
1995/96	£917,200
1994/95	£717,300
1993/94	£565,000
1992/93	£396,500
1991/92	£245,000
1990/91	£203,000

Figure 3.1 Efficiency savings

specifically target future cost savings. Consequently in 1997 a qualified management accountant was employed to develop internal accounting systems and the development of a system of activity-based costing became his first project.

(2) **Product quality.** The traditional and overriding aim of the SNBTS is to provide a clinical support service of the highest quality. This requires the availability of a sound supply of whole blood. Although the use of only voluntary donors contributes greatly to this objective there is also a need to subject all donations to stringent testing for contaminations such as hepatitis. More recently the emergence of HIV and the possibility of a human form of BSE[1] have required considerable modification to existing procedures and increased the costs of testing and processing blood. In order to be able to react to the identification of contamination in the blood supply detailed records of how each donation has been used must be kept. Thus resource use within the SNBTS has been highly dynamic due largely to changes in procedures relating to quality and it has thus proved difficult to maintain accurate and up-to-date information on the structure of their costs.

(3) **Private sector involvement.** Private healthcare has grown in Scotland over the last twenty years. This has created an additional demand for the SNBTS as they are legally permitted to supply the private sector and several private hospitals have made agreements with them to supply blood and blood products. While the SNBTS has had the capacity to meet this private sector demand it has also to consider the issue of making a charge for this service. Donors are, however, potentially highly sensitive to the idea that others may make money from their freely given blood donations and supply could be adversely affected if there were any question of either the SNBTS or other organizations profiting from their altruism. The SNBTS staff representatives have also been concerned that the funding for the service should not be used to subsidize private sector, profit-making businesses. Consequently there has been pressure on the SNBTS management to ensure that a full cost recovery charge for collecting and processing blood is levied on their private sector customers. In this way they can argue that no profit is being made on donations and that no cross-subsidy has been given to the private sector hospitals. The ability to do this is dependent on the availability of appropriate product cost information.

(4) **Stock valuation.** One further source of demand for costing system development lies in the government accountability requirements for the SNBTS which now include a statement of stocks held at the financial year end valued at their full cost (i.e. the cost of collecting, testing and processing the freely donated blood). Accurate stock valuation is also important for one benchmarking/value for money appraisal which is carried out internally. A hypothetical profit and loss account is produced periodically by generating a notional income figure from the products supplied to customers during the year multiplied by their prevailing prices on the international market. Knowledge of the cost of stocks is necessary to compute a cost of sales figure and so complete the profit calculation.

(5) **Existing costing information.** The existing product cost information within the SNBTS was based on a series of specific one-off studies of resource consumption patterns undertaken in the 1980s and early 1990s. These were based on the functional areas of responsibility within the SNBTS (e.g. donor administration, blood collection, blood testing, etc.). The resultant costs were uplifted annually for inflation and were subject to occasional modification for significant changes in procedures.

(6) **Emerging commercial awareness.** The SNBTS has, over time, developed a high degree of expertise in the whole blood transfusion process. Over the last decade there has been an increasing awareness among staff that they have much skill and experience which could be commercially exploited. Consequently there have been several initiates taken to protect and exploit the intellectual property rights which the service possesses. These include joint ventures with commercial undertakings to develop new blood products, the design of new types of bloodbag, the provision of consultancy services to other overseas blood transfusion services in respect of both clinical information and administrative services, the sale of spare operating capacity to other countries and the support of indigenous biotechnology companies.

Developing a new ABC system

It was against this background that the Director of Finance took the initiative to begin the development of an ABC system. To facilitate this a new management accountant was recruited. He had previously been employed by a commercial organization which had used ABC and he had been involved in the design of this system. The management accountant was delegated to lead an ABC project group which contained a further six staff from donor liaison, regional centre administration, blood collection and laboratory services. The Director of Finance, as project director, was also to be an 'occasional' member of the group. Their ABC project work was in addition to the members' normal workloads. Their remit was (a) to develop an ABC system which would cover all areas of the SNBTS with the exception of the PFC which was already experimenting with the ABC approach to costing, (b) to produce not simply product costs but also clear and detailed profiles of how resources were being employed as a basis for monitoring and improving performance. The system was thus expected to extend beyond pure ABC to permit activity-based cost management ABCM. A commercial software package was to be used for the system. However, the project team would be responsible for selecting the key variables, which would characterize the system within a general ABC framework of activity cost pools and cost driver rates. After an initial educational session to familiarize the team with the basics of ABC, a programme of meetings was arranged roughly at monthly intervals between October 1997 and March 1998. At each meeting the progress of the previous month was presented and discussed, outstanding items were identified and a work agenda was set for each group member for the forthcoming month. The management accountant had responsibility for supporting the group's efforts and for translating their work into the computerized ABC model. During the project group's deliberations a wide variety of issues and problems were raised.

ABC system objectives

Although the need for reliable product cost information was recognized as an important objective of their work the group also agreed at the start that they wished to develop a system which would clarify how resources had been employed to deliver SNBTS outputs. The Director of Finance described this as having the facility to start with output costs but then being able to drill down through the layers of the organization to find out how the organization's resources were being used. This is a first step towards being able to use them better.

Support for a system designed to show this level of detail was also strong within the non-accounting members of the group. While they supported the need for reliable cost information they also saw another benefit which would give visibility to an important work issue. This was based on the capability of a detailed activity profile to highlight the time that staff had to spend 'dealing with emergencies and problems', 'coping with new developments', 'managing change' and 'addressing bureaucratic rules'. As one of the laboratory supervisors observed, 'We want a system that will show up what we have to cope with every day. ABC can do this. It can reveal all the things which deflect us from our core work.' Thus for disparate reasons the group established an aim of obtaining a detailed visibility of the cost of work activities as a key feature of the new system.

Defining terms used

Producing an operational definition of 'activity' was not something initially considered by the group and this eventually proved to be a handicap to their progress. Discussions with staff on their work activities resulted in responses describing work activity in terms of 'attending meetings', 'making phonecalls', 'thinking', etc. Activities were viewed at a micro level producing a highly detailed analysis of work. Although insightful, this type of analysis did not suit the product costing objectives of the system as the activities lacked the purpose-based homogeneity needed for activity cost pools in order to compute meaningful cost driver rates. Also, due to the disparate nature of these, it was going to be difficult to ascertain why particular amounts of time had been devoted to specific activities and hence the cost management aims would also be deflected. The group had to spend time explaining the need for a unifying purpose orientation to staff consulted as part of the activity selection process. The term cost driver was another which caused confusion particularly among the non-accounting team members. To assist understanding it was simply classified as a measure of the output of an activity.

Gathering activity data

Choosing the mechanisms for gathering the activity profile data was another early issue which required the group's attention. The task of obtaining information from every staff member on how they spent their work time was considered both too sensitive and too time consuming. Consequently it was agreed that this task would be handled by consulting with supervisory staff only. In addition, many core job descriptions and standard operating procedures which had been previously established were considered suitable as a foundation for this aspect of the system design. Table 3.3 contains some examples of the activities chosen as a basis for one section of the system – blood collection. It was decided that the information gathered on the activity profile would not be obtained on a continuous basis (say weekly or monthly) as it would be impractical. Instead a review would be carried out at least annually and any necessary amendments made to the established activity framework. The group also agreed that idle time should be separately identified in the system and that 'housekeeping' (i.e. predominantly expediting and change management) would be incorporated as a category to cover time spent on change management and problem resolution. As work progressed two significant questions arose concerning the treatment of certain activities.

- Should research and development work come within the scope of the ABC system? While there was a general feeling within the group that the new system should be as comprehensive as possible (and R&D was a significant cost) there was also some recognition that the inclusion of R&D costs could be counterproductive. First, in a product costing context it was recognized that R&D activities primarily related to future products or processing developments. To incorporate it in a system for costing existing products would therefore lead to information distortions. Second, the R&D work was project based with teams of staff devoted to specific research topics for particular periods of time. To base costing on a set of common activities would obscure the project, perhaps the most important cost object from a control and appraisal perspective. Third, the work of R&D was more variable than the mainstream routine operations of the SNBT. It did not lend itself well to a system based on a framework which would only be reviewed annually. For these reasons the team decided, at least initially, to exclude R&D from detailed activity analysis within the ABC system. However R&D costs were to be identified separately and related to future 'outputs' (e.g. specific projects, academic research, etc.). This, together with work activity on strategic planning and intellectual property identification and protection, was to be categorized as 'legacy' activities.

Table 3.3 Example of activity analysis within SNBTS

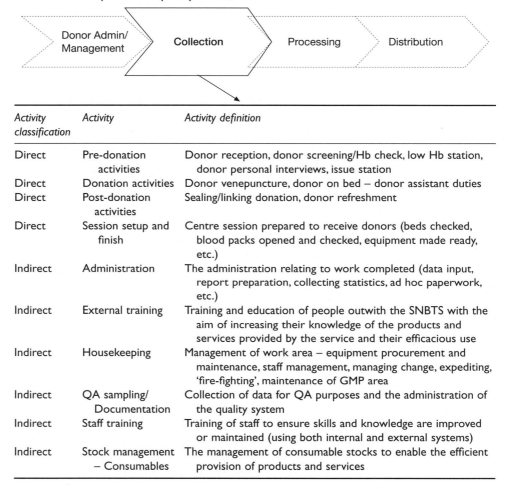

Activity classification	Activity	Activity definition
Direct	Pre-donation activities	Donor reception, donor screening/Hb check, low Hb station, donor personal interviews, issue station
Direct	Donation activities	Donor venepuncture, donor on bed – donor assistant duties
Direct	Post-donation activities	Sealing/linking donation, donor refreshment
Direct	Session setup and finish	Centre session prepared to receive donors (beds checked, blood packs opened and checked, equipment made ready, etc.)
Indirect	Administration	The administration relating to work completed (data input, report preparation, collecting statistics, ad hoc paperwork, etc.)
Indirect	External training	Training and education of people outwith the SNBTS with the aim of increasing their knowledge of the products and services provided by the service and their efficacious use
Indirect	Housekeeping	Management of work area – equipment procurement and maintenance, staff management, managing change, expediting, 'fire-fighting', maintenance of GMP area
Indirect	QA sampling/ Documentation	Collection of data for QA purposes and the administration of the quality system
Indirect	Staff training	Training of staff to ensure skills and knowledge are improved or maintained (using both internal and external systems)
Indirect	Stock management – Consumables	The management of consumable stocks to enable the efficient provision of products and services

- How should indirect support activities be treated? Indirect activities comprised those that did not directly relate to the final outputs of the SNBTS and included services such as computing, finance, personnel and training. Some consideration was given to treating costs such as training as a percentage uplift to direct labour costs but this approach was rejected as it could conceal the costs of important activities. Instead the management accountant obtained the group's agreement to using the notion of a cost 'cascade' (see Case Appendix) as a basis for structuring the system. This involved viewing the costs as flowing from the general ledger to all activities both direct and support. Then the support activity cost pools would 'cascade' into the direct activity cost pools. Reciprocal services (between support activities) was discussed by the group but it was decided not to build them into the ABC model on grounds of practicality (the software adopted did not allow for this facility).

Staff Sensitivities

ABC systems require some level of scrutiny of how staff spend their time and this is potentially a highly sensitive issue for employees and trade unions. Within the SNBTS, budgetary constraint and a history of staff reductions ensured that this was a particularly relevant issue. The project group therefore took time to explain their work and objectives to local management teams and employee representatives and emphasize that the purpose of the exercise was a constructive one to guide the more efficient use of resource rather than simply to eliminate them. Reliance on existing job descriptions as an important data source was also used as a means of alleviating employee fears about the ABC system.

The joint cost problem

Some of the activity at the Regional Transfusion Centres and most of the work at the PFC involved the fractionation of whole blood into components which represented individual product outputs. Thus many of the SNBTS costs were classic joint costs. Figure 3.2 provides a simplified overview of the situation (in reality there are more than two dozen products made from the plasma sent to the PFC).

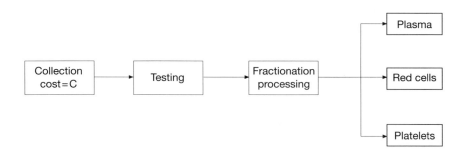

Figure 3.2 Joint costs at SNBTS

While many of the costs of collecting and processing whole blood could be analysed on an activity basis, their attachment to blood component products required the application of some means of addressing the joint cost issue. A number of alternatives for this are open to the SNBTS.

Method 1 – Physical attributes

A physical attribute of the joint products is measured and used as a common denominator for sharing the joint cost among the products. Possibilities would commonly be measures of weight or volume (depending on the nature of the products). However SNBTS outputs include powders, creams and liquids. Currently a variation on this approach is used by the SNBTS to obtain costs for stock valuation. They use a measure of the whole blood input requirement for each product output as the basis for joint cost apportionment. Thus if the output of plasma in a period would normally require 1,000 donations of whole blood, while that of red cells required 250 donations and platelets 750 donations the joint costs would be split 50%, 12.5%, 37.5% respectively.

Method 2 – Sales values

Applying unit sales prices to final product output volumes gives total sales revenue figures which can provide another basis for sharing the joint costs among the products. The results of this method would, in the case of SNBTS, be dependent on the unit selling prices used to determine the product sales revenues. As most SNBTS products are produced for use in the National Health Service, no prices are required. Consequently, to effect this approach sales prices would have to be obtained from the international markets which exist for the products in question. However, SNBTS products in some cases are not exactly comparable with those found in the international markets; they can be of different purity and potency. Market prices are also highly volatile and can exhibit large changes over short periods of time. This can occur in response to shortages of supply (e.g. HIV/AIDS problem adversely affecting donor attendance) or increases in demand (e.g. large-scale catastrophes).

Method 3 – Alternative cost

This method uses the lowest cost alternative means (as opposed to joint processing) of obtaining each joint product as the basis for the joint cost allocation. Alternative bases for acquiring the products do however involve the hypothetical costing of other possible ways of manufacturing or, indeed purchasing them.

Method 4 – Clinical value

This method attributes the joint costs to the blood products on the basis of their clinical values. These are based on the clinical uses which are endowed in the product by each stage of processing. Thus in the above case (see Figure 3.2) the following would hold:

	See Note 1	See Note 2	See Note 3
Red cells	Total cost of collection	+ 1/3 Cost of testing	+Proportion of cost of fractionation based on clinical value
Plasma		+ 1/3 Cost of testing	+Proportion of cost of fractionation based on clinical value
Platelets		+ 1/3 Cost of testing	+Proportion of cost of fractionation based on clinical value

Note 1. After collection the product in a whole blood condition could only ever have clinical value as a red cell product used to restore oxygen carrying capacity and therefore all of the collection costs are attributed to this single product.

Note 2. All products obtain the same clinical value from testing and grouping and therefore carry equal shares of the cost.

Note 3. Processing into different components improves red cell specification by removing impurities. The positive red cell attributes are volume reduction and platelet removal. These have the benefits of reducing the clinical risks of use which would exist if whole blood were used. Plasma simultaneously emerges and is enhanced by being rendered in a form from which other products (e.g. factor VIII for haemophiliacs) can subsequently be more easily extracted. Finally platelets are provided in a more appropriate volume for use and storage and in a form which enables clinical use to be much more effectively made of them. Thus all three products are clinically enhanced by fractionation and should bear a proportion of its cost. The relative clinical value added by fractionation would be estimated by experts for each product as a percentage such that the clinical values of the three products added to 100%.

Postscript on the current situation

At the time of case completion in February 1999 the ABC system is not yet operational as the timing of the SNBTS's original implementation plan was delayed by the diversion of key staff due to the need to conduct a general strategic review. However, all of the data necessary to construct the system has been collected at three of the five regional centres and much of the basic structure of the initial ABC model has been agreed in principle. The process of implementing ABC has also already provided a number of positive insights which auger well for the potential contribution of ABC to the SNBTS operations.

- The activity framework has proved to be highly credible to non-accounting staff in feedback sessions and this has enhanced the accountant/non-accountant relationships in the SNBTS.
- In part this credibility enhancement has been fostered by the educational efforts of the implementation team and has been supported by the demonstration of ABC systems within leading commercial organizations. For example, the retail and distribution activity analysis for a leading supermarket's perishable products was used as an influential example of the potential of activity-based costing to the SNBTS.
- The ABC framework has already been used with success in two specific exercises. First, the cost of donor deferral (donors whose donation has ultimately to be refused on clinical grounds) has been estimated by costing activities identified up to the point of rejection. Second, the implications of changes to existing activities caused by procedural adjustments to cope with the growing CJD problem (see endnote 1) have been costed on a one-off basis by using the ABC framework.
- The activity analysis profiles so far obtained demonstrate clearly the range and depth of technical, clinical and administrative experience and knowledge possessed by SNBTS staff. Indeed it has provided a basis for recognizing staff work contributions and the potential intellectual capital and property rights of the service. In this respect it complements existing accounting procedures and provides what the Director of Finance describes as a welcome and beneficial 'accounting free dimension' to this new development.

These initial benefits have instilled a confidence among the project team that the new ABC system will prove to be extremely beneficial. Moreover there is now some indication from government that the SNBTS current level core funding will be 'ring fenced' in future. Thus the cost savings identified from the new system will be largely available to benefit the SNBTS directly.

Endnote

[1] BSE is the 'mad' cow disease which caused a ban on the export of British beef to European Union countries. Contaminated meat is linked with a fatal illness in humans called new varient CJD. There is no test available to identify carriers of new varient CJD and it is suspected it may be transmittable between humans through blood transfusions.

STUDENT ASSIGNMENTS

1. Discuss the possible benefits which the SNBTS may derive from the development of a new costing system. What are the key characteristics of the new costing system upon which the realization of these benefits is dependent?

2. What do you consider to be the main (a) technical accounting and (b) behavioural and organizational problems involved in implementing an ABC system in the SNBTS? Discuss how you might attempt to resolve them.

3. Draft an outline plan of the steps involved in implementing an ABC system as guidance for the ABC Project Group.

4. Produce your definitions of the terms 'activity' and 'cost driver' in a form which you feel would be clearly understood by the non-accountant members of the SNBTS Project Group.

5. How does a joint costing situation impinge upon ABC?

6. Consider the alternative bases for joint cost allocation. From the perspective of the SNBTS management answer the following questions.
    (a) Which basis would you advocate using if stock valuation was the only reason for obtaining product costs (give a justification)?
    (b) Which basis would you advocate using as a basis for cost recovery charges to the private sector (give a justification)?
    (c) Which basis would you advocate using if SNBTS product costs were used as one means of assessing SNBTS performance (give a justification)?

Appendix   Cost cascade

MEMORANDUM

TO: **ABC Project Team**
FROM: **SNBTS Management Accountant**

ABC Cascade

The cascade is trying to achieve a fair allocation of support costs whose activities cannot easily be linked to organizational outputs – in SNBTS, blood products, lab/clinical services etc.

These overhead/support costs are incurred to enable the departments to run efficiently. For example, Finance arranges the payment of invoices, which ensures that suppliers are being paid. It would, therefore, be fair to allocate the Finance costs of Processing Invoices to those departments using the service.

Whichever way a cascade is drawn up it will be possible to argue it is wrong. In the example proposed, Computing are seen to support all departments, including Personnel (because Personnel use PCs to complete their work). It would be equally fair that Personnel should be seen to support Computing because without Personnel, Computing staff would not have been recruited and their personnel records would not be updated.

It is not possible however, to say Computing support Personnel and Personnel supports all departments (including Computing), because you would then end up in a loop of cost allocations (example below). It is necessary to decide how the cascade is created to prevent his happening.

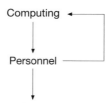

When the department at the top of the hierarchy has been allocated completely, costs may not be allocated into it again by another support function, and so on. It is almost inevitable that there will be a situation where you need to 'bite the bullet' and decide which support department does not receive an allocation from another.

Ultimately, all support costs will be either allocated to activities or to operational departments which will be at the bottom of the cascade. It is likely that these departments will pick up most of the 'support costs'.

Administration cascade hierarchy

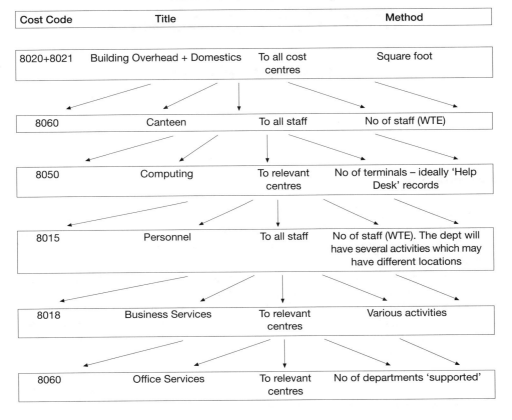

CASE FOUR

—

DIAMED problem

Thomas M. Fischer

Introduction

DIAMED Inc. is a company located in Stuttgart, Germany. The principal partners are the Kleinert family. Mr Kleinert is company founder and managing partner in one. The company consists of two divisions, namely computer tomography (CT) and magnetic resonance (MR) technology. In terms of turnover and number of employees, both divisions are of more or less the same size. In 1987, with 1,200 employees, total turnover was about 600 million Euro.

DIAMED has been in the MR market for five years. Its products to date have utilized 1 tesla-magnets and 1.5 tesla-magnets. The plant in Stuttgart has the capacity to establish two system lines: extension is not possible. Production relocation is not considered to be useful within the company's medium-term planning.

Target costing project COSTO at DIAMED

Currently, the MR business faces problems resulting from Japanese competitive pressure. Given their enormous cost advantage and DIAMED's current cost structure, Japanese pricing of diagnostic appliances could not be matched. As a way out of this situation, there are three possible methods to deal with diagnostic appliances:

1. sell the diagnostic appliances business;
2. shut the diagnostic appliances business down;
3. instigate a turnaround through strict cost management to create a competitive cost structure for new products.

Choosing the third possibility, DIAMED launched a target costing project called COSTO, which aimed at the successful competitive development of a magnet resonance unit (MRU) with the help of target costing and life cycle costing. This concept started with the specific determination of customer requirements to optimize the price/value ratio of the product.

Introduction of magnet resonance technology (MR)

Production of magnet resonance units (MRU) started in the early 1980s. From a radiologist's point of view, magnet resonance technology competes with X-ray technology and computer tomography (CT).

X-ray technology depends on the different X-ray absorption coefficients of bone, muscle and organs. In conventional X-ray images, one looks at a picture of the density of the tissue between the emitter (X-ray tube) and the detector (such as photographic film). One therefore sees all the tissue in the body along the path of the X-ray. Computer tomography is an imaging modality that creates axial images or 'slices' of the human body. To create this image the density of every point is computed from the information gathered from many different X-ray paths.

In contrast to X-ray technologies, *magnet resonance technology* (MR) depends on variations in proton relaxation between tissues in different anatomic structures. Proton resonance is induced by a brief high-frequency impulse serving to rotate the nuclear magnetization so that it is no longer parallel to the magnetic field. Relaxation back into the parallel position causes a resonance signal that is measured with high-frequency antennas. The result is transformed into an image through a mathematical 'Fourier' transform commonly used for digital signal processing.

A significant advantage of magnet resonance technology is the fact that the patient is not exposed to X-rays, which are known to have detrimental side effects. On the other hand, there are some clinical disadvantages of this method when compared to computer tomography; e.g. proton-deficient solid tissue such as bones cannot be well reproduced. Magnet resonance units are being built with magnets which have field strengths between 0.2 and 2.0 tesla, which indicates the magnet capacity (Figure 4.1).

The MR market is characterized by a supply oligopoly of less than ten competitors. Magnet resonance technology (MR) is an industrial plant business; i.e. assembly/installation as much as service/maintenance and product utility are of major importance for both client and supplier. The market cycle is estimated to be about five years. The company planned to enter the market with its new product by mid-1991.

Most reasonably, the market may be segmented according to 'profitability' and 'equipment/function' resulting in three market segments which can be characterized as follows:

1. *Appropriation/performance segment* (M1). Profit considerations are not important. The need is for a unit with the highest performance for research purposes. Unit and performance costs will be paid by public funds or by the hospital institution and thus will be of only minor importance when the system decision is made.
   Examples: teaching hospitals, research institutions.

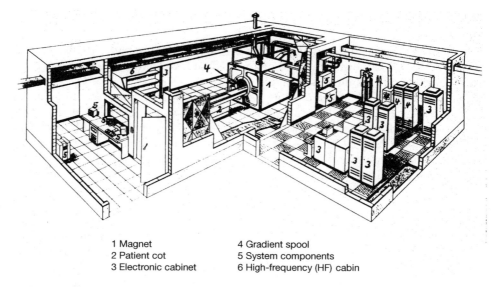

1 Magnet
2 Patient cot
3 Electronic cabinet

4 Gradient spool
5 System components
6 High-frequency (HF) cabin

Figure 4.1 Illustration of a MRU

2. *Efficiency segment with sufficient patient numbers* (M2). Important considerations are system costs per person and system capability, so as to achieve a sufficient level of patient throughput. In order to calculate profitability, system costs are compared to MR insurance reimbursements. The results will show the breakeven point for the number of patients per day.
   Examples: large hospitals, large private group practices.
3. *Low-price/cost-oriented segment* (M3). Absolute system and follow-up costs dominate. Sufficient numbers of patients for profitable management as in M2 is not possible. The breakeven point must be achieved at a small patient number.
   Examples: single practices, small hospitals.

Within the regions mentioned above these three market segments vary with respect to their magnetic field strength (see Tables 4.1 and 4.2). This is a result of the different patient numbers per day which are necessary to achieve a particular breakeven point:[1]

USA:	6–7	patients/day
Japan:	18	patients/day
Europe:	8–9	patients/day
RoW:	8–9	patients/day

The weighted average for all regions amounts to 25% market share for segment M1 and 24% for segment M2. For both segments, DIAMED ranks second after General Electric (Table 4.3). Segment M3 has not been covered so far.

Table 4.1 Product segments per region (current total market share of the different product segments (M1–M3) depending on the field strengths of the magnet and on the region)

	M1			M2			M3		
	Europe RoW*	Japan	USA	Europe RoW	Japan	USA	Europe RoW	Japan	USA
1.5 tesla	80%	95%	50%	20%	5%	50%	0%	0%	0%
1.0 tesla	0%	5%	0%	100%	95%	100%	0%	0%	0%
0.5 tesla	0%	0%	0%	90%	100%	85%	10%	0%	15%
< 0.5 tesla	0%	0%	0%	0%	5%	0%	100%	95%	100%

* RoW means 'Rest of World'

Table 4.2 Split according to MR market segments (M1–M3): (expected total sales units for the different product segments and regions)

M1	1991	1992	1993	1994	1995
USA	58	52	46	44	41
Japan	51	47	46	45	42
Europe	11	15	13	13	13
RoW	9	8	10	12	15
sum	129	122	115	114	111
M2					
USA	147	160	159	157	154
Japan	127	127	129	125	118
Europe	97	111	106	103	102
RoW	47	60	65	67	71
sum	418	458	459	452	445
M3					
USA	85	65	65	58	57
Japan	29	28	28	32	40
Europe	17	21	22	29	31
RoW	22	26	31	35	36
sum	153	140	146	154	164
sum total	700	720	720	720	720

Table 4.3 DIAMED market shares in 1987

	USA	Japan	Europe	RoW
Segment M1	19%	30%	32%	43%
Segment M2	25%	13%	30%	25%

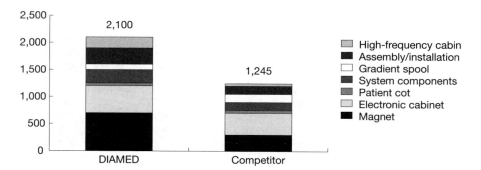

Figure 4.2 Current cost situation in comparison to the strongest competitor (in € thousands incl. assembly/installation)

The most important competitors are:

- General Electric (USA);
- Philips (NL);
- Toshiba (Japan).

Reasons for DIAMED's cost disadvantages (see Figure 4.2) are:

- product features that customers are not willing to pay for ('over-engineering');
- high cost of design of customer-relevant product features;
- lower labour costs of competitors;
- higher process efficiencies of competitors.

New product positioning

Segment M1 remains better served by a system with 1.5 tesla magnets. This brings up the question whether or not to enter into segment M2 or M3. Opportunities to establish oneself in both segments with two different products do not exist, since Stuttgart possesses the capacity for two system lines only. The segment which is not being directly dealt with might be handled as a joint venture with another company.

Segment M2 has been identified as the more profitable market segment for DIAMED. Here, as can be seen above, the market volume is larger than for segment M3, and the Japanese competition with their enormous cost advantage is lower.

Furthermore, market segment M3 shows stronger resistance to computer tomography which is based on X-ray-technology and shows a similar price/benefit relation.

With respect to field strength, a decision needs to be made for 0.5 or 1 tesla. The latter (1 tesla) was considered as the more reasonable decision for the following reasons:

1. stronger differentiation in diagnostic performance relative to segment M3, where mainly 0.5 tesla-magnets are offered;
2. continuity in DIAMED development and distribution strategy, since another 1 tesla-magnet MRU will be developed; and
3. better system capability and efficiency and thus greater chances of future clinical use.

The above-mentioned arguments for a positioning of the new product within segment M2 need to be reconsidered because of the competitive situation within this segment. Therefore efficiency is the most critical issue here. The market performance of the product has to be evaluated relative to its sales price as well as to its acquisition and maintenance costs. This is where DIAMED's main problems arise.

DIAMED's products possess high perceived customer value, but they are overpriced. To resolve this, a market or technology leadership strategy needs to be pursued. In doing so the existing technological capabilities need to be realigned to market conditions. Process efficiency must be improved and overengineering has to be reduced (see Figure 4.3).

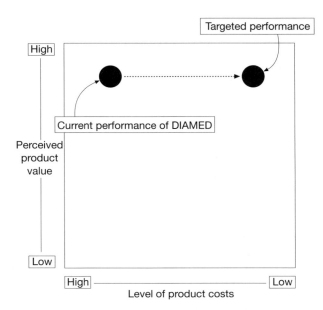

Figure 4.3 Concept of outpacing strategy to illustrate DIAMED's current and future competitive position

Sender: Schuster   **Stuttgart, April 4th, 1988**

The following criteria have been determined as relevant product functions/ attributes for 1 tesla-MRU's. The weighting of the specific user preferences was done by conjoint analysis. Conjoint analysis is a statistical technique using data from interviews in which the respondents are confronted with a combination of various attributes. The survey was carried out by a market research institute. The sample of respondents consisted of 75 medical doctors working in hospitals, large private group practices and single practices located in different regions (North America, West Europe, Japan).

The procedure consists of the following steps:

1. determine the relevant product attributes (functions and price),
2. determine the attribute levels,
3. design the questionnaire,
4. calculate the preference functions,
5. calibrate the demand function.

attributes	attribute levels	part worths
photo quality	(high, medium, sufficient)	(0.9; 0.5; 0.0)
patient throughput	(15/day; 12/day; 6/day)	(0.8; 0.6; 0.0)
reliability	(2,000; 1,800; 1,200 h MTBF)	(0.9; 0.6; 0.0)
space requirements	(40; 50; 60 m²)	(0.5; 0.3; 0.0)
user friendliness	(easy, medium, sufficient)	(0.5; 0.3; 0.0)
assembly time	(10; 14; 20 days)	(0.2; 0.15; 0.0)
3D acquisition	(yes; no)	(0.15; 0.0)
price (€ thousands)	(1,800.-; 2,000.-; 2,250.-)	(0.9; 0.5; 0.0)

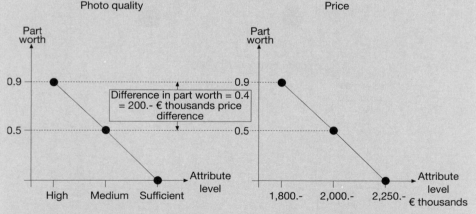

Figure 4.4 Financial impact of changes in attribute levels for one respondent (example)
A switch from medium to high photo quality results in a difference in part worth of 0.4 (left part of this picture). The difference can be transformed into monetary terms by the price/utility function (right part of the picture).

From the sample of attributes three combinations were developed which represent the whole spectrum of realizable product variants: model 1 constituting the 'high-end' type, model 3 the 'low-end' and model 2 the intermediate product design.

Rough cost estimations lead to the following results: Production costs (incl. assembly/installation) of model 2 are about 350,000 Euro less expensive than model 1. Production costs of model 3 are 700,000 Euro less expensive than those of model 2 (see Tables 4.4–4.6).

Table 4.4 Model I (high end)

Attribute	Attribute level	Part worth	Effect on costs
space requirement	40 m^2	0.50	++
patient throughput	15/day	0.80	++
photo quality	high	0.90	+
3D-acquisition	yes	0.15	+
assembly time	10 days	0.20	+
reliability	1800 h MTBF	0.60	+
user friendliness	medium	0.30	Ω
utility of product functions		3.45	++
price (€ thousands)	2,250	0.00	
total utility		3.45	++

Table 4.5 Model 2 (intermediate)

Attribute	Attribute level	Part worth	Effect on costs
space requirement	50 m^2	0.30	+
patient throughput	12/day	0.60	+
photo quality	high	0.90	+
3D-acquisition	yes	0.15	+
assembly time	14 days	0.15	Ω
reliability	1800 h MTBF	0.60	+
user friendliness	medium	0.30	Ω
utility of product functions		3.00	+
price (€ thousands)	2,000	0.50	
total utility		3.50	+

Table 4.6 Model 3 (low end)

Attribute	Attribute level	Part worth	Effect on costs
space requirement	60 m²	0.00	ọ
patient throughput	6/day	0.30	ọ
photo quality	medium	0.50	ọ
3D-acquisition	no	0.00	ọ
assembly time	20 days	0.00	ọ
reliability	1200 h MTBF	0.00	ọ
user friendliness	medium	0.30	ọ
utility of product functions		1.10	ọ
price (€ thousands)	1,800	0.90	
total utility		2.00	ọ

Table 4.7 Summary of the different models

attribute	model 1		model 2		model 3	
	part worth	effect on costs	part worth	effect on costs	part worth	effect on costs
space requirements	0.50	++	0.30	+	0.00	ọ
patient throughput	0.80	++	0.60	+	0.30	ọ
photo quality	0.90	+	0.90	+	0.50	ọ
3D-acquisition	0.15	+	0.15	+	0.00	ọ
assembly time	0.20	+	0.15	o	0.00	ọ
reliability	0.60	+	0.60	+	0.00	ọ
user friendliness	0.30	o	0.30	o	0.30	ọ
utility of product functions (u)	3.45		3.00		1.10	
price	0.00		0.50		0.90	
total utility	3.45	++	3.50	+	2.00	ọ

++: large cost increase; +: medium cost increase; ọ: no cost increase relative to minimal standard

Evaluation of changes in attributes/utility

price $(u) = 2{,}250 - 500u$; u: utility of product functions; price in € thousands

In total, the three selected models show the following relative part worth for their functional attributes (note: except utility of price):

attributes		relative part worth	
	model 1	model 2	model 3
photo quality	26%	30%	46%
patient throughput	23%	20%	27%
reliability	17%	20%	0%
space requirements	15%	10%	0%
user friendliness	9%	10%	27%
assembly time	6%	5%	0%
3D-acquisition	4%	5%	0%
	100%	100%	100%
total utility of product functions	(3.45)	(3.00)	(1.10)

Calibration of the demand function

For the planned start of market penetration of the new product called *COSTO* in 1991 we have developed a demand function of 1 tesla MRU's in our company:

$$x(p) = 80 - 20p.$$

This results in the following combinations of corresponding unit prices and sales volumes:

price (in € million)	0	0.5	1	1.5	2	2.5	3	3.5	4
sales (units)	80	70	60	50	40	30	20	10	0

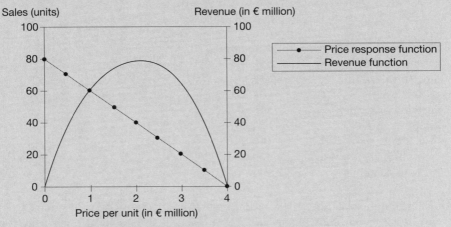

Figure 4.5 Revenue function and price response function

For purposes of profit optimization we always calculate the price/quantity combination maximizing the turnover.

Best regards,

Alfred A. Schuster

Sender: Ritter   **Stuttgart, April 6, 1988**

Dear Ms Frickmann,

due to a computer system crash, I did not succeed until yesterday in sending you all the required data. Still, I hope that the information will reach you in time.

We expect for this project a return on sales of 8%.

Our usual discount rate for investment appraisals is 12%.

Our R&D-costs will be budgeted at a rate of 9.50% of sales revenues. Costs for sales/marketing may be realistically estimated at 25% of sales revenues. Administration costs per project duration (1988–2000) are being calculated with an annual share of 6.25% of sales revenues. This forecast is a result of analyzing various projects during previous years.

Until market introduction, we expect the following cost structure within the total target costs: 95% are consumed by production costs, while assembly- and installation-costs come to 5%.

COSTO drifting costs (i.e. at current (1988) state of technology):

components	(€ thousands)
magnet	650.0
electronic cabinet	577.5
patient cot	57.4
system components	240.6
gradient spool	74.5
high-frequency cabin	150.0
assembly/installation	350.0
drifting costs	2,100.0

The component assembly/installation maintains its independence since COSTO is not being assembled in Stuttgart but at each customer location. As a consequence of productivity improvements, for all calculated cost numbers an annual 5% reduction within the market-cycle can be expected.

Sincerely,
sgd. Markus Ritter

Sender: Altendorf **Stuttgart, April 8, 1988**

Dear Ms Frickmann,

According to the customer requirements regarding the product functions, we have estimated degrees of importance for each particular component as to function fulfillment.
Example of interpretation:
The realization of the product function 'space requirement' is mainly influenced by two components, the magnet (share of 60%) and the high-frequency cabin (share of 40%).

Table 4.8 Components/functions matrix

function / component	space requirement abs.	rel.	patient throughput abs.	rel.	photo quality abs.	rel.	assembly time abs.	rel.	3D-acquisition abs.	rel.	reliability abs.	rel.	user friendliness abs.	rel.
magnet	60.00		65.00		70.00						20.00			
electronic cabinet			30.00		20.00				100.0		20.00		50.00	
patient cot											20.00		10.00	
system components					3.33						20.00		40.00	
gradient spool			5.00		6.67						20.00			
high-frequency cabin	40.00													
assembly/ installation							100.0							
utility of product function	100.0		100.0		100.0		100.0		100.0		100.0		100.0	

Should you have further questions, please contact me prior to April 10. At that time I will be leaving for a two-week vacation.

Sincerely,
sgd. G. Altendorf

Endnotes

[1] This data was gathered from health insurance companies.

```
┌─────────────────────────────────────────────────────────────────┐
│              ┌──────────────────────────────┐                     │
│              │    STUDENT ASSIGNMENTS        │                     │
│              └──────────────────────────────┘                     │
│                                                                   │
│   1.  Discuss the strategic problems emerging from the case of    │
│       DIAMED Inc.                                                 │
│   2.  Describe a method to optimize the product features in       │
│       order to fulfil the customer requirements. Which            │
│       combination of attributes should be recommended?            │
│   3.  Quantify the optimal pricing strategy for the selected      │
│       product variant for the year 1991 on the basis of the       │
│       price response function.                                    │
│   4.  Compute the allowable costs of the product.                 │
│   5.  Calculate the amount of the allowable costs per component.  │
│   6.  Determine the existing cost gap as of 1988 and discuss the  │
│       results.                                                    │
└─────────────────────────────────────────────────────────────────┘
```

Appendix

Stuttgart, July 30, 1991

> Memorandum:
> MR-market after COSTO introduction

Members: Ms Frickmann   (project leader)
              Ms Krause   (project assistant)
              Mr Kleinert   (management)
              Mr Busch   (management assistant)
              Mr Hochdorfer   (production)
              Mr Ritter   (accounting)
              Mr Schuster   (marketing/sales)
              Mr Altendorf   (R+D)

I Situation marketing (redefinition in 1991 compared to the estimation made in 1988)

(a) Market segments

The market segments as identified in 1988 have proved to be constant so that there is no need for redefinition. The composition of market segments in each individual region does not show profound changes either. The forecast of the market segments in relation to each other has barely been altered.

(b) Sales

Here we are looking at a positive development of units to be sold, which for the total MR-market is illustrated as follows:

	1991	1992	1993	1994	1995	1996	1997	1998
USA	497	494	499	500	507	525	535	542
Japan	355	360	375	390	403	417	425	431
Europe	214	262	275	280	294	304	310	314
RoW	134	169	181	220	246	254	260	263
sum	1,200	1,285	1,330	1,390	1,450	1,500	1,530	1,550

This positive development leads to an increase in the forecast COSTO sales as follows:

1991	1992	1993	1994	1995
70	210	220	180	150

(c) COSTO price

The price level achieved for 1991 confirms the 1988 forecast so that no adjustment is necessary.

(d) Market cycle/useful life

Here, too, the 1988 assumptions apply: a five-year market cycle and useful life continue to apply.

2 COSTO cost situation

Currently, in July 1991, the cost situation is as follows:

components	in € thousands
magnet	454.20
electronic cabinet	267.38
patient cot	48.39
system components	95.92
gradient spool	60.17
high-frequency cabin	43.60
assembly/installation	55.59
total costs	1,025.25

The original target cost-splitting did not need to be revised. Costs for R&D/administration/sales/marketing were as predicted in the 1988 forecast, i.e. they amounted to 40.75 % of total sales revenues.

3 Suggestion by Mr Altendorf

Mr Altendorf suggested developing a new software in order to be able to be supplied by a new producer of computer hardware. This would lead to a cost reduction for the 'electronic cabinet' of about 35,000 Euro per unit. He estimated all necessary expenses for software application at 12 million Euro. Completion of new software development can be expected by the end of 1991, so that the 1992 delivery could contain new hardware and software.

4 Further project pursuit

Ms Krause and Ms Frickmann are instructed to process our data in order to create a detailed documentation of the 'turnaround through cost management'.

Ms Krause and Ms Frickmann are furthermore requested to examine Mr Altendorf's suggestion by August 10, 1991 in order to clarify further proceedings.

5 COSTO illustration as of July 1991

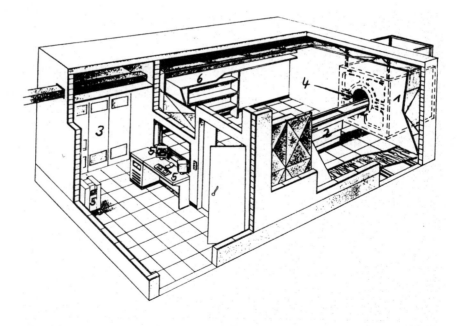

1 Magnet	4 Gradient spool
2 Patient cot	5 System components
3 Electronic cabinet	6 High-frequency cabin

Figure 4.6   MRU layout

Table 4.9 Data for value-added curves (in € thousands)

cycle time (weeks)	total product costs as of March 1988	total product costs as of July 1991	cycle time (weeks)	total product costs as of March 1988	total product costs as of July 1991
1	26,293	0,877	28	545,410	515,719
2	26,293	3,352	29	666,158	515,719/970,171
3	26,293	7,736	30	840,928	979,867
4	26,293	8,458	31	878,931	995,338
5	26,293	19,082	32	939,581	1,005,653
6	26,293	26,199	33	1,022,989	1,025,250
7	26,293	32,490	34	1,104,740	
8	26,293	38,524	35	1,104,740	
9	26,293	47,498	36	1,104,740	
10	26,403	72,716	37	1,104,740	
11	26,624	87,982	38	1,104,740	
12	26,624	109,333	39	1,104,740	
13	26,845	128,002	40	1,104,740	
14	27,176	143,164	41	1,104,740	
15	33,142	239,139	42	1,104,740/1,757,531	
16	34,026	263,842	43	1,790,673	
17	35,794	318,508	44	1,823,815	
18	37,119	350,638	45	1,890,099	
19	42,753	377,042	46	1,912,194	
20	49,603	443,364	47	1,934,289	
21	66,174	473,946	48	1,956,384	
22	85,175	515,719	49	2,000,573	
23	117,655	515,719	50	2,044,763	
24	148,256	515,719	51	2,055,810	
25	169,357	515,719	52	2,066,858	
26	279,499	515,719	53	2,077,905	
27	384,670	515,719	54	2,100,000	

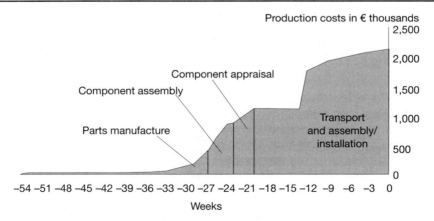

Figure 4.7 Value-added curve (as of March 1988)

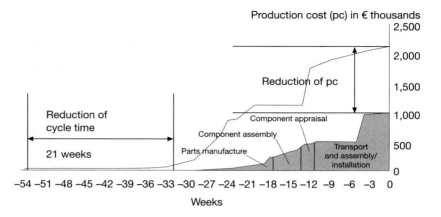

Figure 4.8 Value-added curve (as of July 1991)

Project situation as of July 1991

Table 4.10 Product costs and target costs index (tci)

component costs	€ thousands	cost share (%) (AC)	degree of importance (%)	tci
magnet	454.20	44.30	44.00	0.99
electronic cabinet	267.38	26.08	26.00	1.00
patient cot	48.39	4.72	5.00	1.06
system components	95.92	9.36	9.00	0.96
gradient spool	60.17	5.87	7.00	1.19
HF-cabin	43.60	4.25	4.00	0.94
assembly/installation	55.59	5.42	5.00	0.92
sum	1,025.25	100.00	100.00	

Table 4.11 'Altendorf' suggestion (in € millions)

	1991	1992	1993	1994	1995
cash outflow	−12.00				
cash inflow		7.35	7.32	5.69	4.50
cumulative, nominal	−12.00	−4.65	2.67	8.36	12.86
cumulative, discounted	−12.00	−5.44	0.39	4.44	7.30

At i = 12%, net present value equals Euro 7.3 million.

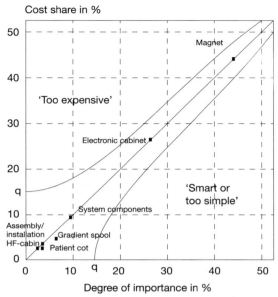

Figure 4.9 Target costs control chart

Table 4.12 Product costs and target costs index (tci) as of January 1992

component costs	€ thousands	realized cost reduction	cost share (%) (AC)	degree of importance (%)	tci
magnet	454.20	–	44.3	44.00	1.01
electronic cabinet	232.38	35	22.7	26.00	0.87
patient cot	48.39	–	4.7	5.00	0.94
system components	95.92	–	9.4	9.00	1.04
gradient spool	60.17	–	5.9	7.00	0.84
high-frequency cabin	43.60	–	4.2	4.00	1.05
assembly/installation	55.59	–	5.4	5.00	1.08
sum	990.25	35	96.6	100.00	

Life cycle costing

For the analysis of project related expenses and revenues, the following assumptions have been made:

(a) COSTO market cycle and useful life are estimated to be five years.
(b) The COSTO development cost, including new development and adjustment, are forecast as follows (in Euro million):

1988	1989	1990	1991	1992	1993	1994	1995	sum
7.10	23.02	19.20	11.00	6.60	2.20	1.60	0.50	71.22

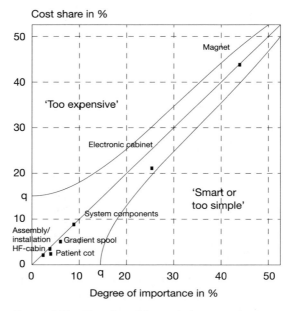

Figure 4.10   Target costs control chart

(c) All necessary production investments are forecast as follows (in million Euro):

1989	1990	1991	1992
2.2	2.86	4.4	4.84

(d) Estimated maintenance revenues/expenditures for 1991 (in thousand Euros):

maintenance revenues/year and unit:	130
− maintenance expenditure/year and unit:	100
maintenance result/year and unit:	30

Maintenance units per year from an installation basis are as follows:

year	1991	1992	1993	1994	1995	1996	1997	1998	1999	2000
units	20	80	170	270	370	400	340	250	150	50

(e) During the market cycle we expect an annual decrease in sales prices of 5%.

Table 4.13 Expenditures of the entire life cycle of COSTO (basis: 1988 forecast; in € thousands)

	1988	1989	1990	1991	1992	1993	1994	1995	1996	1997	1998	1999	2000	sum
cash inflow														
sales revenue				80,000	152,000	180,000	171,000	163,000						746,000
maintenance				2,600	9,880	19,945	30,094	39,178	42,354	36,001	26,471	15,883	5,294	227,700
cash outflow														
investments		2,200	2,860	4,400	4,840									14,300
production				36,060	71,145	85,021	80,627	76,453						349,306
assbly/install.				2,050	3,895	4,625	4,394	4,174						19,138
R&D	7,100	23,020	19,200	11,000	6,600	2,200	1,600	0,500						71,220
administration	1,000	1,000	1,000	7,500	7,500	7,500	7,500	7,500	1,000	1,000	1,000	1,000	1,000	45,500
marketing/sales				20,000	38,000	45,000	42,750	40,750						186,500
maintenance				2,000	7,060	15,343	23,149	30,137	32,580	27,693	20,363	12,218	4,073	175,156
total nominal	−8,100	−26,220	−23,060	−0,410	22,300	40,256	41,074	42,664	8,774	7,308	5,108	2,665	0,221	112,550
total discount.	−8,100	−23,411	−18,383	−0,313	14,172	22,842	20,809	19,299	3,544	2,635	1,645	0,766	0,057	35,562

At a discount rate of $i = 12\%$ (representing the WACCs), the net present value is € 35.56 million.
The internal rate of return equals 25.76%.

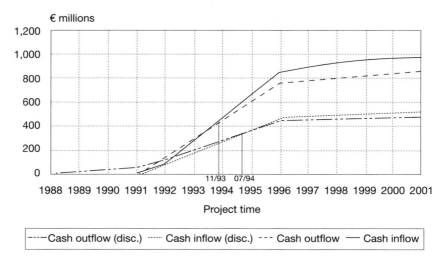

€ millions

- The non-discounted pay back equals 5.9 years
- The discounted pay back equals 6.6 years

Figure 4.11   Pay back (non-discounted, discounted)

ADDITIONAL STUDENT ASSIGNMENTS

Referring to the Appendix:

7.   Which measures were taken to reach the improved situation as of July 1991?

8.   Evaluate the quality improvement project suggested by Mr Altendorf!

9.   Is DIAMED able to realize a return from the project that would compensate their capital costs? How do you judge the project risk point?

—

The Royal Hotel*

Peter J. Clarke

Introduction

It is said that the difference between an Irish summer and Irish winter is that in summer the rain is warm! Recalling this, Pascal Burke smiled as the rain drops gathered on and lazily meandered down the window pane outside. It was mid-afternoon but the dark, heavy rain clouds outside necessitated the use of desk lamps for those working indoors. Pascal had not expected to be at his desk this Friday afternoon. Indeed, Pascal had not expected to be at any desk at this time! He should have been on holiday. He had just finished his MBA degree, as a full-time student and had graduated near the top of his class and had been voted by his fellow students as 'the person most likely to be famous'. While the award was made slightly tongue in cheek, Pascal, nevertheless, took it seriously. Pascal took most things seriously – especially work.

On leaving school, seven years earlier, he studied for and earned a degree in hotel management. His father owned a hotel in a provincial town in Ireland in which Pascal spent most of his school holidays working. He developed a keen interest in the hospitality industry and his decision to study hotel management was a logical progression from his schoolboy times. His studies were a combination of theory and practice and he acquired good experience both within Ireland and Europe. On graduation, he joined the Smith Group which was a family run hotel chain in Ireland. It was a private company, unlike Irish publicly quoted hotel chains of Jurys Hotel Group plc or Ryan Hotels plc. After three years he had progressed as far as he could and felt it was time to broaden his horizons. A full-time MBA offered the greatest challenge and opportunity. After one year of study his perspective had been considerably expanded and changed. He enjoyed his time studying in Dublin and looked forward, after a brief holiday, to a job search in the area of promoting the Irish tourism industry to the European market. However, it was not to be after the recent phone call from his mother. . .

* The permission from Horwath Bastow Charleton to quote from their *Ireland and Northern Ireland Hotel Industry Survey 1996* is gratefully acknowledged.

The scenario

A few days earlier his mother had phoned to convey the bad news of his father's heart attack. Thankfully it was not fatal and his father, even at sixty years of age, was expected to make a full recovery in due course. In the meanwhile, the hotel was effectively without a manager, so Pascal promised to return home immediately to try to sort things out. Before he left for home he phoned his girl friend to apologize for the cancellation of their holiday. It was a 'special offer' holiday so he didn't lose too much money – he didn't have much money to lose.

The Royal Hotel is situated in a provincial town on the east coast of Ireland, about an hour's drive from the capital city, Dublin. The town is situated in what the tourist brochures describe as 'the Garden of Ireland'. The hotel is an ideal location for exploring the Dublin/Wicklow mountains. The hotel is only a short distance from the sea although only a few of the town's hardy souls swam during summer months. Rather, walking along the sea front with the invigorating ocean air was the preferred option for many. The town had a population of about 5,000. This population, coupled with a significant hinterland and number of tourists, provided a reasonable trade for the other three hotels in the immediate vicinity. The Royal, like the three other hotels in the locality, is a fifty bedroom, two star hotel and can be described as being in the mid-price range. Each guest room is comfortable, includes a telephone and most have a private bathroom. With its traditional Irish pub – named the 'Lady Gray' after a rather notorious inhabitant of the town during the previous century – together with the restaurant and function room, the Royal Hotel offers the cost-conscious guest excellent value and good food. Unlike the other hotels, the Royal Hotel was situated in the town. A few years ago, most of its gardens were replaced by tarmac in order to provide ample parking space for its patrons. Thus, its physical scope for expansion was restricted and any proposed developments to the hotel were likely to encounter resistance from local residents and the planning authorities.

Some immediate problems and issues currently occupied Pascal's mind. Over the past few days he had introduced himself to employees as the acting General Manager of the hotel. He had also read or at least glanced at all the correspondence and reports on this father's desk. The one that interested him the most was the summarized management accounts for the year ended 31 October 1996 (Table 5.1). Although it was only mid-October, Pascal had asked the hotel accountant, Pat Doyle, to prepare them for the past year, including projections for the last weeks in October. Pat Doyle was not a qualified accountant and his role in the hotel was effectively that of bookkeeper. He operated, with a good degree of accuracy, debtors and creditors ledgers, the payroll function, and prepared bank reconciliation statements. He was also responsible for tax compliance of the hotel, mainly the operation of VAT and the deduction of payroll tax under the PAYE system.

At first, Pascal did not absorb the financial data since his mind wandered to the taxation side of the hotel and tourism industry. A VAT rate of 12.5% applies to accommodation as well as meals in hotels, whereas alcohol and soft drinks are rated at 21%. Such legislation places hotels at a relative disadvantage. For example, in Ireland, food is exempt from VAT if purchased, say, in a supermarket, while meals served in a hotel (or restaurant) are subject to VAT at 12.5%. Similarly, hotels must charge VAT on accommodation services, while bed and breakfast establishments and self-catering facilities normally avail of VAT exemptions which apply to small businesses. While the imposition of VAT on tourism activities is a positive boost for the Exchequer, it can also be argued that it is discriminatory since, for example, most other export industries are not required to charge VAT on their exported goods. Thus, in macro-economic terms, there is a conflict between maximizing tourism tax revenue (nearly 3 billion Euros per annum), or minimizing the cost of holidays in Ireland to encourage more visitors. Generally speaking, tourists have a wide choice of international destinations and cost is often an important factor in their decisions. Currently, around 22% of tourist spending is on accommodation, 10% on shopping, 32% on food and drink, 8% on entertainment and 12% on transport (Business and Finance, 1997). Furthermore, as a service industry, most tourism enterprises do not qualify for manufacturing tax status in Ireland. The Irish Hotels Federation believes that as tourism is an export sector there is a strong argument that it should be treated as favourably as export manufacturers and computer software developers who pay a reduced rate of 10% corporation tax.

The tourism industry is highly seasonal and very dependent on factors, such as, weather, the political situation and the economic climate, both in Ireland and internationally. For example, in 1995, the excellent summer weather, the peace process in Northern Ireland, and economic stability in Europe, created a tourism boom in Ireland. It is also rapidly becoming one of the world's largest industries accounting for some 5% of world national product and around 6% of the world's workforce. As a highly labour intensive industry, tourism growth has a significant employment impact. Almost 100,000 people are employed in the tourism industry in Ireland representing 7.5% of total employment. Perhaps, not surprisingly, payroll costs constitute the largest single expense item for most tourism businesses. Also, the industry is the most successful sector in the creation of new employment. Since 1987, tourism has created almost 30,000 new jobs in the Irish economy. This represents more than 50% of all new jobs created in Ireland during that period.

Generally speaking, the current worldwide trend away from sun destinations and towards cultural and activity-based holidays has proved to be very beneficial to the Irish tourism industry. Recognizing this, the National Development Plan 1994–1999, sets three key targets for the tourism sector. It aims to increase foreign tourist revenue by about 1.5 billion Euros, to increase visitor numbers to Ireland by 1.7 million and to create 35,000 new jobs in tourism. Indeed, the Irish Tourism Board (Bord Fáilte, 1994) hoped to attract 4.4 million visitors per annum to Ireland by 1999. The climate for development of the tourism industry in Ireland is ideal at present. For example, government funds are available under the National Development Plan and there have been recent beneficial changes in tax legislation. Tax incentives are particularly important to the hotel and tourism industries, because of low profit margins and volatile earnings. The most pervasive and

Table 5.1 Management accounts for year ended 31 October 1996 (€ thousands)

		Revenues				Expenses			
	Total	Rooms	Food	Bar	Functions	Laundry	Maint.	Admin.	Other costs
Turnover	1,554	400	551	541	62				
Less: Departmental costs									
Labour	355	85	127	133	10		29	96	
Goods for resale	680	–	326	354					
Other direct costs						100		39	
Departmental operating profit	519	315	98	54	52				
Other costs									
Advertising									3
Depreciation: Fixed assets									30
Insurance									40
Light and heat									31
Miscellaneous									30
Rates (property tax)									18
Repairs (materials)							101		
						100	130	135	152
Reapportionment: laundry	100	25	25	25	25	(100)			
maintenance	130	91	13	13	13		(130)		
administration	135	45	45	45	–			(135)	
other costs	152	38	38	38	38				(152)
Profit/(Loss)	2	116	(23)	(67)	(24)				
Profit/Sales (%)	0.13%	29%	(4%)	(12%)	(39%)				
Room occupancy	65%								

attractive tax incentives were introduced by the 1995 Finance Act. The government's objective for the scheme is 'to revitalise and update the tourist amenities and facilities in the resort areas designated'. The pilot scheme is exclusively targeting *seaside resorts* and the scheme has hence become known as the 'seaside resorts scheme', but the Finance Act does not refer to the scheme being specifically for seaside resorts. The incentives available for resort areas include (a) accelerated capital allowances, (b) double rent allowances and (c) relief for expenditure on certain rented residential accommodation. In addition, financial support is increasingly available from banks and financial institutions, and the industry itself is experiencing the effects of growing maturity and independence (Ernst and Young/AIB, 1995). However, Pascal realized that the hotel sector is as vulnerable to painful shakeout as any other industry. He remembered that in the US and UK during the 1980s there was a huge increase in the supply of hotel rooms followed by a dramatic contraction in demand. Declining tourism numbers were certainly a factor. In the UK alone, hundreds of hotels became insolvent in the early 1990s. Resale values of hotels collapsed.

Pascal's thoughts returned to the summarized management accounts prepared by Pat Doyle (Table 5.1). Pascal was slightly amused that what were referred to as the 'management accounts', were so simple but they made grim and surprising reading. The hotel reported a profit of only 2,000 Euros for the year. Clearly, the overall profitability of the hotel would have to be improved. In his father's temporary absence this would be Pascal's responsibility and he intended to upgrade the hotel to three star status. However, this aspiration would require significant expenditure to ensure that all guest rooms had a private bathroom with a bath and/or shower. *Table d'hôte* and *a la carte* menus would be introduced to provide a high standard of cuisine in relaxed surroundings. In general, the Royal Hotel would need to offer a range of services to satisfy the cost-conscious client. Closing down the hotel for the forthcoming winter season might allow some changes to be made. Another alternative would be to sell the hotel as a going concern. Either way the decision would require clear and unambiguous thinking and this was what Pascal was resolved to do. But, first he had to get a better overall picture of the situation.

The management accounts had been prepared to conform with the Uniform System of Accounts for Hotels. The Uniform System originated in the USA and was first published in 1926. It sets out recommendations on how particular transactions should be dealt with in accounting terms. Results of hotels are reported in a particular way, using standard formats, and are therefore comparable with results of other hotels. One of the main principles of the Uniform System is that results are reported by each department of the hotel, in line with the traditional organization structure which is found in most hotel operations. All expenses that are attributable to (and controllable by) a particular department are allocated against the revenue of that department to arrive at a departmental operating profit. The allocation of revenues and costs enables the General Manager to allocate responsibility for results to individual department heads who can directly influence, and be accountable for, the results of their department.

For management accounting purposes, the Royal Hotel operated four departments, i.e. Rooms, Food (Restaurant), Bar and a Function Room which generated rental income for weddings, social and other functions, including business meetings. Any revenues generated by such functions from food or bar sales were directly attributed to their respective departments. This function room, tastefully decorated, offers a much-needed facility for local business and commercial clients. It can accommodate up to 200 guests in total.

The various cost headings used in the management accounts were relatively straightforward and self-explanatory. The bulk of cost items (excluding the direct costs of the four revenue departments) were charged to one of four cost headings, i.e. Laundry (which was an externally purchased rather than in-house service), Maintenance, Administration and Other Costs. In turn, these costs were re-apportioned by Pat Doyle to the four revenue departments as follows:

Cost item	Basis of re-apportionment
Laundry	▪ Equally to all four departments.
Maintenance	▪ Space occupied by four departments i.e. $^7/_{10}$; $^1/_{10}$; $^1/_{10}$; $^1/_{10}$.
Administration	▪ Equally between three departments.
Other costs	▪ Equally between four departments.

The resulting net profit figures indicated that rooms were the only profitable section in the hotel. They returned a profit of 116,000 Euros after all expenses. To Pascal's surprise, the Restaurant, Bar and Function Room all reported losses for the year of 23,000 Euros, 67,000 Euros and 24,000 Euros respectively. It was easy for anyone to see that the hotel would find it difficult to remain profitable in future years unless costs could be controlled and unless overall turnover and occupancy levels could be significantly expanded.

What were the good features of the situation, Pascal asked himself? For one thing, the hotel had no borrowings and its long-term finance was represented entirely by shareholders' funds of some 750,000 Euros. The hotel was carried at a book-value of 600,000 Euros but its current market value was considerably in excess of this figure. In addition, the hotel was in excellent condition as evidenced by spending in excess of 100,000 Euros on maintenance during the previous year. His father, Pascal always remembered, would never compromise on quality – either in terms of physical appearance or level of service. As a result, the hotel enjoyed a reasonable reputation for good fare in the town. Staff morale was high and nobody could remember any formal industrial dispute of any consequence in the establishment in recent years.

The decision

In the gathering gloom of the evening, Pascal turned his thoughts towards two possible alternatives – to close the hotel down for the winter season or to keep it open and try to improve things. Either way, a decision needed to be made quickly.

In some ways, closing down the hotel for the six winter months (and re-opening in May) was the easy option and should be a significant cost saver. Closing down would result in significant cost savings on laundry, maintenance and administration costs. However, staff would have to be notified, so that they could make other arrangements, although he did not know employment law in this area. Also, he would have to notify patrons, who had made advance bookings, that the hotel was closing down during the winter months. Confirmed bookings (for rooms and various functions) for the forthcoming winter season currently ran at a level of 150,000 Euros. Such trade could easily be transferred to nearby establishments. On average, 25% commission would be received for such referrals. This, he had confirmed, on an informal basis, with James Dunne, the owner and general manager for the Bay Hotel, just two miles away. Pascal and James knew each other – a familiarity extending back to school days together. In current times they kept in touch with a round of golf on the nearby course every few months. Since the illness of Pascal's father, James had been in regular telephone contact offering to 'assist' in any way possible.

As an alternative, Pascal considered staying open for the winter months. From his student days he still retained some good contacts in the advertising industry. They should be able to advise him how to spend an additional 15,000 Euros – about 1% of annual turnover – promoting the hotel. He was confident that this would allow the hotel to achieve a 50% occupancy level during the winter months. Taking last year as a whole, the hotel operated at a 65% occupancy level. This would normally fall to 40% during the winter season (1 November–30 April). Anyone in the hotel industry knew that overall room occupancy was a critical factor in determining overall profitability. Pascal realized that very serious thought should be given to the various cost and revenue elements in the financial planning process. Apart from the additional advertising spend, he anticipated that some of his operating costs were 'fixed' in the sense that they would be incurred regardless of the level of activity (i.e. room occupancy) and covered a twelve month rather than a six month period. He anticipated that any possible increase in the level of fixed costs would be so marginal in the context of total costs incurred that they could be ignored for computation purposes in the initial draft of his calculations. He realized that his preliminary cost analysis would be a little unscientific and imperfect. He wanted to get a 'first draft' ready in a format that would be suitable for spreadsheet purposes. This would allow him to change his assumptions about the next six months and to, instantaneously, see the immediate financial impact. He was confident that he could get a fairly good picture of the various financial implications. The option to stay open would have to be financially viable.

Pascal realized that financial planning could not realistically take place in a vacuum. There were many external factors to be considered, such as, the existence and level of competition. Pascal had received the 1996 copy of the Irish Hotel Industry Survey (Horwath Bastow Charleton, 1996). This survey represents useful guidelines (rather than standards) for comparing the operating results of hotels in different classifications (e.g. mid-price, luxury, etc.), Region (e.g. Midlands & East) and size (number of rooms). Pascal was interested in other hotels in the Midlands & East Region and also those hotels in the mid-price range.

Reviewing the material, he was aware of the huge amount of comparative data on:

Departmental analysis per available room   (Table 5.2)
Market data   (Table 5.3)
Services and facilities offered   (Table 5.4)
Marketing information   (Table 5.5)

Table 5.2   Departmental analysis per available room: Region – Midlands and East

Room occupancy	65.5%	
Average size of property (rooms)	51	
Actual average daily room rate[1] per room occupied	€ 47.61	
Revenue per available room	€	%
Rooms[2]	10,603	23.7
Food and beverage	31,104	69.5
Minor departments[3]	1,591	3.6
Rentals and other income[4]	1,431	3.2
	44,729	100.0
Departmental expenses:		%
Rooms	2,715	
Food and beverage	23,759	
Other departmental expenses	1,106	
Total departmental expenses	27,580	61.7
Total departmental profit	17,149	38.3
Undistributed operating expenses:		
Administration	3,142	7.0
Marketing	852	1.9
Energy	1,279	2.8
Property operations & maintenance	2,443	5.5
	7,716	17.2%
Gross operating profit	9,433	21.1%
Fixed charges	5,302	11.9%
Profit before tax	4,131	9.2%

Source: Horwath Bastow Charleton,
      Ireland and Northern Ireland Hotel Industry Survey, 1996, Dublin.

(1) Total room sales divided by number of rooms *occupied*.
(2) Total revenue divided by number of rooms *available*.
(3) Revenues generated from health club, gift shop and news-stand when occupied by hotel.
(4) Income from rentals of space.

Table 5.3 Market data (Region – Midlands & East)

	Midlands & East (%)
Source of business	
Northern Ireland	8.5
Republic of Ireland	60.0
Foreign	31.5
Total	100.0
Composition of market	
Business travellers	31.5
Independent tourists	45.5
Tour groups	13.3
Conference participants	6.6
Other	3.1
Total	100.0
Percentage of advance reservations	80.9
Composition of advance reservations	
Direct enquiry	69.7
Own reservation system	11.5
Independent reservation system	2.1
Travel agents	3.7
Tour operators	8.5
Other	4.5
Total	100.0
Method of payment for hotel services	
Cash sales	56.3
Credit card sales	28.5
All other credit sales	15.2
Total	100.0
Credit card sales by card type (percentage of revenue)	
American Express	13.2
Diners Club	5.0
MasterCard	33.6
Visa	41.4
Other	6.8
Total	100.0

Source: Horwath Bastow Charleton,
Ireland and Northern Ireland Hotel Industry Survey, 1996, Dublin.

Table 5.4 Services and facilities offered (by classification)

	All hotels (%)	Mid-price (%)
Guest services offered		
Executive floors	22.1	23.7
Non-smoking rooms	51.5	52.3
Facilities for disabled	64.7	65.8
Health Club	47.1	39.5
Car rental services	51.5	47.7
Multilingual staff	29.4	18.4
Safety deposit box	66.2	57.9
Frequent guest programmes	51.5	47.7
Business centre	38.2	31.6
Fax for guest use	94.1	94.7
Teleconference facility	11.8	10.5
Audio visual equipment	72.1	65.8
Fire detectors	100.0	100.0
Sprinklers	16.2	18.4
Direct dial telephone	95.6	94.7
Guest room facility		
Electronic card key system	19.1	13.2
Hairdryer	94.1	89.5
Bathrobe	32.3	18.4
Shampoo	98.5	97.4
Conditioner	82.3	78.9
Iron	41.2	36.8
Newspaper	32.3	28.9
Coffee/tea maker	80.9	81.6
Mini bar	16.2	2.6
Cable television	97.1	97.4
VCR	7.3	5.3
Room fax facility	36.8	28.9
Radio/alarm clock	48.5	47.4
In-room safe	11.8	7.9
Turn-down service	50.0	26.3
Telephone	100.0	100.0
Technological information		
Computer reservation system	82.3	78.9
Yield management system	19.1	18.4
Point of sale equipment	55.9	55.3
Microcomputers for guest use	16.2	10.5

Source: Horwath Bastow Charleton,
Ireland and Northern Ireland Hotel Industry Survey (adapted), 1996, Dublin.

Table 5.5   Marketing information (Ireland – Midlands & East)

	Midlands & East (%)
Advertising utilization	
Print advertising	100.0
Radio and TV advertising	61.5
Outdoor advertising	61.5
Promotions	69.2
Merchandising	38.5
Direct Mail	61.5
Telemarketing	23.1
Offer weekend discounts	100.0
Average weekend discount	14.4
Percentage of rooms sold at a discount (all rooms)	23.0
Percentage of room nights by day of the week	
Sunday	7.3
Monday	13.7
Tuesday	15.2
Wednesday	15.8
Thursday	15.5
Friday	16.1
Saturday	16.4
Total	100.0

Source: Horwath Bastow Charleton,
Ireland and Northern Ireland Hotel Industry Survey, 1996, Dublin.

Burke appreciated that not all this information could be relevant to his decision but it was up to him to determine what was and what was not. He also realized that his observations and recommendations would have important implications for himself and certain individuals within the hotel. He stretched across his desk, cluttered with a vast amount of paper, for his calculator . . .

STUDENT ASSIGNMENTS

1. What are the critical success factors for the Royal Hotel? Specify why you have chosen them.

2. What are the financial implications of the two alternatives contemplated by Pascal Burke (i.e. staying open or closing down for the winter months)? Your assumptions should be clearly stated. What are the non-quantifiable factors that should be taken into consideration? Which alternative do you recommend? Be specific.

3. Based on the comparative information provided, undertake a benchmarking exercise for the Royal Hotel with other comparable hotels in the industry segment and suggest methods for immediate profit improvement. Project the financial consequences of your conclusions for the next six months, assuming that the hotel stays open.

References

Bord Fáilte (1994). *Developing Sustainable Tourism – Tourism Development Plan 1994–1999.* Dublin.

Business and Finance (1997). Are we building too many?, Belenos Publications, 1 May, Dublin.

Ernst and Young/AIB (1995). *Tourism 2000 – Growing Your Business.* Dublin.

Horwath Bastow Charleton, *Ireland and Northern Ireland Hotel Industry Survey 1996.* Dublin.

—

Cost control in product design and development: the Volvo Car Corporation experience

Urban Ask[1]

Introduction

The Volvo Car Corporation (VCC) is part of the Volvo Group that has 72,900 employees, production facilities in more than 20 countries, and worldwide sales. VCC is the largest single operation in the group, with about 28,000 employees.[2] Its operations include R&D, design, production, marketing and spare parts handling. Headquarters and the R&D function are based in Sweden, while production is carried out in Sweden, Belgium and the Netherlands. Cars are also assembled in Botswana, Indonesia, Thailand, Malaysia, and the Philippines.

Volvo cars are characterized by a strong identity, which is based on features grounded in the Volvo core values of safety, environment, and quality. VCC occupies a prominent position in the family car segment, but is trying to enhance its competitive position by expanding its customer base and introducing new models more frequently. The recent introductions of exclusive convertible, coupe and cross-country models are good examples of that. By these introductions VCC has entered the speciality car segment to meet the needs of customers before and after the family car segment.

The sales volume in 1997 was 386,440 (invoiced) cars and the sales value was SEK 96,453,000. VCC has the objective to reach an annual sales volume of 500,000 cars by the beginning of the 21st century. The market share today is only about 1% of the world market and the domestic market makes up about 15% of total sales, which means that VCC operates in an international environment where competition is fierce.

The product context

Historically, VCC has had a relatively limited product programme, with a small number of product models available in several variants. From the start of mass-production in 1944 the models have been characterized by long life cycle time with a large volume of sales that has been maintained through a number of model upgrades (normally on an annual basis). From the start of car production for 'common' people in 1944 to the early 1990s, one may argue that Volvo has only had seven models in production (Table 6.1).

Table 6.1 Car models produced, their lifetime and volume produced (to 30/6/98)

Model	Lifetime (year)	Number of cars produced
PV 444/544	1944–1965 (22)	440, 000
Amazon/120	1957–1970 (14)	667,323
140/160	1966–1975 (10)	1,351,119
340/360	1976–1991 (16)	1,139,119
740/760/780	1982–1992 (11)	1,239,222
240/260	1974–1993 (20)	2,862,415
440/460/480	1986–1996 (11)	703,257
900/90	1990–1998 (8.5)	656,644
850/70	1991–	1,027,773
40	1996–	285,024

Since 1990, we have witnessed the introductions of the 900 (1990), 850 (1991), 40 (1995), 70 (1996), 90 (1996) and 80 (1998) models. Thus, in seven years Volvo has introduced four completely new car models. They can be deemed as only four because the 70 model is an upgraded version of the 850 and the 90 is an upgraded version of the 900. However, the development activities of the 70 and 90 models were extensive, as they had a large number of new features (for example, in the commercials for the 70 model it was said that there were 1,800 new features in comparison to the 850 model). The introductions are part of a product development programme that includes the introduction of a new car model every year for the near future.

The product programme includes a compact model and a large model (or platforms) that appeal to different customer segments. Today, the product programme consists of the S (Sedan), V (Versatility), and C (Coupe/Convertible) product lines. The S and V product lines include the 40 and 70 models, while the 80 model is available as Sedan only and the C-line is available only for the 70 model.

The strategic context

In 1979 Renault and Volvo came to an agreement to co-operate on research and product development. This was the first attempt to co-operate with Renault. The second attempt started when ideas of an alliance between the companies formed in 1990. Doubts were raised from both shareholders and employees concerning whether or not the merger was positive from their respective perspectives. The doubts turned into negative views of the alliance plans, which finally had the effect that the alliance was never realized. Thus, in 1993 the alliance plan broke down, and the CEO and the board of the Volvo Group had to resign. The breaking of the alliance plan with Renault in 1993 was a turning point for Volvo. This was a traumatic event for the whole organization, and still seems to affect Volvo in many ways. Volvo had put great trust in the alliance and formulated their strategies accordingly, and they had also reorganized several organizational functions. For example, the reverse engineering and competitor surveillance functions in Volvo were minimized, since Renault had this competence. Several co-operative product development projects that had been going on for some years had to be terminated. Years of joint product development work were, more or less, wasted and their own product development portfolio could not fill the void. Obviously, it was not only necessary for VCC to change their strategy and to establish a new product development portfolio, but also to reinvest in important competencies that had been lost.

In the spring of 1994 the Volvo top management formulated eight strategic issues (presented in the annual report of 1994), which contained the Volvo strategy for the future. The basic strategic issue was that the company should move from being a conglomerate to being in the transportation industry. This was a step towards what, historically, had been the core operations of Volvo. The company should also strive to have full control over their core strategic businesses, and to have a strong balance sheet. A more customer-oriented business, with a high level of product development and cost efficiency were three other issues of high priority in the new strategy.

The new strategy also initiated activities in other areas. In late 1994 a new 'Volvo Company Philosophy' was established. It was centred on a customer orientation perspective, in which the goal was to work in the best interest of the customer. Customer satisfaction (which also became one important performance measure that was scrutinized by top management) should be fulfilled by the company-wide adoption of a holistic view of the business. A holistic view is seen as a view of operations that helps employees to understand how theirs and others work contributes to customer satisfaction. The company philosophy document reads:

> We create added value for each customer by focusing all our product development and operations on existing and perceived customer requirements, and satisfying those needs with maximum cost efficiency.

According to the philosophy, customer satisfaction should be fulfilled while still being highly cost efficient. Achieving cost efficiency requires a commitment to profitability at every level in the organization.

The increased need for product development gave rise to a new product strategy. At the beginning of the 1990s the company launched their platform strategy. Its cornerstones were product and process development functions that made possible the development of several car models based on the same basic design. By the use of a common platform and a number of integrated modules the same components would be used for a number of models (which is referred to as commonality). Also, their production would make use of the same production system. The strategy strove to combine differentiation (one platform brings several models into the market that are valued differently by customers) and low cost (by using the same components in different models costs can be reduced). It was with this platform strategy that VCC was aiming at broadening their product range to meet increasing specific customer needs and to target new customer groups. As already mentioned, the strategy included the intention to release a new product model every year in the foreseeable future. Thus, a situation of a stable product programme and long product life cycles belonged to the past. There was then a great challenge for the organization to cope with the increasing pace of product development.

The platform strategy not only induced a change in the product development function with regard to, for example, organization, process, time, and timing aspects, but would also increase the need for flexible production systems and cross-functional working methods. Also, it had increased the company's product development costs. However, based on the anticipated larger volumes of sales, the product development cost level was expected to remain stable at approximately 5% of annual sales.

The development of cost control in product development

In this section about 20 years of cost control development is described. The first section describes how the 'first' system of cost control in product development came into being, and what its basic focus was. The second section details the current cost control process and the third section describes how people at VCC today discuss the changes they see as necessary to match the current and future situation (and the strategy).

The project control system (PKS³)

In the early 1980s four management accounting representatives from Volvo made two visits to Renault. The purposes of the visits were to get ideas and to discuss how Volvo could benefit from the way Renault planned and controlled product costs in the early stages of the product development process. There were two major driving forces for Volvo to make the benchmarking visits to Renault. First, VCC had experienced considerable overspending in their latest product development project. This led to an internal audit of the work procedures used to control product development project costs and future product costs. The conclusion drawn was that there was an urgent need for a better control system for product development.

Some of the major flaws identified in the internal review were (from an internal VCC report written in 1980):

- little use of economic goals as a means of control;
- too diffuse economic goals that could not be attached to responsibilities;
- a build-up process (not market-driven) derived from goals and budgets;
- too long a lead time in the cost follow-up activities (cost reporting every sixth month and a very rough cost summary every third month);
- the economic consequences of technical solutions often came as very late surprises to project management and other cost-responsible persons;
- the long time taken for cost effects became visible to the project made it very difficult to change decisions already taken;
- the cost control work had very low priority, and the 'control' performed was based on summarized historical cost figures;
- low discipline in the updating of cost figures led to difficulties in the analyses of cost variances; and
- low level of detail and many deficiencies in the information on which cost figures were based.

Another reason for the benchmark visit was that Renault, in this sense, was considered a best practice company (remember that contacts already were established between the companies). Renault had been successfully developing its cost control competence, methods and routines since 1961 (according to a Volvo report from the visit). Thus, they had twenty years of experience of cost control in the early stages of product development.

Inspired by the visit and by a book on how Ford Motor Company (Europe) developed their Ford Fiesta ('Let's call it Fiesta'), a project group (mainly consisting of controllers) at Volvo started to develop a new system for planning and controlling project development costs and future product costs. The outcome, partly an adaptation of the Renault system, was the project cost control system (PKS). It was introduced in a manual in August 1981, and slightly revised in 1984.

The PKS manual

A PKS manual was developed to serve as a guideline for cost control activities during all stages of product development. It was to be used for new car development and for upgrading existing models. Several premises for cost control were established in the manual. For profitability calculations a product life cycle perspective should be adopted. PKS and its activities should be integrated with the work methods established for the product development process. It was mentioned that the implementation of PKS required a more proactive cost control than had been the case in earlier product development projects. The 'costs' that should be included in the early calculations (control activities) were the so-called 'standard factory cost', and the 'entry ticket costs' (i.e. investments, costs for special equipment, and product development costs) (Table 6.2).

Table 6.2 Standard factory cost and entry ticket costs

Product cost calculation	Variable	Fixed	Total
Volvo Group material costs			
+ External material/components costs			
= *Total cost of material*			
+ Logistic costs			
+ Manufacturing and assembly costs			
= *Standard factory cost*			
+ Vendor tools			
+ Purchase overhead			
+ Price difference material			
= *Production cost*			
+ External work			
+ Factory levelling			
+ Freight and insurance			
= *Reference cost*			
+ Warranty			
+ Development engineering costs			
+ Indirect variable man. and assembly costs			
+ Indirect variable material costs			
+ Indirect variable other costs			
+ Operating expense			
+ Start costs, new projects			
+ Currency difference			
+ Other VCC costs			
= *Full cost VCC*			

Entry ticket costs
Soft costs (man-hours for construction/development work)
+ Industrial start-up costs
+ Product specific investments (tooling costs)
+ Investments in production process/equipment
= Entry ticket costs

According to the manual, cost control should consist of the following three steps (see also Figures 6.1–6.4 for some points of departure from PKS):

1. Establishment of cost targets
   Cost targets should be worked out at the lowest possible level that is relevant for cost control and it should always be possible to relate to the responsibility distribution in the organization.
2. Commitment to the cost targets
   To gain acceptance from responsible persons was of importance, and this should be achieved through information sharing and dialogue.
3. Cost follow-up
   The main responsibility for cost follow-up should be at the same level as the cost targets were set.

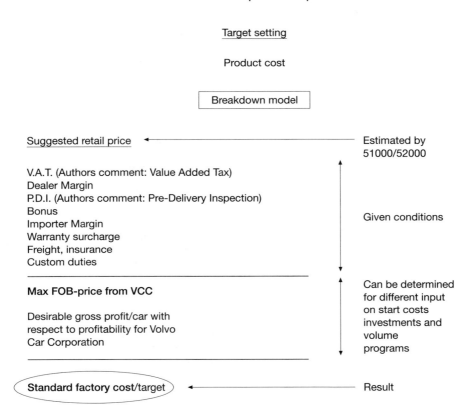

Figure 6.1 Target setting (breakdown model)
(Transcribed by the author from original documents written by hand in 1980. 5100/5200 refers to the organizational numbers for the Product Planning functions.)

The cost control activities were related to the two major stages of product development; the pre-study stage and the product project stage. In the pre-study stage, the major concern was the overall profitability of the new project and the level of detail with regard to costs was low. Several sensitivity analyses had to be conducted to include simulations of prices, volumes, product development costs, investment levels, product variations, product costs, and profitability. Results from simulations were used as inputs to a breakdown calculation for the vehicle in question. The starting point for that calculation was the assumed revenues and long-term profitability goals of VCC (i.e. return on the average capital employed). The calculation was performed 'backwards' as below:

+ Assumed revenues, based on assumed sales volume and sales price to customers and on assumed spare parts profit
− Required return on the average capital employed
− Investments and vehicle specific equipment costs

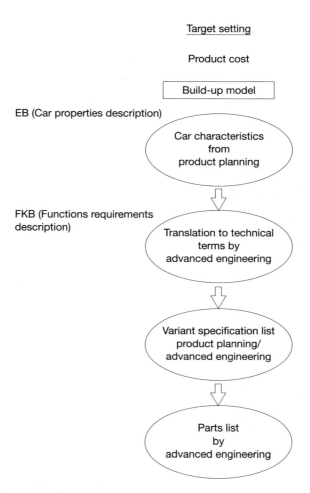

Figure 6.2 Target setting (build-up model)
(Transcribed by the author from original documents written by hand in 1980. 800627 refers to the date of the document, and 50440 to the financial planning function.)

- Product development costs during the whole life cycle
- Investments in stock
- Warranty costs
- Sales costs
= Cost target for standard factory cost

The calculation resulted in the cost target (allowed cost) for the standard factory cost. Cost targets were also set for car variants, i.e. for several specifications of the new car model that were to be the cost objects (in VCC they are called calculation variants). It was recommended that several calculations should be performed in

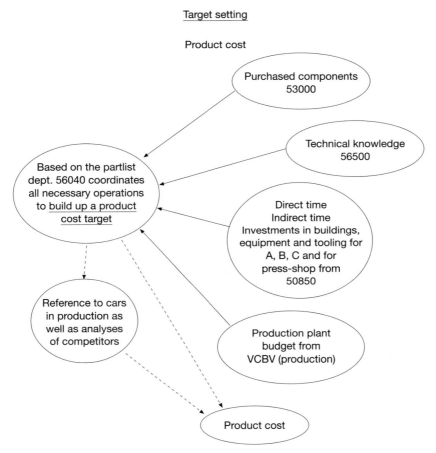

Figure 6.3 Target setting
(Transcribed by the author from original documents written by hand in 1980. 53000 refers to the purchasing function, 56500 and 56040 to product development functions, 50850 to a production staff function, 800627 to the date of the document, and 50440 to the financial planning function.)

order to find the most realistic alternative. The backward calculation was revised at the end of the pre-study stage.

At the end of the pre-study stage verification of the cost target (for standard factory cost) was to be done by a build-up calculation for the same car variants as in the backward calculation. Also, assumptions made concerning investments and product development costs should be verified. The verification calculation of the cost target was based on preliminary specifications of product properties and production methods. The calculations should also include the assumptions made regarding annual volumes of components, and carry-over details (i.e. components carried over from cars already in production). When the assumptions were

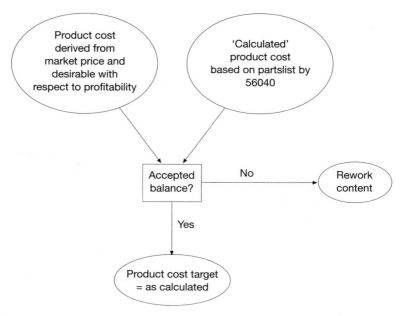

Figure 6.4 Target setting
(Transcribed by the author from original documents written by hand in 1980. 56040 refers to a product development function, 800627 to the date of the document, and 50440 to the financial planning function.)

clarified, reference cars and car systems were chosen as cost benchmarks (both internal and external benchmarks were used). An incremental cost analysis was then carried out for each proposed system in the new car, i.e. cost increases compared to the reference system were identified. Calculations of the manufacturing cost (the costs for manufacturing in the stamping, paint shop, and assembly factories) and the overhead cost rates for logistics and product development should also be done.

When the build-up calculation was finalized, the estimated standard factory cost, i.e. the result of the calculation, was compared with the revised breakdown calculated cost target. If there was a negative gap between the costs (i.e. build-up cost > breakdown cost) the top management group of VCC had to decide if a lower profitability target was allowed or if the product (project) content had to be changed. In the latter case the pre-study leader was assigned to find out how the cost targets could be met and had to present an action plan (including cost reduction potentials) to the group. He (at that time all project leaders were men) had an array of potential product- and process-related actions available that could lead to fulfilment of cost targets; for example, changing design, product properties (features and functions), materials, and suppliers, and improving engineering processes. When a balance or a positive gap between the costs was achieved, (i.e. build-up cost = or < breakdown cost), the product project received acceptance for start-up.

At the project stage cost targets were to be further broken down into targets for both organizational functions and car systems. Cost target follow-up should be performed on a regular basis. The development of standard factory costs and product development costs should be reported every quarter, while profitability reports were scheduled for twice a year (or when needed due to cost target deviations). However, less formal reports on the development of product development cost and product cost should be presented every fourth week.

The implementation of PKS

Several attempts were made to implement PKS and some of the ideas in PKS. The last (latest) trial was made during the development of the 850 model in 1986–1987. Entrepreneurial spirits with their heart and soul in management accounting carried out the PKS project and the related implementation work. These were mainly project controllers from the product development function and people from the central management accounting staff that were using the PKS manual for cost control. Central management accounting staff were focusing their efforts on the breakdown calculation in PKS, while the project controllers focused on the build-up calculation. They were trying to get acceptance and involvement from the engineering (and purchasing) managers for increased and improved cost control in the product development function. In particular, controllers tried to get engineers to accept and commit themselves to cost targets through information sharing and dialogue (i.e. step number 2 in the PKS manual, as described above).

The ideas of PKS became accepted among most fellow management accountants and controllers, but were not accepted by engineering professionals engaged in product development activities. Thus, the implementation attempts were not very successful, even though management support was available for tests of PKS ideas in action. This was mainly due to the strong resistance from the engineering profession to commit themselves to cost targets. The mentioning of cost targets created a lot of frustration and they were seen as major obstacles to innovative product development work (which was seen as the major aim by the engineering professionals). At meetings, where the ideas of PKS were either described or tested in action, engineers loudly expressed their frustration by claiming that the use of cost targets was merely an attempt to strengthen the accounting regime in the company.

The tough resistance from the engineering functions to tighter cost control had the effect that the entrepreneurial spirit faded away after far too many setbacks to implementation efforts. To a large extent, PKS became no more than a paper tiger. In an interview with one of the 'founders' of the PKS manual the following explanations for the implementation failure were presented:

- VCC was at the time doing financially well, which made cost control a low priority area for the organization as such.
- The engineering profession had strong influence over product development activities, and the engineers were committed to targets such as high quality and safety which they perceived as incompatible with low costs (potentially expressed in the cost targets that they had to commit to).
- PKS was built upon cross-functional working methods, but the organization was not mature enough to work across functions (and/or across professional borders).
- The organization had too little experience in starting their cost control activities from a market orientation and from customer values. This led to poor input data on market and customer value dimensions in the implementation try-outs of the PKS system.
- The project group assumed that Volvo already had resources and competencies for the proposed cost control approach, but suitable people where scattered around the organization. The starting point, from their perspective, was to re-organize the cost control function. However, at that point in time they did not find support for a reorganization. It turned out that there was a lack of competent persons that could participate in the implementation activities (i.e. competence was available, but it was employed in other management accounting activities than cost control *á la* PKS).

Despite the problems with the implementation of PKS at the beginning of the 1980s, most of the basic premises formulated in the PKS manual have, over the years, received some acceptance and are today spread throughout the organization. However, the origins of cost control ideas or activities are often not referred to as stemming from the PKS manual.

The current system

In 1991, a major organizational change took place in the development function. At that time the cost engineering function (see description below) was established. During a two-year period the cost engineering function had to consolidate the existing competence of cost control in the early stages of product development. The current manager of cost engineering says that without the work done in PKS it would have been much more difficult to establish the current system and its processes. Thus, the current system is partly an updated reflection of PKS.

Product development activities and related cost control activities are carried out in the following stages: (1) the concept development; (2) the pre-study; and (3) the project stage.

Most product development and cost control activities in the early stages of product development are organized around a 'project gate system'. The gate system is used to ensure that a whole range of quality requirements in product and process development activities as well as product upgrading activities are fulfilled

Table 6.3　The project gate system

Gate no	Description	Main activity between gates
0	Start of pre-study	Pre-study
1	Start of project	Definition of project
2	Project book	Product and process development
3	Tool design	Product and process development
4	Tool manufacture	Product and process development
5	Verification test series	Verification
6	Pre try-out series	Verification
7	Try-out series	Verification
8	Start of production	Production
9	Product release	Production
10	End of project	Production continues

(Table 6.3). The use of the concept gate in the system reflects a metaphor where the fulfilment of requirements is the key that opens the gate. It may sound rigid, but there is reasonable flexibility built into the system in order not to fully stop the development process if some requirements are not met.

The gate system includes eleven defined gates.[4] Ten of them (1–10) are related to the project stage, while one (gate number 0) sets the conditions for the start of a pre-study. In the gate system several cost control activities are prescribed and cost requirements (notice that the concept of cost target is not used, which is an adaptation to the gate system) that have to be fulfilled are established. All requirements are stated in one of four status terms that should support identification of the current status of the project. The terms used are initiated, preliminary, finalized, and verified (Figure 6.5).

Three organization functions provide specialists to the cost control activities. They are cost engineering (cost engineers), cost management (project controllers), and platform organization (business controllers). It is, however, seen as everyone's responsibility to control costs in a product development project. A major part of the control work takes place in cross-functional settings, where people from the cost control functions interact with engineers responsible for design and/or construction work.

> . . . of course, the cross functional groups have the competencies that are needed for solving their tasks and one of their tasks is to achieve the product cost targets that are set, and to ensure that the project is in control of the costs . . . the Cost management function is of course a very natural part of the product development organisation and they are part of the product development team where they are the project leader's right hand when it comes to the handling of project costs over time.
>
> (The President of Product Development)

First, in the late concept development stage, pre-study and early in the project stage, the *cost engineering function* provides cost engineers that support the

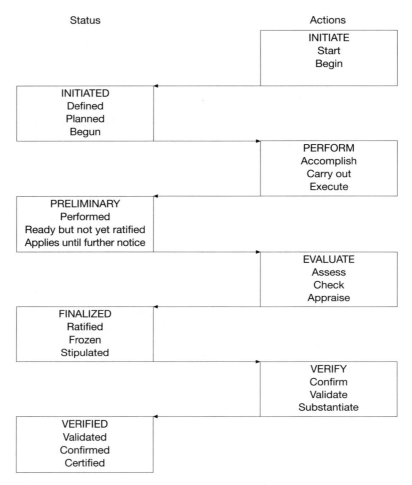

Figure 6.5 Status terms and actions in the gate system

product development organization with cost analyses and, especially, the setting of cost requirements. The cost engineers' involvement starts just ahead of gate 0 and ends at gate 2. The function is performed by persons with long-standing experience of product development and construction work. They are engineers who have developed experiential skills in costing and cost control. It should be noted that no management accountants are engaged in the setting of cost requirements. Cost engineering's activities are, basically, organized in accordance with the competence profiles possessed by the cost engineers. Each cost engineer performs cost analyses and establishes cost requirements for a limited range of functions/systems in the car (e.g. one person may support the exterior team, while another the engine team).

The second function involved is the *cost management function*. This provides the project or project leaders with project controllers (assisting the technical project leader). Also, when needed, controllers of larger systems tasks and/or components tasks are appointed to support the technical project leader. The engagement of cost management starts at gate 2, when cost engineering has established cost requirements that are accepted by the project leaders. The project controllers then have to verify the cost requirements, i.e. ensure that the actual costs are in accordance with the requirements. To be in control, they frequently set up cost review meetings in which the cost-responsible persons have to report the cost status of their systems and/or components tasks.

The basic task for the *business controllers* is to control and verify that the development project stays profitable (i.e. they need to adopt both revenue and cost perspectives of the development project, while the cost engineering and cost management functions basically only need to adopt a cost perspective). Business controllers report to the business area manager (e.g. one business area consists of all '70' models). The business controllers are responsible for profitability during the entire product development project. In the stages ahead of gate 2 they co-operate with cost engineering personnel, and in the later stages with cost management personnel. The business controllers conduct reviews of the development of the different market assumptions that have been set in the early stages and reviews of the cost at vehicle level. They use sensitivity analyses for calculations of alternative scenarios, and give early warnings to the business project leader and the business area. They thus have the possibility to demand special revenue and cost analyses that may be needed.

> You also must have in mind that we have not carried out that many product development projects before the platform strategy was launched. We are therefore inexperienced in the controlling of this kind of product development, which is a quite new way of development for us. . . . I am responsible for the cost targets that are set by the Cost engineering function. My role is to compile all the cost data from the technical side and to compare it with the revenues estimated by the business area in order to evaluate the project profitability.
>
> (Business Controller)

The major differences between the persons involved in cost control activities can be summarized as below:

	Timing of involvement	*Major focus*
Cost engineers	Gate 0 to 2	Setting cost requirements
Project controllers	Gate 2 to 10	Cost follow-up
Business controllers	Gate 0 to 10	Profitability reviews

The *concept development stage* is not, officially, included in the gate system. However, the stage has its gates, and it normally starts at gate −3 and ends at gate 0. The main purpose of the concept development stage is to provide technological and technical solutions to functions and systems of the future product. The inputs to ideas for a future product are many, e.g. market, competitor, and trend (customer and technology trends) analyses, design studies, generic R&D achievements, and internally developed experience. The information is brought together in a letter of intent, which should include performances, attributes and features (i.e. product properties) that are needed in the new car, and price information. Early in the stage, several car concepts are considered, and later in the stage a final concept is chosen. The choice decision grounded in the core values of Volvo, the overall business and competitive strategy, and in the product and technology strategies.

In the concept development stage, cost engineering people start their cost control activities just ahead of gate 0. Cost engineering receive a lot of input data for their activities, such as the allowable cost (i.e. price less required profit), estimated sales volumes, commonality targets, reference data on Volvo cars and competitors' cars, best practice (cars and/or companies), and in-house R&D etc. Also, cost engineering people receive specifications on the product properties for the car variants that should be developed. That data is used in a Value Function Deployment (VFD) exercise. VFD is only used for properties that are considered necessary to stay competitive in the car industry. VFD is a structured matrix approach used to distribute relative cost increases among car properties and systems. The starting point is to identify a relevant reference car that can be used as a benchmark (often this is the car that is going to be replaced by the car under development). Then the current cost per system for the reference car is established and the improvements are analysed from a cost perspective. For example, technological change, customer requirements, competitors' action, etc. may trigger improvements. Finally, the total vehicle cost increase, due to the improvements, is established and distributed among the car systems and properties. This gives cost engineering guidance on how to set cost requirements. When the VFD exercise is finalized, a VFD cost summary matrix is established. In the matrix the cost increase for each property improvement is compared to the estimated customer value for the same property. The purpose of this is to determine if the cost increase has a corresponding customer value increase, i.e. if the money is spent on the right things from a customer perspective. However, there is a belief in VCC that customer values are too subjective, being based on limited market research, subjective knowledge, sheer guesswork, and/or options price lists.[5] Furthermore, there is some scepticism about the precision and relevance of customer values that are broken down for each car property or car system.

After performing the VFD, cost engineering establishes the preliminary cost requirement for the whole vehicle and the initiated cost requirements for the systems. Cost requirements are set for both standard factory cost and entry ticket costs. In this development stage cost engineering starts to communicate the cost requirements to the pre-study leader in order to gain acceptance for the cost requirements.

In the *pre-study stage* (from gate 0 to gate 1) the specific business goals, corresponding to the long-range plan and to the strategic product plan, are established for the development project. These are, for example, goals concerning profitability, customer segment, market shares, quality, and manufacturing. Also, the project content and product properties have to be defined, and the principal technical solutions have to be specified. In this stage a preliminary estimation of revenues is done by business controllers through simulation of alternative scenarios which take changes in volumes, prices, price levels, currency fluctuations, and market shares into account. Simultaneously, cost requirements for the standard product factory cost, product development costs, and investments needed are established for the product project by cost engineering. At this stage there is a preliminary cost requirement available for the product. The cost is a combination of the estimated achievable cost from a build-up calculation and a top-down established cost requirement (i.e. a cost requirement established from the market conditions that take long-term company profitability into account).

During the first gates in the *project stage* (from gate 1 to gate 2), cost engineering has to establish the finalized cost requirements. This is done through a dialogue with the project leaders. From gate 2 and onwards to gate 10, the system's task and/or the component task managers are responsible for attaining the cost requirements (i.e. to achieve verification status of the requirements). In this work they are supported by a project controller, who is assigned to the cost management department, but is appointed to the project. The basic means for attaining the requirements are the cost review meetings, in which every item (with an own identity in the project accounts) is analysed with respect to its cost status.

A need for changes in cost control methods and activities

Recently, many arguments have been put forward for a change in the current cost control activities and systems. In the document 'Volvo Group Philosophy' of 1994 it is stated that, due to the rapid changes in business environment, there is an increasing need to adapt the management control systems. It is said that there is a need for more proactive cost control and a need for accountants/controllers working 'on-line' in the cross-functional meetings that take place in the product development process. They cannot just report what happened last month.

> In general, we have too many transaction oriented accountants today . . . I think that we need to find new ways now, and to change that picture so we become more business oriented in the future.

> (President of Finance)

In order to be cost-effective in the future (which was one of eight issues formulated in the new strategy of 1994), Volvo realizes that many of the cost control activities need to be redirected from the manufacturing stages to the early stages of product development. Volvo is, in this sense, no exception to the cost commitment phenomena. According to the manager of cost engineering, when production starts, some 80% of the product cost is already committed.

> . . . often in a product development project the order of priorities is such that the task to find a technical solution comes first, then should you spend as little time as possible

to bring the solution into place. When this is done you tell the project management the cost for the solution. That is, the costs are more or less the sum of the consequences of the two others . . . I cannot accept that we see the cost as a consequence . . . now we talk a lot about management by objectives and target costs, but that will only be nice words if we don't put them into action . . . Target costs need to be set when the project starts and there shall be a commitment to the target costs from the project members. The project controller has no chance to affect the costs, he is just an instrument for cost control. It is the constructor who specifies the product, the tool maker, and the supplier and so on who really determines the costs and these people need to have very clear rules and goals . . .

(President of Product Development)

. . . and in the early stages of product development, that's where we commit our future costs.

(President of Finance)

Also, as the proportion of external components in the cars is high, and as out-sourcing issues are high on the agenda, the importance of suppliers is recognized.

This is a great challenge to us. If you look at the whole value chain, you will find that our costs to a large extent are determined by the suppliers, so that's where the big money is.

(President of Finance)

Today (1998), in several different arenas, discussions and activities are going on that have the purpose of changing the work and methods of cost control in the early stages of product development. One stream of activities is concentrated on a business process refinement and information system development project. The project was initiated in 1996 as part of a process orientation[6] of the entire Volvo Group.

Also, internal needs and distrust in the old systems of management accounting and management control are other factors mentioned that prompted the project to redesign the currently applied cost control system. In the process project the cost requirement process (i.e. the cost control activities described above under the heading 'The current system') is being mapped (as one out of four management control processes) and proposals for a future process are being put forward. In the mapping, several internal 'customers' (mainly managers with an engineering degree in the product development function) were questioned about what requirements or needs they have of the cost control process. Below is a summary of what was said (from an internal Volvo document, 1998):

Cost targets are very important for our work but they must be established very early in the product development process, otherwise there is risk that designers and developers do not accept them. Also, if they are not established early, costs are already committed for in the design process.

There is great need for support to perform cost estimations and calculations in the early stages. Today, there is not enough resources or competence that can support this work.

It must be outspoken that focus should be on the early stages, and all our decisions that commit costs must be made visible to us. There is also a need for clear and consistent definitions of what should be included in the target cost.

All functions/professions that are active in the development work need to be involved in the calculation and need to be aware of how they can affect the costs.

Cost engineering need to be organised together with the module teams in order to get a better involvement in the cost control work/process.

We need to be better in the communication of cost targets, and to be more precise on the relation to company profitability.

Also, the cost engineering function, which is responsible for the activities performed in the cost requirement process, has identified several improvement areas and ways in which they would like to work with cost control in the future.

The bases of their proposed cost requirement process are the establishment of target costs (they write target costs, cost targets, and cost requirements interchangeably) in two subprocesses. One is a top-down process, which starts from the market assumptions made and the profit margin requirements set by top management. The other subprocess is a bottom-up approach, starting from the component level and then being aggregated to the higher levels, in which the estimated achievable cost is established. In both processes benchmarking (external and internal) is seen as a very important input. Cost targets are set for a complete vehicle and for major car functions or groups of functions. This should be done at the very early stages of the product development process (from gate −3 to gate 0). At this stage the cost engineering function wants to engage in several cost control activities.

Between gates −3 and −2, they would like to analyse the chosen product concept by bringing all the underlying assumptions together, with regard to, for example, customer categories, sales volumes, production sites, unique and other features, budget frame and budget restrictions, profitability requirements, timing, etc. Once a clear picture of the future car is established, reference data from their own cars, competitors' cars, best practices (cars and/or companies) and in-house R&D, is collected. The reference data is used in benchmarking activities for the purpose of establishing cost targets for the future car. Also, at this point in time Value Function Deployment (VFD) is used for the same purpose. VFD is conducted with those persons responsible for the properties (e.g. performances, attributes and features) of the future car. After the benchmarking activities and the first round of VFD, cost targets are established for the standard factory cost and the entry ticket costs. The cost targets are communicated to and discussed with the concept leader, who at this stage, is responsible for the total cost of the vehicle.

The first improvement area relates to timing, thoroughness, and how the cost requirements could be better integrated with other requirements. In order to gain acceptance in the organization, the cost requirements need to be better balanced with other major requirements such as product properties. Cost engineering people see a need to work through the technical solutions and their cost consequences before cost requirements are established and accepted. By this they hope to improve cost consciousness among designers and constructors. Thus, they see a need to be involved at a much earlier stage than they are today and to work through the cost requirements more often than is the case today (also before passing gates 0, 1, and 2, instead of only at gate 0).

Improving the dialogue between the involved functions in the product development work is seen as another important area. Through earlier involvement and more communication and dialogue, cost engineering hopes to create better respect for the cost requirements among responsible individuals (i.e. project leaders, systems and/or components task managers). They also perceive an ownership of the cost requirements as important, and propose that project management sign the acceptance and taking over of responsibility for cost requirements in a more formal way than is done today.

Another stream of change activities is a recently started 'target costing project'; led by an experienced controller who was also deeply involved in the development of PKS. Several initiating factors are at stake here. First, a project leader of the small platform expressed a need for support to reduce costs in the early stages of development. Second, two influential persons, after having attended a target costing seminar in the US, now support a test of the target costing philosophy in the product development organization. Also, some transparencies, originating from the CEO of the Volvo Group, that had been circulated in the VCC organization have triggered change (of, at least, attitudes). In the transparencies it is, among other things, stated that target costing is an important challenge for the development functions at the Volvo Group.

Endnotes

[1] The author wishes to thank the Swedish National Board for Industrial and Technical Development (NUTEK) (grant no: 8520P-96-05970), and the Tore Browaldh Foundation for Social Science and Education (grant no: T7/95), for financial support. The author is also grateful for the support received from several people at the Volvo Car Corporation, especially Sten-Olof Gustavsson, Lars Johnson-Sabel, Kjell Månsson and Thomas Nyvall.

[2] The other parts of the Volvo Group are Volvo Trucks (22,520 employees), Volvo Construction Equipment (8,560), Volvo Buses (4,220), Volvo Aero (4,170), and Volvo Penta (1,400).

[3] The acronym PKS stands for the Swedish word 'projektkostnadsstyrning', which translates as project cost control in English.

[4] This applies to the official gate system as the VCC Quality Department documents it. To add to the confusion, I use minus gates later in the text. This is due to the fact that VCC also uses minus gates (−3 to −1) during the early concept development stage. However, the minus gates are more loosely defined and used in a more informal way than those included in the official gate system.

[5] An option price list specifies the prices for extra equipment that you may want to have on your car. For example, in such a list you would find the price of an air-conditioning system that is not a standard feature.

[6] A process can be defined as a series of interdependent activities that are performed to achieve a specific objective (e.g. to deliver customer value). In this case becoming more process-oriented means a change of the organizational structure and control apparatus towards a focus on the organization's activities as they flow across functions. Process orientation (management) is implemented to encourage cross-functional interaction and more flexible ways of working. This will provide the employees a more holistic perspective of the business and help them understand their role and contribution in the organization. Process orientation discourages working in isolated specialist functional units.

STUDENT ASSIGNMENTS

1. Identify the major triggers for change and barriers to change that are present in the case.

2. Compare the situation in 1980 and 1988 in relation to the arguments put forward for a change of the system used for cost control. Discuss similarities and/or differences in the arguments used and whether you think a change may be more successful today.

3. Compare both the features of the PKS-system and the current VCC-system to control costs with how Target Costing is described in the literature. Would you consider any of the Volvo systems as a Target Costing system? Put forward the arguments for your viewpoints.

4. In the current system for cost control, three different functions are involved: the Cost Engineering, the Cost Management and the Business Controllers functions. Discuss what you think is needed for effectively controlling costs at Volvo.

5. The Cost Engineers use three different cost concepts: target costs, cost targets and cost requirements. What do you consider as differences in these three concepts? Which concept would you prefer to use and why?

6. Volvo uses different statuses on their cost requirements. What benefits do you perceive in having different statuses on cost requirements?

Appendix I   Further points of departure in the development of PKS

(Transcribed by the author from original documents written by hand in 1980)

Document number 1: Cost Target Follow Up (G1)

Basic decision rules:

1. *Within targets* (including unspecified) = Volvo Car BV responsibility (authors comment: this means that the production function of Volvo takes over the cost responsibility).
2. Follow-up calculations *lower than targets* = No change of committed targets
3. Follow-up calculations *exceed targets* = Car committee responsible for decision
800627/50440

Document number 2: Project Cost Control

Major differences between the proposed system and the actual system for project control:

1. Detailed cost targets.
2. Cost targets related to responsibility areas on detailed level.
3. Cost targets on realistic level (reference material).
4. Several VCG-HQ staff units involved in target setting in early phases.
5. Commitment of targets emphasized and formalized by assignment.
6. Formalized follow-up system where target deviations are related to responsible departments with the main purpose of stimulating action-programmes to reach targets.
7. Production plant budget simulation for first year of full-scale production.
8. Clearly defined decision rules for using 'unspecified' of cost targets.

Appendix 2   Information to aid interpretation of Table 6.3 and Figure 6.5

As mentioned in the case, Volvo uses a project gate system (Table 6.3), with four different status terms, in the product development process. The status terms (Figure 6.5) are used to assess the project situation with regard to the following seven main categories (statuses are, however, set for their subcategories): (1) Business, (2) Project Management, (3) Product, (4) Materials and Components, (5) Production Process, (6) Marketing, and (7) Aftersales.

For example, at Gate 0, Gate 1, and Gate 2 the subcategories of 'Business' should have reached the following statuses:

Category		Gate 0	Gate 1	Gate 2
1.	Business			
1.1	Strategies			
1.1.1	Business strategies	Preliminary	Finalized	Verified
1.1.2	Business responsibilities	(term not applicable)	Finalized	Verified
1.2	Goals, requirements			
1.2.1	Business goals	Preliminary	Finalized	Verified
1.3	Programme			
1.3.1	Product programme	Initiated	Preliminary	Finalized
1.4	Financing			
1.4.1	Financial plan	Preliminary	Finalized	Verified
1.5	Profitability			
1.5.1	Cost requirements	Preliminary	Finalized	Verified
1.5.2	Estimated revenue	Preliminary	Finalized	Verified
1.5.4	Profitability	Preliminary	Finalized	Verified

The status terms are used to decide whether the next project gate may be opened or not. Between the gates the status of the subcategories should be further improved by actions taken necessary to reach the next status term (see Actions in Figure 6.5). For example, you need to have taken some evaluation actions (assess, check and appraise) before you can go from a preliminary status to a finalized status (see Actions in Figure 6.5).

—

Wisapaper: the role of management accounting in managing customer relationships[1]

Vesa Partanen
Marko Järvenpää
Tero-Seppo Tuomela

The purpose [of the ABC project] was to see the causal relationships [between activities and costs] and to look at them also customer by customer. But it is very laborious to do the follow-up at such a level that you define every single activity. On the other hand, the system must be reliable . . .

It is difficult to make people see that costs do not necessarily accumulate at a specific cost center. To get people to accept this, it is simply tough. As we come to the process management, costs should be traced within processes, but we are afraid that it means too much work. Is there value added?

(Mikael Vikström, Manager of Financial Planning and Accounting)

Introduction[2]

UPM–Kymmene Group

In the early 1990s, Finnish forest and paper companies seemed to be in trouble. There was a total mismatch between the timing of heavy investments in the latter part of the 1980s and the global economic decline at the beginning of the following decade, which hit Finland especially hard. The paper industry made losses of hundreds of millions of Euro even though two considerable devaluations of the Finnish Mark were made, not least in order to relieve the difficulties being experienced by Finnish companies operating in the forest industry.

At the same time, competition was becoming more and more intensive. Although, from a Finnish point of view, the forest industry had been one of the most open sectors of the Finnish economy after the Second World War, the globalization of competition set new challenges. While the cost efficiency of the Finnish forest industry has traditionally been considered very good, this was no longer sufficient. Other methods of improving profitability were needed.

Major reorganizations were considered to be one way to reduce the excess capacity and to respond to the competitive challenges. The announcement of a merger between United Paper Mills (UPM) and Kymmene in 1995 gave birth to the biggest forest industry enterprise in Europe. At the end of the year 1997 the UPM–Kymmene Group had a total of 33,814 employees.

The company's turnover in 1997 was well over 8 billion Euro (USD 9 billion). The Group markets its papers through its own marketing network and converted paper products are sold mainly through the Group's own sales companies.

UPM–Kymmene is aiming at solid profitability and a stronger balance sheet over the next few years. The management of UPM–Kymmene has set a long-term profitability target of 15% return on capital employed by the divisions and their units. This aims at giving a return on equity which exceeds risk-free returns by a clear margin. The Group has set a target for its equity to assets ratio of at least 40%. The main goal in the immediate future is to reduce indebtedness, which has had a major impact on the company's share prices. According to Juha Niemelä, President and CEO of UPM–Kymmene, the company will strengthen its market position although it already has a strong position in Europe and in EU markets. Because it is difficult for UPM–Kymmene to increase its market share in Europe, it has started to move beyond Europe and made significant acquisitions and established joint ventures both in Asia and in the United States in 1997. Mr Niemelä sees the future of UPM–Kymmene as quite promising:

> In any case, we are ready for the tightening competition within the forest industry. From our own standpoint, we can come up with considered decisions whose goal is satisfying the needs of our customers and the market. We watch the signals of the market, but do not react compulsively.

Wisapaper

UPM–Kymmene has four business units at Pietarsaari, a small town on the western coast of Finland: a sawmill (Wisatimber), a pulp mill (Wisapulp), a paper-converting mill and a kraft paper mill (Wisapaper; see Figure 7.1). The kraft paper mill is called Wisapaper and it operates as an independent business unit in UPM-Pack, the Packaging materials division. Wisapaper employs about 230 people and its annual turnover is about 120 million Euro.

The value chain at Pietarsaari comprises also a pulp mill, which is an important supplier of raw material to Wisapaper, and an integrated paper-converting mill, which is an important customer of Wisapaper (see Figure 7.2). Wisapaper manufactures packaging material for further conversion and other industrial use, the main products being white sack, brown sack, white kraft and brown kraft. To a

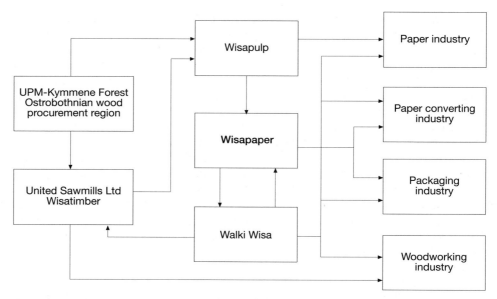

Figure 7.1 The conversion of raw materials for industrial use at the Pietarsaari units of UPM–Kymmene

certain extent, products are customized according to customer needs. Compared to printing and writing papers, demand and prices have been stable, although there are significant differences between individual products. During recent years the market for packaging materials has grown steadily and this good demand is expected to continue.

During the 1990s the profitability of Wisapaper varied considerably. 1995 was a tough year, as the price of pulp was extremely high. In 1996 the price of pulp went down, which allowed some flexibility in the pricing policy of Wisapaper. Better efficiency in terms of improved utilization of capacity resulted from the high demand, with the whole packaging materials division operating at 99% of capacity. Since the overall efficiency was very good at Wisapaper, return on capital employed rose to over 40%, well above the long-term 15% target of the Group. Such figures allow company managers to claim that Wisapaper is not only the biggest but also the most profitable kraft paper mill on the globe.

Currently, managers at Wisapaper see their unit as a leader in cost efficiency in Europe. A specific strategic target for future years is to maintain this number one position. However, the management of customer relationships is, at the moment, perhaps even more important than cost efficiency. This is reflected in the critical success factors and their relative importance that have been identified by Wisapaper managers:

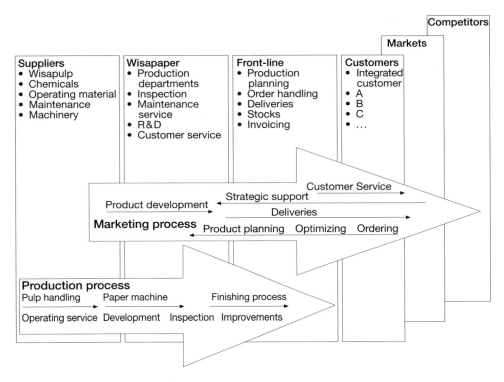

Figure 7.2 The core processes of Wisapaper

Cost efficiency	35%
Quality	35%
Customer service	20%
Image	10%

Cost efficiency and customer service are also interconnected. For example, in the autumn of 1998, paper machinery will be further modernized. While one objective relates to improving efficiency, another aim is to enhance quality and overall image, i.e. to have a positive effect on the way customers perceive the company and its products:

> [As] we are modernising the machinery, production *efficiency* will improve . . . And while we do it . . . *quality* will also improve; this investment has a direct impact on many things. Naturally it will affect our *image*: customers know that this new UPM-Kymmene also invests in the packaging materials business . . . The fact that they are investing in this business affects our credibility, we will be in this business.
>
> (Sören Slotte, Marketing Director of Wisapaper, emphasis added)

The modernization of production machinery involves a stop in production. This break, lasting for several weeks, imposes challenges on customer relationship management. Customers should be served according to long-term agreements even though production volume is insufficient. So it is both strategic imperatives and operating pressures that make excellent customer relationship management a key success factor for the company.

The management of customer relationships

The end of joint marketing

Until the beginning of the 1990s all Finnish paper products were marketed through the Finnish paper marketing association, Finnpap, founded in 1918 to handle the joint marketing of Finnish paper. However, the keen competitive situation in the market-place made some Finnish paper companies question the merits of belonging to a joint marketing organization. While Finnish companies had increased their product range, the battle for market share had become relatively stiff. In 1991 Kymmene left Finnpap and started to market its own products.[3] The aim was to find new markets and to address a particular customer portfolio. Wisapaper, being part of the Kymmene Group, was forced to acquire first-hand information about customers and to make direct contacts with them. While the notion of customer had already gained some momentum in Wisapaper, the resignation from Finnpap was the final motivator to adopt a true customer focus. Sören Slotte, Marketing Director of Wisapaper, describes the situation:

> [I]n my opinion, customer focus has suffered from the fact that we in Finland have had all these [joint sales companies]. The salesman has been somewhere else, far from the factory . . . Likewise, we here have been far from the market place. At the moment we want to balance this situation. To understand that what we do here has a direct impact on the customer who pays the bill. At the same time as this has become more visible, there is no such filter as [a joint sales company]; the customer and our factory play together and we are becoming more conscious of all this.

The marketing department of Wisapaper operates both directly with customers and through separate country- or area-specific sales offices. Sales offices are located worldwide selling products from the whole Group and providing customer service in their region. On the one hand, the challenge is to serve sales offices well enough that they provide excellent customer service so as to create long-term relationships with customers of strategic importance. On the other hand, it is crucial to obtain information about customers from sales offices and to distribute it throughout the organization.

In search of customer focus: TQM and process management

As the years have gone by, new management ideologies have been introduced that have direct links to customer focus. The ideas of total quality management (TQM)

Table 7.1 TQM/standards for customer service

Area	Target	Next step	Responsible	Time	Measure
Customer segments	To choose our customer/customer segments	* Check and test working accordingly	SS	April 1996	Working accordingly
Technical ass. before sales	Complete database available for all	* Decide project * WE-group's test case * On-line connection	SS/FW	1995	Report/ Customer contact
Marketing ass. before sales	Communicated strategy Database for all	* On-line connection * Project	SS/VTP	1995–1996	To decide
Customer retention	Order size and frequency follow-up	* SPOS follow up	CW	1995	−30% deviation 4 times/year
Handling of claims	Simple, fast controllable system	* Lotus Notes handling	VTP	1995–1996	All handling in Lotus Notes
Services index	Right service per customer segment	* To create and communicate service targets	SS/CW	1995–1996	To be decided
Order changes	To minimize changes	* Check SPOS * Set target	VTP/SS	1996	To start follow up

have been promoted. Within this ideology the need to define quality from the customer perspective has become prominent. In order to address total quality management principles, different kinds of standards and action plans have been set (see Table 7.1). Some years ago, a project related to TQM, called 'Wisateam', was initiated to empower employees by establishing teamwork principles. In a sense, the Wisateam project failed as true adoption of team-based working methods was hindered by functional organizational structures.

While struggling with problems of TQM, another related management ideology has gained increasing attention. In fact, it was the Wisateam project that highlighted the need to adopt process-based thinking. The Quality Manager of Wisapaper, Carl Westman, participated in a management course and was convinced that only by focusing on processes could quality be truly improved. Also within this process management ideology customers are of key importance. All processes have customers, either internal or external. Process management is considered to be a key tool in establishing total quality thinking within Wisapaper.

Overall, the implementation of process management principles is proceeding little by little. Core processes have been identified and ownership of these processes has been set. Processes have been classified as either core processes or supporting processes. Core processes at Wisapaper are paper production and paper marketing (see Figure 7.2). The purpose is not to end up with re-engineering; in contrast, the idea is not to break traditional functional borders. The aims are more abstract: to change the way of thinking, i.e. to improve understanding of the functions and processes of the entire company and to see the linkages between different processes and individual actions. The need to adopt a process-based way of seeing things has not yet been communicated to the lower levels of the Wisapaper organization. Mr Westman considers it very important to avoid incorporating unreasonable expectations among employees, especially after the failure of the Wisateam project. Related to this is the fact that the use of consultants is avoided: top managers are afraid that projects may expand too fast and too widely if consultants play a key role.

The selection of process owners is a critical task in the implementation of process-based thinking. Typically, top managers in the functional hierarchy have also been put in charge of processes. While some managers have uttered their concern about 'sitting in different meetings all the time and not really doing what they should do', the design of process management implementation is firmly in the hands of the core management team, especially in those of Mr Westman, Quality Manager of the firm, who explains:

> Our way of appointing the process owners has been that we have selected the functional manager who is closest to the specific process area, so that we have not initiated any contradictions. It is a very simple solution. Processes follow these functional responsibility areas to some extent . . . [For example] joint processes are still being defined, what are the correct names and so on, but the functional managers are in charge even though the processes do go further than the functional areas.

Successful adoption of total quality principles requires the effective use of performance measures. In order to establish a total quality mentality, performance measurement should also be aligned to processes. Mr Westman stresses the crucial role of measurement:

> [Q]uality management requires performance measures. I think that the only way of developing measures is through processes. Whatever [measurement] tool you use, processes are always there, in the background . . . The point is that we define these measures and they start to guide action. Then we initiate improvement projects and we see whether things have been improved or not.

> . . . We have simplified, or I have, these measures into a model so that I talk about owner's measures, customer's measures and personnel's measures. Every time we define a process we begin by thinking about the owner's requirements with respect to this particular process and then we should deduct what are the objectives and the measurement formula. We test the measures whether they work or not, and we should find such a comprehensive measure that really appreciates the process owner's [needs].

As the processes of Wisapulp and Wisapaper are tightly interconnected – and these units also have some common processes – managers of Wisapulp and Wisapaper have developed process management principles together. Management accountants play a key role in the development of performance measures within process management. Johan Högnabba, the Vice-president of Finance and Information Management, has defined a 'balanced scorecard' that is based on the three sets of measures: owner's measures, customer's measures and personnel's measures. He considers that such a performance measurement framework is a tool of high potential in managing total quality and processes within. Measures in the scorecard have been defined and the calculation of most measures began during year 1998 (see Table 7.2).

Owner's measures are calculated monthly, including a sub-ROCE (return on capital employed) figure for the two core processes: marketing and production. The purpose is to identify on which components of the ROCE figure a core process has an effect. The impact of (from the process owner's point of view) uncontrollable components of the ROCE measure is eliminated.[4] The aim is to extract the controllable part and see trends of development within it. Customer satisfaction inquiries regarding both products and services have been chosen to represent the customer perspective of the marketing process. For the production process, customer's measures are still undefined. Personnel interviews will also be conducted once a year in order to calculate personnel's measure for both the core processes. Different measures for common processes have also been set.

The development of performance measures is not an easy task without conflicts. Mr Högnabba agrees with Mr Westman that the adoption of process-based thinking has, overall, proceeded too slowly. But there are some differences in opinion with respect to the measurement:

> [Mr Högnabba] thinks you should have ROCE up here, [at the business unit level], and then you divide it into sub-ROCEs, but I remain sceptical. I want that we calculate measures only at the process level. Even though we speak about sub-ROCEs they are not additive.

> . . . The ROCE measure as such does not count, it is the trend. Have we improved according to the measure or is our performance getting worse. You should not take it too solemnly. (Carl Westman, Quality Manager)

Customer segmentation

At the same time as (total) quality related ideologies have gained momentum, structured approaches have been adopted in the management of customer relationships. One of the most valuable frameworks in establishing customer-oriented thinking has been the division of customers into five groups: Partners, Key customers, Special, Bulk and Others. Customer segmentation has been made with regard to customers' strategic importance. For example, customers that are not strategically important, but are needed to generate sufficient production volume are labelled Bulk customers (see further details in Table 7.3).

Table 7.2   Main measures of the processes

Wisapaper	Owner's measure	Customer's measure	Personnel's measure
Production	ROCE with external influence eliminated (once a month)	Under construction	Inquiry based on personnel interviews (once a year)
Marketing	ROCE with external influence eliminated (once a month)	Customer satisfaction regarding both products and services (once a year)	Inquiry based on personnel interviews (once a year)
Wisapulp			
Pulp line	ROCE with external influence eliminated. Follow up of fixed costs (once a month)	Customer interviews (once a year)	Inquiry based on personnel interviews (once a year)
Lye circulation	ROCE with external influence eliminated. Cost trend of the lye circulation (once a month)	Quality measures of white liquor Availability of white liquor (once a month)	Inquiry based on personnel interviews (once a year)
Common processes			
Human resource	Cost/employee (once a month) Inquiry for the efficiency and need of the products (once a year)	Inquiry for the efficiency and need of the products (once a year)	Inquiry based on personnel interviews (once a year)
Finance & IT	Cost index of both personnel and systems. Time schedule and budget follow up. Maintenance cost/working hours.	Inquiry for the efficiency, availability and need of the products (once a year)	Inquiry based on personnel interviews (once a year)
Technical processes	Cost/ hour of work. Amount of capital employed.	Inquiry for the efficiency, availability and need of the products (once a year)	Inquiry based on personnel interviews (once a year)
Energy production and distribution	Change in electricity and fuel costs at a constant unit price level regarding the situation of production (once a month)	Availability of energy (once a month)	Inquiry based on personnel interviews (once a year)

Sören Slotte, the Marketing Director, describes the meaning of customer segmentation or classification as a way to effect organizational thinking:

> [I]t is one of those 'spiritual' things. That people know it is the way it is. It is control with a vision. It is a communicative tool, so that we have a common view of customers.

Table 7.3 Different customer segments of Wisapaper

	Partners	*Key customers*	*Special*	*Bulk*	*Others*
Number of	3	67	15	177	38
Definition	Strategic customers, ideal product structure	Strategic customers, not always ideal product structure	Prospects with strategic importance	Not regular long-term customers	Not suitable for Wisapaper of strategic or profitability reasons
Profitability	(quite) high	high	from negative to positive	moderate/high	negative
Role	profitable long-term relationships	the base of profits	potential future partners or third-party references	important with regard to economies of scale	evening of volatility in demand/to get rid of
Comments	'They are the partners, the rest are customers'	'With them we are willing to develop'	'The profitability is bad, but in the long-term they might be something else'	'We might raise the price but that might turn out to be more expensive than what it should'	'If we have to make up our mind, to whom we will supply, they will be left out'

However, this segmentation does also have an impact on some specific actions. In the long run, *Others* will be substituted with customers of higher ranking and profitability. On specific occasions, when demand exceeds capacity, production is targeted to *Partners*, *Key customers* and *Special customers*, while *Bulk customers* and particularly *Others* are not provided with all the goods they would like to have. Mr Slotte goes on:

> [The group of *Others*] can hang on and especially when there is not [enough] demand, they can hang on longer but they are not provided with equivalent service compared to those who operate in our primary business areas . . . The classification is important when [production is] booked up, when we face a choice regarding who we do supply and who we do not supply; then we try to take care of our regular customers and those who are in the group *Others* will be left out in the first place.

In the case of excess capacity there are basically two options: products can be sold also to *Others*, or the paper mill can be stopped for lay days. Both of these alternatives have been tried in recent years. The classification of different customers is checked twice a year. Sören Slotte gathers the sales managers together and they go through the list customer by customer and decide whether each customer is in the correct segment.

A reason for customer retention may also stem from the need for a presence in certain foreign countries. There are countries in which all customers are currently unprofitable and no changes are foreseeable in this respect. The motive for the retention of customers in such a country is usually the need to gain information about competitors' actions in that market area. Another explanation could be that these customers are allied with customers in another country who are highly profitable or are of strategic importance.

Acquiring information about customers

Personal contacts between salesmen and customers' procurement personnel form a valuable basis for gathering information about the behaviour and thoughts of customers and competitors. During the past couple of years several other, more systematic methods for acquiring information about customers have been established. First-hand information about customers is highly valued and this is why customers are requested to make an evaluation of projects carried out by the company. Customer surveys and interviews have been carried out systematically since 1993. The making of in-depth interviews has been outsourced in order to get reliable results. Specific image analyses are also made in about three countries every year. The marketing department itself surveys its customers and also collects information about customers' views of major competitors. In the spring of 1998 this information was connected to other performance measures in the process-based 'balanced scorecard' (see Table 7.2). Customer interviews and surveys are not, however, problem-free:

> It is not good enough. We are listening now, but . . . it is very difficult to say that I
> do not like something. Usually you are cautious with these issues . . . That's just
> the way it is. I believe that we are in a learning phase. Just keeping it up is laborious,
> it is expensive and there will always be room for interpretation. But this is the way we
> do it until we find a more efficient way of doing it. (Sören Slotte, Marketing Director)

There are also internal performance indicators of customer service, both quantitative measures and more qualitative issues. Quantitative performance measures include changes in orders ratio, order confirmation ratio, confirmed time of arrival ratio (CTA), mean response time to orders, mean response time to inquiries and mean response time to claims (see Figure 7.3 for details of the most important non-financial performance measures in customer service). Specific targets have been set for all of these measures. Plans for seminars for different customer groups, product plan charts and the co-ordination of R&D co-operation between *Partners* and possibly with *Special customers* are examples of issues that are systematically monitored but not measured as such.

Another internal source of customer-related information is the costing system. Managers consider customer profitability information an important tool in managing customer focus. Management accountants have contributed to the control of customer relationships by providing this information. In the future management accountants intend to take a more active role in making analyses instead of purely number crunching. Their aspiration is to be true 'business partners':

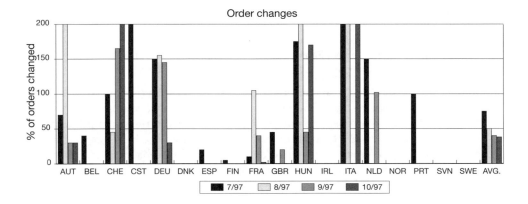

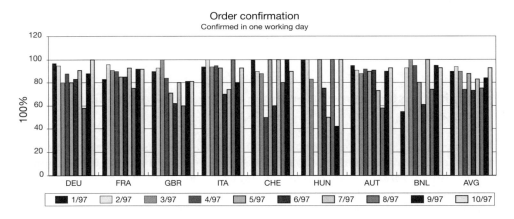

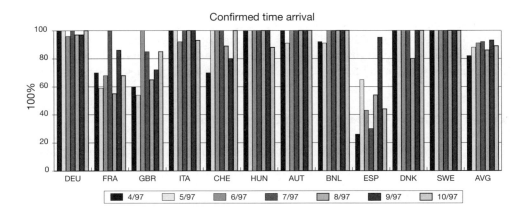

Figure 7.3 A progress report of customer service measures

Our role is to produce information and to analyse it . . . This analysis thing, that is what
we are heading for. So that you do not just give the figures but you also analyse it . . .
How to create the knowledge and how to get it out . . . it should be like key figures
about the customer. Now these figures are in five databases and in twenty reports . . .
(Mikael Vikström, Manager of Financial Planning and Accounting)

Currently, there is an attempt to combine different sources of customer information
into an 'early warnings system'. The major contribution of this system is its alleged
ability to anticipate the future. The aim is to gain reliable and real-time information
based on changes in buying behaviour patterns of customers, in order to identify
emerging trends and changes in the market-place. Another objective is to identify
customer-specific trends concerning customers who are treated incorrectly by the
company (e.g. repeatedly late deliveries) or conversely, customers that are not
behaving according to agreed contracts (e.g. payments are continuously late).
While the overall responsibility for development is in the hands of marketing
people, the role of management accountants is to incorporate financial aspects of
customer relationships into this system. This system, at least in some form, should
be in use before the end of 1998.

Managing customer relationships: customer profitability information

The calculation of customer profitability information has a long tradition at
Wisapaper, however, the need for improved reliability and accuracy of customer
profitability information has become evident as the adoption of customer focus has
become more prominent.

Early systems of customer profitability information provided only crude and
sometimes distorted information. The recently implemented activity-based model
provides more accurate information about customer profitability to Mr Slotte,
Mr Högnabba and other Wisapaper top managers. Sales offices are also informed of
their customers' profitability. The full potential of this system will be realized
when refined customer profitability information, based on activity-based costing
principles, is distributed to individual salesmen throughout the sales organization.

Earlier systems for customer profitability analysis

As the proportion of raw material costs in the industry is high, for many years it
seemed appropriate to use only direct costs for customer profitability calculations.
This natural emphasis on material costs is evident in the relative cost structure of
Wisapaper, which can be described in terms of four cost categories:[5]

Raw materials	64%
Direct and indirect production costs	20%

Sales and General Administration (S&GA) 8%
Freight   8%.

At the beginning of the 1990s only direct material costs and freight costs were traced to different orders and thereby to different customers. Conversion costs, marketing costs and administrative costs were not recognized by this system. However, this variable costing system covered most of the costs at Wisapaper and it was simple and easy to use.

In 1993 the customer profitability calculation was changed, so that production and administrative overheads were allocated to orders/customers according to machine hours. Machine hours were considered as appropriate cost drivers because they are the crucial resources which are 'sold' to different customers. Sales (and marketing) costs were not, however, allocated at all: instead, a fixed amount was charged for every order to cover sales costs. Customer profitability based on this full costing system was reported on a quarterly basis.

However, even the revised reporting system caused doubts because managers felt that on some occasions it produced results which were not in line with common sense thinking. In small orders the manufacturing time per ton is relatively long due to set-up time, which means that the cost per ton should be higher. This was not reflected in the standard costing system. In addition to this, the relatively large amount of effort put by sales people into getting small orders could not be seen in the customer profitability information. Managers had the impression that these issues have an inevitable effect on costs, consequently, they considered small customers to be less profitable than shown in the profitability reports.

In these earlier systems, customer profitability reports were not regularly distributed to sales offices, since these reports indicated only the overall profitability of individual customers. As the same customers operate in different countries with local sales offices, customer profitability information at country level or at different sales offices was unavailable in these reports.

Origins of ABC-adoption

Johan Högnabba, the Vice-president of Finance and Information Management, became very interested in the fresh ideas of cost accounting and cost management at the beginning of the 1990s. He had read seminal books and articles related to activity-based costing (such as Johnson and Kaplan, 1987, *Relevance Lost*) and he would have liked to introduce ABC at Pietarsaari units. Other managers, however, argued that activity-based costing was perhaps applicable in companies like Ericsson or Kanthal, but not in the forest industry because of the low proportion of overhead costs and the relatively low process and product diversity. Högnabba made further investigations and found out that 'Competitor A' was using ABC in some business units. Högnabba contacted this company and received further information. He also contacted a couple of well-known ABC consultants and invited them to lecture about ABC. The purpose was to convince other managers of the usefulness of ABC in their specific context. He was not, however, able to sell the idea to other managers until Wisatimber,[6] the sawmill at Pietarsaari, was faced with a financial crisis due to a severe decline in demand by its customers operating in the construction industry. At that time, Wisatimber was chosen as a pilot case for the ABC project.

The ABC system at Wisatimber was designed mainly by a M.Sc. (Tech.) student, Mikael Vikström, as part of his Master's thesis. Improvements in production processes resulting from the use of ABC information were considerable. First, some products were found to be so unprofitable that their production was cut down permanently, the excess material being used as raw material in other business units. Second, two production stages were automated. Similarities between the manufacturing processes of several products were identified and their production was synchronized. Finally, the capacity of a drying plant was increased through major changes in working methods.

At Wisatimber, the adoption of activity-based costing also made it possible to calculate customer account profitability in a meaningful way. It was found out that those customers who were purchasing sawn goods with higher value added were usually very profitable, while customers buying goods having less value added were often unprofitable. Customer profitability was also analysed with reference to the size of customers and whether they were domestic or foreign customers. The profitability of small customers was questionable both in and outside of Finland. Medium-sized customers were typically very profitable, while major differences were found among large customers. While large overseas companies contributed to the profitability of Wisatimber, two of the three big domestic customers were clearly unprofitable. Small and frequent deliveries were seen as the most important single factor resulting in poor profitability. Contracts with these two large Finnish customers were re-negotiated in terms of larger and less frequent deliveries. ABC calculations were used as arguments in these negotiations. New operational modes had clear effects on the sawmill's overall profitability. All these actions took place over a two-year period, after which Wisatimber was recognized as the most profitable sawmill in the Group. This chain of events convinced Mr Högnabba that the introduction of ABC would be of great benefit also in the case of Wisapaper.

The introduction of ABC for customer profitability analysis

In the strategic planning process for the years 1996–1998 at Wisapaper, the adoption of activity-based costing was accepted as one particular objective. This initiative was taken by Mr Högnabba, who was greatly encouraged by the earlier success of ABC at Wisatimber. As a result, an ABC development project was launched in February 1996 and the task of designing the practical solution was, again, delegated to Mikael Vikström, who had by then been promoted to Manager of Financial Planning and Accounting at Wisapaper. The plan was to establish a more accurate costing system and carry out customer, country and product level analyses to check the correctness of impressions about the relative profitability of customers.

The first step was to identify different activities carried out in the company. In the production process the most important aspect was to recognize the set-up activity. This identification made it possible to use 'actual' manufacturing time (i.e. processing time + set-up time) instead of pure processing time in allocating manufacturing (and administrative) costs.

In the sales and marketing function, the activity analysis revealed that there are basically five different activities:

- sales order
- order handling
- invoicing
- transports
- sales general.

The most critical part of the activity analysis was the allocation of time to different activities. When conducting time consumption analyses, a valuable finding was that different customers used these activities in significantly different ways. It was estimated that, for instance, compared to a domestic customer, it takes four times longer to invoice an export customer with an irrevocable letter of credit. On the other hand, an integrated customer consumed only 30 per cent of the invoicing time required by other domestic customers. Therefore, based on these time consumption analyses – and sometimes also on crude estimates – specific weights were defined to assign activity costs to different kinds of customers (see Table 7.4). If necessary, these weights are revised quarterly.

The first activity-based calculations in 1997 showed that most costs (up to 90%) had previously been assigned to the right customers. However, at the level of some individual customers, differences were found to be very significant. Changes in calculated profitability were marginal with respect to large customers, but many small customers were found to be less profitable than had earlier been thought. Also some middle-sized customers were found not to be profitable (see the example in the Appendix).

An additional improvement in the new system is that it allows a wide range of comparisons and analyses. While the previous version of customer profitability calculation produced information only customer by customer, the new system gives also country-specific information. Product and customer groups have been defined in a more relevant manner, which gives a reasonable basis for assessing their impact on overall profitability.

The role of the improved customer profitability information

At first glance, the usefulness of refining customer profitability information with ABC principles may seem to be lacking. Mikael Vikström, the designer of the

Table 7.4 Weights for marketing activities in the ABC system

Weights for different orders according to different criteria	Weight/order	Euro/order
Sales order		
Integrated customer	0.15	12.61
Sales department – domestic group customer	0.80	67.28
Sales department – domestic customer	1.00	84.09
Sales department – export group customer	1.80	151.37
Export customer	1.50	126.14
Order handling		
Integrated customer	0.30	10.09
Sales department – domestic customer	1.00	33.64
Sales department – export customer	1.30	43.73
Export customer	1.50	50.46
Export customer with irrevocable letter of credit	3.00	100.91
Invoicing		
Integrated customer	0.30	2.52
Domestic customer	1.00	8.41
Export customer	2.00	16.82
Export customer with harbour stocks	3.00	25.23
Export customer with irrevocable letter of credit	4.00	33.64
Transport		
Integrated customer	0.10	2.52
Domestic customer	1.00	25.23
EU customer	2.00	50.46
EU customer with irrevocable letter of credit	2.50	63.07
Non-EU customer	3.00	75.68
Non-EU customer with irrevocable letter of credit	3.75	94.61
Sales general		*Euro/ton*
All customers	none	8.41

system, himself questions the use of ABC for fine-tuning the assignment of certain production costs:

> Sometimes I wonder the usefulness of making these allocations. Because also in my opinion, eh, is there any sense that you allocate all kinds of costs ... if we would calculate the cost per ton it would be about 40 pennies and I have not even taken pennies into account in the system . . .

In the same vein, the users of customer profitability information see the impact of the 'better' system as quite marginal:

> It is difficult to say, how this [refined customer profitability information] contributes to decision-making. . . We had this follow-up also earlier; it just is more accurate and easier to communicate. It is quite seldom that we have the production booked up;

usually the machine has to be kept going and then we have accepted orders from customers with poorer profitability as well. (Sören Slotte, Marketing Director)

Customer profitability information serves, however, both strategic and operational purposes. It gives a strategic frame of reference when, for example, segmenting the customers. Non-strategic customers with poor profitability are likely to be labelled as *Others*. The classification of customers is not, however, solely dictated by profitability. Large customers with moderate profitability but reliable payments can be important, since they relieve risks and even up volatility in demand. Time frame is also taken into consideration: some unprofitable firms could be labelled as *Special*, as they might turn out to be very profitable in the future because of new innovations. Nevertheless, customer profitability information serves as an important basis for such considerations.

The operational use of customer profitability information is also important. Overseas sales companies are informed about their customers' profitability. Lowered customer profitability triggers discussions with the sales company in question, leading to negotiations with the customer about price or delivery terms (quantities and frequency of single orders) according to instructions received from the marketing department of the company. It is, however, not possible to achieve any upward price changes by a one-sided decision, since the competition is keen. Competitive strengths are relatively even and no clear market leader exists. The changes in quantities and frequency of deliveries (for example by producing monthly only one lot instead of two) are thus seen as good options to improving unprofitable customer relationships.

Refined customer profitability information is seen as a tool to be used in preparing for the future. It is quite likely that the importance of customer segmentation will increase as Wisapaper moves towards addressing the needs of strategic customers. The activity-based system has already assisted in moving some customers from one category to another. In addition to this, the activity-based system is also expected to make it possible to legitimize permanent abandonment of unprofitable customers. So far, decisions with such radical consequences have not been made, but in order to make such decisions, it is necessary to have reliable supporting information:

> In order to make people feel that accounting is reliable, accounting figures should be reliable also in the case of small customers or products. Mistakes should be abolished. If accounting results are contradictory to one's sense, the overall confidence in accounting information suffers. If we notice that a customer is not a good one, we can now rely on management accounting system and it is therefore easier for us to make the decision. (Mikael Vikström, Manager of Financial Planning and Accounting)

Mr Högnabba sees the implementation and use of activity-based costing as an important tool in questioning the current state of operations:

> We have tried to analyse different cost drivers and to see how they have an impact on the profitability of an order . . . to see how we deal with different customers. We need to know whether we are doing the things right or wrong, in a profitable or loss-making manner. (Johan Högnabba, Vice President of Finance and Information Management)

The improved accuracy has also an indirect impact on the usefulness of customer profitability information. The new system with reliable results allows wider distribution of customer profitability information (it could be now distributed also to the sales offices) which in turn increases the visibility of specific actions:

> We have 'always' had [customer profitability information]. We should remember that we had it already before the adoption of activity-based costing. The purpose is not to provide totally accurate information of product or customer profitability. The most important thing is that we get this ranking, a relative comparison. The new thing is that we print it out and distribute it more widely. We trust that it is correctly calculated. This way we can use it to affect the behaviour of salesmen in point of sale and sales negotiations. They know that [some particular customer] is a problem child . . . I think that it trains the sales personnel to think like managers do. (Sören Slotte, Marketing Director)

Endnotes

[1] The authors would like to thank the reviewers of the case, Tom Groot and Kari Lukka, for their constructive comments on the case text. We also would like to thank Markus Granlund for his insightful comments of an earlier version of the case. Most of all, we are indebted to Johan Högnabba, Mikael Vikström, Carl Westman and Sören Slotte, the key players in the story. Without their effort and assistance, this case would never have seen the daylight.

[2] The events described in this teaching case have been updated to April 1998. Any changes beyond this point of time have not been taken into consideration.

[3] At this time UPM was the dominant player in Finnpap. Finnpap ceased operating as a joint paper marketing organization at the end of 1996 and became a UPM-Kymmene subsidiary. Currently Finnpap is part of the sales company network of UPM-Kymmene.

[4] To give some examples, with regard to both production and marketing process the volatility of the price of pulp is eliminated. The stock of finished goods and receivables are excluded from the controllable capital of the production process.

[5] The proportions have been slightly modified.

[6] All units at Pietarsaari were at that time controlled by the joint finance function. Nowadays Wisatimber belongs to the other operational division of UPM-Kymmene and thus it has a separate finance function of its own.

STUDENT ASSIGNMENTS

I   The management of customer focus

1. Evaluate the connection between TQM, process management and customer focus. Did these popular management 'ideologies' support each other at Wisapaper?

2. Describe the tool set used at Wisapaper for managing customer relationships.

3. How were these tools used and for what purposes, i.e. were these tools used in order to enhance customer orientation or to control customer focus (or both)?

II   Customer profitability analysis and activity-based costing: reasons for adoption

1. Do you think that the circumstances in which Wisapaper operates is a typical context for ABC adoption?

2. Why was customer profitability reporting refined with activity-based information? What do you think about Mikael Vikström's opinion that accounting results should not be against one's senses?

III   Customer profitability analysis and activity-based costing: the new system

1. How do the three ways of calculating customer profitability differ from each other? Why did the profitability figures of customers A, B and C change in a different way (see the Appendix)?

2. Evaluate the pros and cons of the latest form of customer profitability analysis.

3. How should Wisapaper managers use customer profitability information? What should they do with customers B and C (see the Appendix)?

IV   The role of management accountants

1. How important is the role of management accountants in managing customer focus at Wisapaper?

2. What do you think about management accountants' aim to become true business partners? What is required from management accountants and other organizational actors in order to facilitate such a role change?

Appendix An example of customer profitability analysis

Customer A: Medium-sized, domestic group customer
One order in the period (72 tons)

Customer B: Medium-sized, export customer with harbour stocks, United States
Five orders in the period (2, 3, 3, 6 and 10 tons)

Customer C: Small, export customer, Great Britain
Two orders in the period (0.5 and 2 tons) with irrevocable letter of credit

Variable costing system

	A	B	C
Sales (€)	70,800	24,200	2,292
Direct materials (€)	49,560	15,730	1,535
Freight (€)	1,062	847	57
Profit (€)	20,178	7,623	699
Profit %	28.5%	31.5%	30.5%

Full costing system

	A	B	C
Sales (€)	70,800	25,200	2,292
Direct materials (€)	49,560	15,730	1,535
Freight (€)	1,062	847	57
Manufacturing (€)	10,620	3,388	275
Sales and Marketing (€)	84	420	168
General Administration (€)	2,124	678	55
Profit (€)	7,350	3,137	201
Profit %	10.4%	13.0%	8.8%

Current ABC system

	A	B	C
Sales (€)	70,800	24,200	2,292
Direct materials (€)	49,560	15,730	1,535
Freight (€)	1,062	847	57
Manufacturing (€)	10,089	5,082	344
Sales and Marketing (€)			
– sales order	67	631	252
– order handling	34	252	202
– invoicing	8	126	67
– transports	25	378	126
– sales general	605	202	21
General Administration (€)	2,018	1,016	69
Profit (€)	7,331	−65	−382
Profit %	10.4%	−0.3%	−16.7%

—

Introducing the commercial manager: management accounting support for the sales function of Bass Brewers, UK[1]

Thomas Ahrens

Introduction

At the time of the case research, in 1996/97, Bass Brewers Ltd was the second largest British beer brewing company with a market share of about 23%. Among its brand portfolio was Carling Black Label, the best selling British lager beer. Bass Brewers sought to maintain their leading position through the continued internal creation of strong brands and the provision of high levels of customer service. Their most successful recent market introduction was Caffrey's Irish Ale, a premium ale sharing some of the characteristics of stout, that reached high levels of sales very quickly.

Bass Brewers distributed nationally, as did the four largest competitors. Prior to the government's Beer Orders the then eight largest brewers were vertically integrated organizations that controlled production, distribution, and tied retail outlets. They had grown through successive mergers with regional brewers. The Beer Orders limited the number of public houses[2] brewers could own. Public houses were sold to independent operators or large retail organizations without production facilities of their own who put pressure on margins. In 1996, with an overall shrinking market for beer, the brewing business was characterized by over-capacities in production and heightened competition for beer taps on the bars. Pressure for mergers had reduced the number of large national brewers to five.

Bass Brewers was part of Bass plc, quoted on the London Stock Exchange with a market capitalization of approximately £6.9 billion.[3] Bass plc had grown from its origins in brewing into a leisure group with interests in hotels (Holiday Inn Worldwide), restaurants (Toby, Harvester), bars (O'Neill's, All Bar One), soft drinks (Britvic), and entertainment such as bingo halls (Gala) and betting shops (Coral).

147

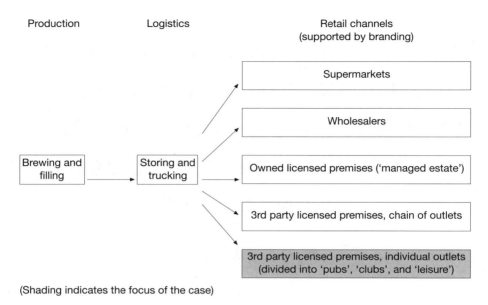

(Shading indicates the focus of the case)

Figure 8.1 The commercial process in British brewing

Corporate head office was in London. The brewing division in Burton-on-Trent, England's most famous brewing town in the Midlands, had to compete for capital with ventures that generated very high returns on investment, such as Gala and Toby.

In 1996 Bass Brewers employed 4,300 people in the UK (and 4,000 abroad) and returned profits of £159 million on a turnover of £1.78 billion. The principle areas of activity were beer production, distribution, branding, and marketing. Beer retailing was the task of its sister division, Bass Leisure Retail. The main retail channels were supermarkets and wholesalers, the managed estate of licensed premises[4], and licensed premises owned by third parties, falling into large chains and small independent operators. This case focuses on the latter (see Figure 8.1).

Tradition and change at Charringtons

Charringtons has been the traditional trading name for Bass Brewers' distribution in the South East of England. Before the Beer Orders, the sales regions were almost run like independent companies and Charringtons was one of them. Controlling the entire value chain, Bass, like the other big brewers, had had little reason to fully exploit economies of scale. For example, it had not been uncommon in the industry to operate more than one distribution depot in the same town when they were inherited through merger. The Bass Brewers sales regions had individual management structures and non-standard local accounting and management information systems. In 1994 this was about to change.

Peter Swinburn, Bass Brewers' Sales Director, and Paul Thomas, Finance Director, introduced a programme entitled the Commercialization of Finance. Previously implemented by Paul Thomas when he was working in the Bass Leisure Retail Division, it sought to modernize regional brewing management by redefining the tasks of the finance function. Competitive pressures were conducive to those efforts. Since the Beer Orders had forced the large brewers to sell many of their public houses, large retail organizations had sprung up in the field demanding discounts on their purchases from the brewers. The brewers felt the pressure on their margins all the more because national beer consumption in Britain was falling. Overcapacity became a serious problem. The big brewing companies closed large brewing sites. The trend towards merging the large brewers continued.

The Commercialization of Finance had implications for the provision of management information. For example, where management accountants would traditionally show sales performance as a £ contribution margin per barrel of beer sold, they now calculated contribution margin per sales £ in order to be able to calculate the percentage return on sales. But more importantly, it had implications for the way in which financial expertise was organized with Charringtons and Bass Brewers to support sales.

Traditionally, the accountants at the Charringtons head office in Silvertown, in the London Docklands, provided the complete financial support function for their regional sales. Ray Jones, commercial support manager for Charringtons until May 1997 explained:

> You are asking the one person who is a commercial support manager within Bass who's come from outside of Bass. [. . .] maybe I should highlight what the role was and how it was perceived to be a change and an addition to what was already here within the region or in all the regions before this change took place. There was more what I would call a traditional structure with a finance department, a sales information planning department, a customer accounts department, and a loans processing and credit control department. So we had these departments working in little boxes doing the more traditional jobs. It was felt that that was not particularly adding value to the business. It was more processing, back office, not seen by the sales organisation. So a decision was taken at board level, I presume, it came off the back of a project, a review project, to focus this much more on value added, customer facing issues rather than a back office. And that drove the creation of a commercial support department, which was, if you want, the amalgam of loans processing and credit control, customer accounts and finance and sales information.

The finance department dealt with the traditional financial accounting tasks, such as making and receiving payments and calculating regional profits. The sales information planning department kept records of sales targets and plans. Customer accounts handled orders and was responsible for payments to and from customers. The loans processing and credit control department administered customers' credit status and calculated the profitability of loans given to them.

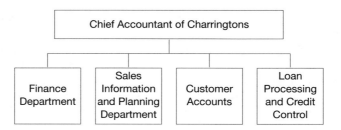

Figure 8.2   The old structure of the finance department

This loan function requires more detailed explanation. Traditionally, brewers sought to secure trade with independent outlets through loan ties. Since the Beer Orders forced brewers to reduce the number of public houses owned, loan ties increased in importance for securing sales. Often independent operators lacked the means for refurbishment and maintaining adequate working capital. Bank loans were usually unavailable for lack of collateral. Instead, brewers would offer loans in return for distribution rights knows as loan ties. Loans could also be structured in a way that allowed the operator, who might initially lease the property from the brewer, to acquire ownership of the property over the duration of the supply contract.

Usually, the loans offered by brewers had interest rates below market rates. Sometimes loans might carry no interest at all. Such subsidies were compensated by higher beer prices charged to the independent operator. Therefore, the financial success of a distribution contract that included a low interest loan came to depend on the realization of forecast sales volumes: if volumes were lower than predicted, the higher unit selling price for beer could not compensate for the cheap capital loaned to the outlet. If volumes were higher than predicted, the brewer benefited more than expected from the high unit selling price charged to the outlet. The loan subsidy was overcompensated. As a financier, the brewer played a more active role than a bank. It took a share in the risks and rewards of the retail performance of individual outlets. This meant that the brewer would evaluate outlets on their overall commercial performance. Sales were of course the central variable, but with outstanding loans at risk, the brewer would be interested in the long-term viability of an independent operator's business. Many factors, such as the character and history of the operator, sales volume, product portfolio, product prices, characteristics of the clientele, local competition from other licensed premises, the presentation and state of repair of the outlet, dispensing technology, etc., had to make sense for the outlet as a whole in order to make a good selling proposition to customers. A salesman who visited an outlet would observe it through the eyes of a critical customer from the moment he drove into the car park:

They need to do something about those weeds over there . . .

The view from head office

The centralization of administrative and reporting functions and the heightened focus of regional management accountants on commercial issues had been planned for a while. The reorganization followed a vision that Kevin Rhodes, Operations Development Manager at Bass Brewers' head office in Burton, explained in February 1997. Central to the plan was

> to drive a lot of the reporting and the standard reporting out of a central point that we can produce each period in a standard format and not need lots of people in the regional bases that produce reports that can be produced from a computer system at the push of a button. [. . .] What we then want the regional [management accountants] to do is be able to answer the regional questions, the ad hoc type questions and to help the commercial managers. They could be there to do their inquiries from the database and do the what ifs from the data provided [. . .]

Score-keeping and retrospective analysis were to be separated from the business advisory function. The finance function was to be split into a management accounting role and a commercial role. If management accountants were to provide ad hoc analyses to regional questions, commercial managers should fill a different gap:

> There was nobody out there actually helping newly appointed salesmen understand what was behind the deal structure how to put it together in terms of this type of customer, this is the sort of risk, these are the sort of financial criteria that you should be thinking about. [. . .] let's get out there in the field which is where the commercial manager should be 70, 80% of their time actually working alongside those people driving the deals, make sure they're taking action. So I guess that was the driving force in creating their jobs and it was finance that was pushing for this to be created because I feel . . . we were producing the information, finding that the action that was coming from it was not really of the desired type. [. . .] We have salesmen saying that is great having someone out here that I can talk to, that is available and understands the workings in my area, understands the customers, actually visits my customers, seeing real people and not some numbers on a . . . profit and loss account. So we've humanised finance people I guess. . .

The view from the new commercial support manager

Half a year later, in December 1997, Andrew Bailey, the new commercial support manager explained that the restructuring had been taken even further. Charringtons had no more regional management accountants at all. The credit control and credit processing function along with the servicing of individual customer accounts had been centralized for all of Bass Brewers in Leeds. Also, financial reporting had been standardized throughout the regions and was now centrally operated in Burton-on-Trent,

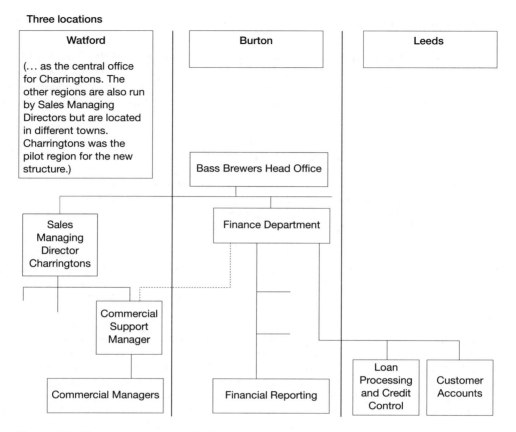

Three locations

| Watford | Burton | Leeds |

(... as the central office for Charringtons. The other regions are also run by Sales Managing Directors but are located in different towns. Charringtons was the pilot region for the new structure.)

Bass Brewers Head Office

Sales Managing Director Charringtons

Finance Department

Commercial Support Manager

Commercial Managers

Financial Reporting

Loan Processing and Credit Control

Customer Accounts

Figure 8.3 The new structure of the finance department

which really leaves [only] commercial support in the region [. . .] providing the link really between financial information, loans, credit-control people, with sales. [. . .] We've now got three [people working in commercial support], from what would have been a [Charringtons finance] department of about thirty. It's because we've moved all the loads around, but it's now very much more sort of remote and virtual teams, rather than functional teams. So, while people in Leeds in the customer accounts area don't directly report to in this region, there are people up there, certainly people work on customers and accounts within this region. So, if you like, they're reporting to us and to their own line manager in Leeds at the same time. [. . .] they'll go direct to individual sales people for the sort of day-to-day operational things. You know, we [in commercial] are very much about looking at the business in total, trying to move things forward, coach, develop people, look at processes and systems rather than individual issues with individual customers, which is very much more a sort of sales issue.

The pace of changing to the new structure with a much reduced finance function in the regions was not without risks, but he felt that customer relations had not suffered:

There were risks in terms of number of people still in the business, taking people out of the business before necessarily we'd put all the processes in and there are issues around control and things like that. But generally, things have worked out well and it's not been a huge issue for us.

At Charringtons the independent sales that the commercial managers supported were divided into 'pubs, clubs, and leisure'. 'Pubs' were traditional public houses. 'Clubs' were also known as 'working men's clubs'. They were a traditional form of association that offered licensed premises for socializing, for members only. The clubs were non-profit organizations with the aim of supplying cheap beer to their members, still mainly men. Usually, they obtained better contracts from brewers than public houses because of their much higher sales volumes. They were typically managed by committees. 'Leisure' comprised commercial outlets that were more fashionable than public houses. Examples would be bars and nightclubs. Independent restaurants and hotels also fell in this category.

The view from a newly appointed commercial manager

The new commercial managers welcomed the new organization:

> What happened a few years ago was, you had the sales operation and finance operation, and basically they were run more or less independently, so it was a 'them' and 'us' situation. The sales team could go out, sell the beer, and basically finance would report on a monthly basis the sales, how they were doing against budget etc., what the variances were and suggest ways in which they could claw back money etc. [. . .] So every month they'd attend maybe one or two sales meetings, present figures, put forward a few suggestions and that would be it. And what they decided was, really that wasn't a very good way of influencing the business, because your contact with the sales teams is quite minimal.

He felt that in his old role score-keeping and retrospective analysis took up too much of working time. Under the new organization structure the commercial managers dealt with the customers' wider commercial issues. One commercial manager gave an example of a working man's club that had difficulties in paying Charringtons for deliveries:

> The problem with the account [outlet] was the people that are running [. . .] that are on the committee have been there quite a while. And they're reluctant to change the way they operate. And the costs in the club were quite horrendous. They had people behind the bar and they were paying them phenomenal amounts of money. Their wage base was very, very high. . . Their accountants were charging them quite a lot of money [. . .] A lot of their costs had not been controlled, the contracts that they had. . . The increases from the previous year were just phenomenal, like cleaning etc. etc. Basically we just went in there and said that they did really need to organise things better and negotiate the terms of all the contacts that they had [. . .] We put forward various suggestions and they've actually taken those on board. The cash flow has increased, they are in a better position now. They had a massive stockholding, [. . .] they had

something like two and a half, three weeks worth of stock when they should only really keep 6 or 7 days worth of stock. [. . .] We were quite lucky, because they did realise that unless they made the changes, they'd come into big problems, there probably wouldn't be a club there in about 6 or 7 months time. [. . .] I spoke with the person that pulled together all the financial information and they gave me a list of creditors and things and I ran through them and looked at exactly what they were and how they were being paid. [. . .] They were paying bills for services they didn't really need. And what you've got to bear in mind is that these people are, this is a social thing for them, [. . .] they viewed it as a place where they could go to meet their friends and have a cheap drink and have a chat. They knew that things were going wrong for them, but they didn't know really what to do and how to overcome those problems. So it was quite good, I think, the fact that they were quite open-minded and they let us come in. They didn't view it as: why are Bass coming here and telling us how to run a business? They actually viewed it as: all right they've actually put the time in to come and talk us through all. It was quite constructive.

He saw this example as symptomatic of a more 'partnership-oriented' style of dealing with accounts:

It's really now more customer focused, and more getting involved with the customer and their business, because you're showing them how much they can make on selling your brands. And a lot of the brands we sell are high demand products [. . .] like Caffreys or Carling Premier. These are premium products for which we can command a reasonably higher price. And obviously the account can do the same. So rather than selling, a product like Carling Black Label, say at £1.60 a pint in the club, they can sell Carling Premier or Caffreys and charge £2.00 or £2.10 [. . .] [Still] the prices are a lot lower than if you went to a pub. But they've still got to be high enough so that the customer can make a reasonable return, in terms of servicing its own debts, and also providing an environment that's nice for the club members. Because they've got to actually think ahead all the time [. . .] maybe every 2 years, they've got to refurbish. It could be that they need money to make an extension, and they might need to take on a loan to do that, and then need money to service the loan.

Personally, he preferred the work of a commercial manager to that of a management accountant:

There's a lot of satisfaction in going to an account that's not been properly run and then walking away say two months later, knowing that you've asked for changes to be made and they've made them, and the pub's now running quite well.

The view from the sales force

Those examples would indicate that commercial managers could support the sales process by addressing questions that go beyond calculations of financial returns. The Charringtons sales force seemed to welcome the role changes in the finance function. Allan Pearce, the account manager[5] for a sales region in East Anglia, explained that his job had become a lot more interesting. He felt that in the past he just sold beer and that now it was more 'professional'. Whereas previously he had concentrated on maintaining friendly relationships with his accounts, occasionally handing out free beer, now every financial advantage given to a customer was included in the account calculation to evaluate its profitability. The customer relationship had become regularized. 'Private deals', where account managers gave favours to the accounts, could no longer by-pass the new IT systems.

Supply deals with customers were struck on the basis of presentations. A presentation to an outlet was built on a service package that the account manager thought profitable and attractive to the account. Such a package comprised a volume target for the account, a range of brands to be supplied at certain prices, a discount structure that was often tied to volumes achieved, defined standards of product delivery service and emergency engineering service for the beer cooling and pumping equipment, and often a subsidized loan and its repayment schedule with periodic payments or higher prices for beer. The presentation would highlight to the manager of the outlet or the club committee the points that the account manager thought made the proposal attractive to the customer. Account managers would prepare one or two presentations with different service levels or loan and repayment structures.

Allan was very proud of his recent presentations. He thought they worked because they demonstrated to customers that he had sat down and thought about how best to structure a deal to meet their needs. Presentations used to be photo-copied for the committee meetings. Now he used PowerPoint on a sizeable, portable computer screen. He demonstrated to me a presentation for a large foot-ball club.[6] The slides came up flashing in different colours, dancing in from left and right. He found PowerPoint much better than photocopies because it looked more professional and he could control what people could read at any one time. He and a colleague had videoed their presentation to the football club to check how they did. He was particularly proud that during the presentation he did not once men-tion the word 'discount'. Instead they highlighted to the club the gross and net profit in which their proposal would result. Emphasizing discounts made his products look cheap. Instead he preferred to emphasize the brand quality of the products and the margin that the account could make on them.

The presentations required considerable financial expertise. The structuring of the loan agreements, in particular, was a traditional domain of the finance function. They had also administered the legal documentation to ensure that Charringtons had a charge on the agreed collateral. With the newly introduced laptop computers in the sales force, financial expertise was made available to the account managers. Sitting in the company car, after talking to the manager or committee chairperson of an outlet, they could make rough calculations on the financial feasibility of proposals. The laptops were also used to make notes of changes in the business relationship with an account, for example, changes to the delivery schedule, credit status, or the volume agreements. They also entered points for action, such as record updates, equipment repairs, or special payments into the laptop. Every evening the laptops were connected to Bass Brewers' central computer system by modem to transfer the information of the day. On one visit to a club the committee chairman tipped with his forefinger on the closed laptop on the bar to indicate that he wanted to see action on a point he had raised: 'Why don't you type it in here?'

While presentations were important, they needed preparation through the continuous development of the account relationship. Every day the account manager would visit a number of outlets. Most visits were regular 'courtesy calls' to show the manager's availability for question and problems. Even though there was a central customer help line, many customers preferred to deal face to face with their familiar account manager. Alternatively they could ring him on his mobile telephone. Only rarely did such calls result in emergency visits. It was more likely that the account manager would co-ordinate deliveries or repairs from the Bass Brewers service departments.

The regular calls also had the function to 'keep in touch'. Account managers wanted to be informed about the personal circumstances of the committee chairperson or manager, have an eye on the appearance of the outlet, check how many and what sorts of customers frequented the bar, in short, know about any obstacle to the commercial success of their accounts. Particularly with clubs it was valuable to know all the committee members, not just the chairperson. This way the account manager could sound out committee members' different opinions and concerns in order to position Charringtons as the brewer best suited to address them.

The account manager's personal credibility often played a role in that. Customers were not necessarily interested in obtaining the financially most attractive deal. They also wanted credible brands and reliable delivery and equipment servicing. In the case of club committee members an overriding concern was often the secure future of their club. All large brewers would offer similarly attractive deals to a high volume club. The trustworthiness of the account manager was important to convince committee members that the brewer would stick to their promises and, if necessary, support the committee in the case of unforeseen cash problems or management difficulties.

Outlook

Looking back on the changes, Charringtons' commercial support manager was reasonably confident that they had produced the desired outcomes:

> I think the essence of what we've tried to do, is to say we've got hundreds of people in this business controlling things and producing reports that don't make any difference at all, and trying to firstly reduce that number of people, because that's an enormous amount of people who spend time churning pieces of paper and things out. But also change the focus so that finance [gets] closer to sales people [. . .] because sales people are the ones who influence performance, 'cos they're doing the deal with the customer and affecting what happens. If their finance skills are better and there's finance people working closely with them, then there's more of a chance that we can actually influence things, while at the same time putting new systems and processes in that actually reduce the number of people you need to do those reporting jobs . . .

The overall headcount in the finance department could be reduced. With the re-organization in place, commercial managers hardly generate any reports at all. Exceptions would be ad hoc issues on which they feel they need to collate comparative information to shed light on the commercial success or potential of their region:

> We won't produce any reports other than the ones that we want to produce ourselves, any analysis or investigation, that's the only time we really start reporting. [. . .] It's very much looking to where the issues are, and then just hoping you can go in and do something about it, rather than reporting everything and anything. [. . .] So our commercial managers now don't really get involved in processing-type issues, they're much more involved in adding value to the deal itself . . . and monitoring that deal to make sure it's delivering what we said it was going to deliver rather than putting the thing together in the first place.

Score-keeping and retrospective analysis were left to the management accountants at Bass Brewers head office in Burton. He felt that the roles of commercial manager and account manager were becoming more similar but they could still be distinguished:

> While the commercial manager needs to get involved with individual sales people at a detailed level, we're trying to begin to move towards commercial managers looking at the business as a whole as well, as a whole region [. . .] the edges between what an Account Manager would do and a commercial manager, are beginning to get closer and closer together, which is partly why we're trying to get commercial managers to look more at regionally-based initiatives, not simply looking at issues relating to customers in particular business units, but trying to take a view of what's happening in the business as a whole. [. . .] One exercise we're doing at the moment is looking at local accounts that aren't performing as we would expect them to, and we kick that off now when we're actually looking at every account across each business unit for the whole south-east region, rather than individual commercial managers doing something with a business unit we'll extend that out and do it for the whole region at the same time, as a regional issue rather than you know just one business unit.

A central task for commercial managers is to 'add coaching for people on commercial and finance issues'. Coaching should become an important part of the commercial managers' role, vis-à-vis sales managers and customers alike. They should be made aware of obstacles to business success and strategies for addressing them, but coaching should also raise their awareness of commercial potential. Therefore commercial managers can benefit from diverse career backgrounds:

> [They] either have a sales background or a finance background and wanted to get more involved in other things. [. . .] Commercial manager skills are more about the business rather than finance or sales, they're a mixture of things really.

Charringtons' commercial support manager himself

> spent a few years in logistics, running distribution operations from area group project work, [. . .] and then moved into sales [. . .] before moving into finance. [. . .] I think

we're moving more towards commercial skills rather than true finance skills within commercial support. And our concentration of qualified accountants would be in our finance department and financial control in Burton, obviously where they need that element of expertise. And then for people out in the field like myself, commercial managers, it's more about the relationship between sales and finance and marketing and commercial issues, rather than pure finance, technical issues. I don't really get involved in the sort of statutory reporting, tax and things like that. [. . .] It's more about brand mix, margins, loans, credit, that sort of thing. So it's more commercial than pure finance really.

As the commercial function spreads, different types of career path become possible.

The finance people can either stay in finance and get involved in financial reporting, financial control, corporate finance, and those sorts of issues, or they can take a different branch and get involved in commercial issues which will then get them involved more in sales and marketing. So, it probably provides a couple of different options for them and it means that people who aren't accountants can actually get some finance experience at the same time.

Endnotes

[1] I would like to thank Paul Thomas, Kevin Rhodes, Ray Jones, Andrew Bailey, Indy Kenth, and Allan Pearce from Bass Brewers for making the writing of this teaching case possible. This case is written to familiarize students with management accounting practices and stimulate class room discussion. It is not a comment on best practices.

[2] 'Public houses' or 'pubs' are traditional British bars that sell beer as well as other alcoholic and non-alcoholic drinks in an informal atmosphere. Traditionally they were the most important sales channel for beer, but supermarkets and wholesalers have recently gained in importance.

[3] On 12 January 1999 the pound traded at Euro 1.40.

[4] Licensed premises include public houses, restaurants, hotels, clubs, etc.

[5] Account managers are sales managers who are responsible for sales to a certain number of customers (also known as 'accounts'). They are in regular contact with their customers and occupy the most junior position in the sales hierarchy.

[6] See attached PowerPoint file of such a presentation to support multi-media teaching.

STUDENT ASSIGNMENTS

Summary and explanation:

1. What services did management accounting provide traditionally to the sales function in Charringtons?
2. What were the reasons for changing the traditional organization of the management accounting function?
3. What benefits were expected?
4. What were the risks associated with the change?
5. How was financial expertise to be relocated within the new organization structure?
6. What tasks would you still call 'management accounting' within Bass Brewers?

Analysis:

7. Within Bass Brewers, what used to be called 'management accounting work' was split into three sub-functions. How would you label those newly separated sub-functions?
8. What are the characteristics of a successful sale for Charringtons and how can sales managers achieve them?
9. Suggest different ways in which the three new sub-functions of management accounting can support the sales function.
10. Many interviewees express the view that commercial managers can better concentrate on 'adding value' to the organization. Explain what they mean when they use the term 'adding value' in this way. Are there other ways in which the finance department could 'add value' to the organization?

Discussion and speculation:

11. Is the new organization with commercial managers an improvement over the old structure?
12. Should management accounting be separated from, or integrated with, commercial management?

CASE NINE

—

KCI Konecranes: developing non-financial measures in a global crane company[1]

Kari Lukka
Markus Granlund

Introduction

KCI Konecranes is a supplier of cranes and services for vertical transport and materials handling in various manufacturing and transportation industries worldwide (Figure 9.1).[2] Its strategy is to achieve high growth by capitalizing on a global market approach and increasing service revenue. As a result of a number of acquisitions during the 1980s and 1990s, KCI currently operates in 30 countries around the globe, including a strong presence in the fast growing Asia-Pacific economies. The service business – currently over 40% of group sales – is based on firm

Figure 9.1 Examples of KCI's products: a standard crane, a paper mill crane, a goliath gantry crane

Table 9.1 Key volume and profitability figures by business area in 1996

Key figure / Business area	Maintenance Services	Standard Lifting Equipment	Special Cranes	Total
Sales (€ million)[4]	195	152	103	450
(% of total)	(43%)	(34%)	(23%)	(100%)
Operating income (€ million)[5]	15.9	16.3	16.1	48.3
(% of total)	(33%)	(34%)	(33%)	(100%)

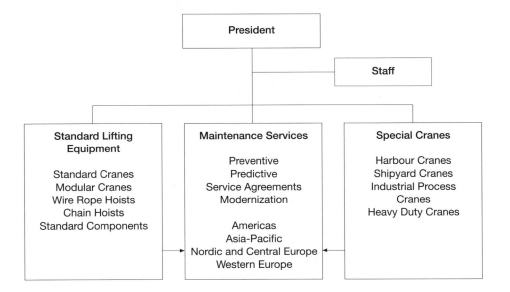

Figure 9.2 KCI Konecranes business areas

maintenance agreements with customers. With over 90,000 cranes under such agreements, KCI is the largest service provider of its kind in the world. In lifting equipment, KCI is a technology leader with over 90% of its sales coming from products launched since 1986.

The net sales of KCI for 1996 were 413 million Euro.[3] The number of personnel is more than 3,500. KCI Konecranes' shares are listed on the Helsinki Stock Exchange.

KCI's products and services form three principal business areas: Maintenance Services, Standard Lifting Equipment and Special Cranes. The key volume and profitability figures by business area in 1996 are given in Table 9.1. Subsidiaries are grouped into four geographical regions: Nordic and Central Europe, Western Europe, Americas, and Asia-Pacific, covering in principle all business areas. However, geographical segmentation plays a particularly important role in the Maintenance Services business (Figure 9.2).

Maintenance services business

The crane business in general is a mature industry in Western economies. In Europe and the US, investment in new industrial infrastructure, leading to a need for new cranes, is related to growth in GNP. The crane maintenance business is, however, a relatively new one. This service business is still in its early stages of development; crane maintenance as a professionally run specialist business does not have a long history. KCI has attained worldwide market leadership in crane maintenance and modernization, and is able to service all kinds of cranes, regardless of their original manufacturer.

KCI's objective in its Maintenance Services business (with almost 1950 employees in 1996) is to focus on prevention and prediction, rather than on repair when a failure has occurred. The aim is to reduce to a minimum unexpected downtime and other surprises caused by crane faults, and, as a result, to create cost advantages for their customers. The company stresses particularly the planned nature of their maintenance activities, and its high technical competence, due to the fact that KCI is one of the largest players in the crane manufacturing industry in the world, and the largest in industrial process cranes.

Tightened legislation has led to more and more rigorous rules on safety, increasing complexity but also the potential liability risk for the crane operator. Currently some 70% of crane maintenance is performed by customers' in-house maintenance teams that are typically responsible not only for cranes but also for a variety of other types of equipment. KCI management believes that KCI's preventive maintenance approach is particularly appropriate in this kind of situation, offering KCI a competitive advantage over in-house maintenance teams, leading to increased outsourcing of these services by crane users. Also, it is an approach that the other significant group of competitors, the local service providers, are seldom able to copy because of insufficient resources to offer performance guarantees, inherent to the KCI preventive maintenance concept.

The Maintenance Services business is operationally divided into two major subareas: Field Services and Modernization. The latter refers to large projects, replacing existing crane technology by new technology, and typically related to the capital investment budget of the customer. Field Services cover all other types of crane maintenance activities, such as preventive maintenance programmes, inspection and service contracts, on-call repairs, small-scale field modernizations, and the sales of replacement parts. In the area of Field Services, KCI aims at increasing the number of long-term service contracts with their customers.

In 1996, the performance of the Maintenance Services business was primarily characterized by growth: both sales and order backlog increased considerably during the year. Field Services' performance – best described by the number of cranes with annual maintenance contracts – exceeded 90,000 cranes. The business volume of modernizations of old equipment increased as well. The total increase in sales of Maintenance Services, at fixed exchange rates, was 22% and in orders 21% (14% in sales and 13% in orders in 1995).[6] The operating margin stayed a little below the 1995 level because of accelerating expenses with the fast growth. In absolute terms the operating margin increased to EUR 16 million (EUR 14 million 1995).

Field Services in Finland

Crane Services Finland (CSF), a profit-centre headed by Mr Rauno Haapanen, is responsible for maintenance field services in Finland. Mr Haapanen reports to Mr Harry Ollila, who is in charge of the Nordic and Central Europe Region of KCI, and responsible for all KCI activities in his geographic area. However, as KCI operates a partial matrix structure, Mr Ollila shares this responsibility with two other directors: for the Standard Lifting Equipment business with Mr Arto Juosila, who is globally in charge of that business, and for the Special Cranes business with Mr Antti Vanhatalo, who also runs that business segment globally.[7] Crane Services Finland, operating in the Finnish domestic market only, is divided into four geographical service branches – South, West, East and North – each of which again includes several service districts. The four service branches operate with a profit-centre responsibility as well as CSF itself. The organizational position of CSF is outlined in Figure 9.3.

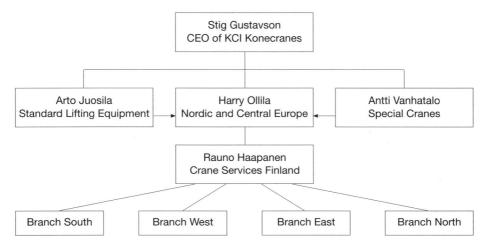

Figure 9.3 The position of Crane Services Finland in the KCI organization

CSF, with personnel of 170 in 1996, is regarded as the most developed profit centre in the Field Services business of KCI. It has operated for a relatively long time and has managed to gain a large market share. In other countries, where KCI has operated for a shorter period of time, a large proportion of sales often comes from on-call type services; CSF has already managed to gain a large number of long-term service contracts on a fixed price basis. As a result, CSF has established a solid position in the Finnish maintenance services market, and its yearly sales figures tend to remain relatively stable. In many other countries, the field services units of KCI currently have much larger growth potential.

The development of non-financial measures: the headquarters perspective

The development project involving non-financial measures at KCI started in 1991, during a top management conference of the crane division of Kone Oy,[8] dealing with quality issues. Stig Gustavson, who was in charge of Kone Oy's crane business at that time (the current CEO of KCI) was the primary initiator of this development project. The notion of reliability, understood from the customer's viewpoint, was raised as the key issue to be managed, and it was felt that factors contributing to reliability had to be made visible through systematic measurement. Teuvo Rintamäki, at that time the controller of Kone Oy's crane business and today the CFO of KCI, was made the 'owner' of the project and given the responsibility for the practical development of those measures. He describes the reasons for this solution:

> One attempted to ascertain preciseness, functioning and the practical handling of reporting, and accounting people are used to report internationally and strictly. Also the consideration of the practical form of these measures was left to me.

Through the notion of reliability, KCI's top management attempted to capture the major strategic issues of the firm: the goal, to sell and maintain safe cranes which function without breakdowns and therefore do not cause costly down-time to customers. Reliability was regarded as important for the global business concept of KCI as well. Top management felt that – even though KCI can gain significant competitive advantage through economies of scale in production and product development, and by spreading acquired know-how internationally – being global also involved considerable costs. One of the popular slogans at KCI is the aim to be 'globally local', meaning that KCI has to be able to respond to local competitive pressures and meet local demands all over the world. KCI has to be globally flexible in order to survive – and this applies particularly to its Maintenance Services business. Consequently, it was felt that KCI had to be superior to competitors in quality issues. Rintamäki puts it as follows:

> We cannot afford to make mistakes in doing business similar to local service providers . . . In order to survive in this business in the long run, we have to be number one in quality. Reliability is of vital importance to us, since we are not a local well-known establishment but just some KCI from somewhere. Our customers have an inherent tendency to doubt whether we can operate effectively.

Even though a few non-financial measures, such as delivery reliability, cycle times and various measures of productivity, had been developed and used in some local crane business units before 1991, CFO Rintamäki felt that such prior measurements had been very unsystematic. On the other hand, financial reporting has always tended to be comprehensive and well-organized at KCI. The key financial indicators at KCI are those very typical of Finnish industrial firms, including various measures of selling activity (e.g. realized deliveries; orders received; order backlog), profitability (e.g. value added and other different contribution margins; operating result; return on assets), and certain balance sheet and cash flow based measures (e.g. working capital items; fixed assets; operative cash flow). According to Rintamäki, even though financial measures have always been, and still are, the core of measurement at KCI, their relative importance somewhat decreased after the implementation of the new non-financial measurement system. However, the development and implementation of non-financial indicators did not cause any change in the financial measurement system applied at KCI.

Based on the strategic importance of being reliable in the eyes of customers, CFO Rintamäki started the development process by identifying the critical success factors both for the two new equipment business areas and for the Maintenance Services business. In the latter case, the critical success factors were considered to be:

1. Instead of selling repair services, KCI aims at selling the availability of cranes, based on fixed price, long-term maintenance services contracts, in which proactive maintenance activities are the key element. The goal is that cranes will always be in working order, and no down-time will be caused by broken cranes. KCI considers this focus to reflect a differentiation strategy, since there is practically no competition using this service approach.

2. Highly developed technological know-how, based on the fact that KCI is, in addition to being a service provider, a manufacturer of new crane products. KCI aims to consider the maintenance needs at the product development phase, for instance, by the current standard of installing a condition monitoring device in all new equipment (whether the customer likes to pay for it or not).

As both of the above issues may appear costly alternatives for the customer in the short run, the true challenge of these two approaches is to persuade both current and potential new customers to include in their crane maintenance cost analysis the losses caused by down-time and other problems due to broken cranes. KCI management feels it is up to them to educate their customers in this regard, a task which has so far turned out to be rather difficult.

In addition, while developing non-financial measures for the Maintenance Services business, the CFO paid particular attention to motivating service unit managers to take advantage of existing growth potential in their respective markets. In Rintamäki's view, it is of vital importance to continuously obtain new customers under service contracts, even if they might appear small in the beginning: according to his experience, all new customers tend to create sales of about five times their initial order size in the course of time.

The applied non-financial measures in the Maintenance business

Given the above two major success factors, Rintamäki started to develop the non-financial measures to be used, a task he did not find particularly simple. In that phase of the process, he consulted a couple of high-ranking, experienced Maintenance Business managers, encountering, however, no significant differences of opinion.[9] Rintamäki's major aim was to develop measures which stimulate growth. The end result was three non-financial performance measures (see Appendix), to be applied in the Field Services units of the Maintenance Services business area.

Lost Contract Ratio

$$\frac{Number\ of\ lost\ service\ contracts}{Number\ of\ new\ service\ contracts} * 100$$

- discontinued orders initiated by KCI itself are not counted, nor are renewals counted as new contracts;
- a ratio value of 100% means that KCI has lost (number-wise) as many old contracts as it has been able to win new ones during the period;
- the ratio is intended to stimulate growth by winning new customers;
- high figures typically indicate problems.[10]

Service Hit Ratio

$$\frac{Total\ orders\ received}{Total\ quotations} * 100$$

- measured in monetary units, on a monthly basis;
- both very low figures (KCI is not considered an attractive service provider) and very high ones (can be a sign of lost growth potential) may indicate problems;
- should be interpreted together with volume and the development in contribution margin.

Pricing Ratio

$$\frac{Sales\ or\ orders\ quoted\ at\ (pre)fixed\ prices}{Total\ sales\ or\ orders} * 100$$

- high percentages are considered favourable, since in the long run services based on fixed prices are in the interest of both KCI and its customers.[11]

These three non-financial measures were implemented in 1992 in a straightforward manner. No pilot tests were made, the CFO simply circulated a motivation letter and reporting instructions around the organization in order to start the non-financial measurement immediately. Rintamäki commented upon the issues linked with data registration and standardization as follows:

Well, it was not a question of a very complicated issue. We did not waste time on that, we didn't make it that difficult. Of course, some people wondered how to count all these things in practice, what should be registered, what not. Registration systems differ a bit in different parts of the organisation . . . We thought the measuring of these issues is anyway relevant, even though we had to overlook some problems of comparability.

In fact, some parts of the organization seemed to take seriously the difficulty of comparing the resulting figures of the non-financial measures. In one French unit the CFO even had to promise in writing that the non-financial measurement results from the unit in question would never be compared with those from other KCI units. However, at KCI Headquarters, comparability was regarded as an irrelevant issue. According to Rintamäki, the most important things are, instead (i) the ability to follow the trend of development in each profit centre, (ii) to secure a positive development trend, and (iii) to conduct measurement on an honest basis overall.

In 1994, the CFO noticed a declining activity level regarding the provision of non-financial information from operating units. Therefore, he once more circulated a reminder, together with reporting instructions. In 1996, he felt that the process had reached a state in which he himself could start playing a smaller role: he had the impression that reports of non-financial measures were discussed monthly in profit centres following demands of the managers in charge. Non-financial measures are part of the routine monthly reporting (see Figures 9.4 and 9.5), and they are raised as a discussion topic about twice a year within the top management of KCI.

The consequences of non-financial measurement: the headquarters perspective

CFO Rintamäki felt that the main positive effect of non-financial measurement in the Maintenance Services business so far has been the increasing emphasis on long-term service contracts. This contributes to the changing image and growing importance of the service business in KCI's business portfolio. In fact, KCI top management has invested in getting rid of the traditional idea of maintenance as being nothing but 'after sales' for the 'more important core business' of selling new cranes. Consequently, at least officially, the traditional state of affairs has indeed turned upside down: currently, Maintenance Services is regarded as a business area at least as important as the new equipment business.

No significant dysfunctional effects were felt to be caused by the non-financial measurement system. The randomly emerging arguments and conflicts linked to it are regarded as a natural element in this kind of development – that is, as a useful means to shake up the prevailing structures. 'Of course those who look bad in the light of a certain measure do not like the measure itself', Rintamäki comments.

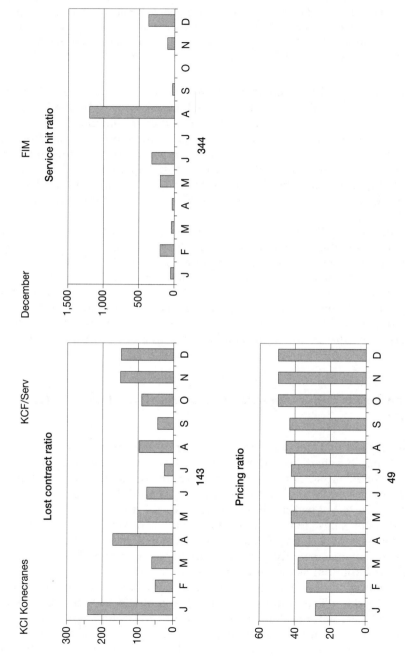

Figure 9.4 Non-financial performance measurement report/Crane Services Finland (1996)

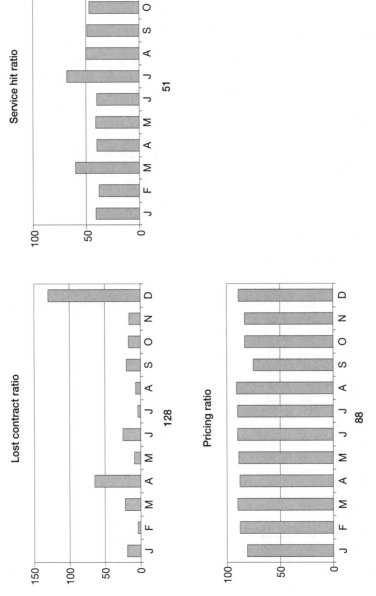

Figure 9.5 Non-financial performance measurement report/Crane Services USA (1996)

Recent developments of non-financial measurement: the benchmarks of performance

In 1995, a new development project in the Maintenance Services business was started, again initiated by CEO Gustavson and owned by CFO Rintamäki. This project, under the heading of 'Benchmarks in Maintenance services', aimed at developing the operational practices in this business area, to improve support for the global business image of KCI. A consultant was hired who spent months travelling around the world visiting KCI's maintenance business units in order to get a picture of their current practices. He reported to KCI top management that service practices often differed significantly from one place to another, and that much had to be done in order to create global, homogenous maintenance business practices at KCI.

One part of this benchmark project has been to develop new performance measures for the Maintenance Services business. The CFO felt that, of the three non-financial measures in use, the Service Hit Ratio, in particular, did not work properly. At the moment there is a list of six (partly) new benchmark measures, five of which are non-financial in nature, the remaining one being a financial one. These suggested control measures are:

Staff to Operatives Ratio

$$\frac{Number\ of\ staff\ personnel}{Number\ of\ operative\ personnel} * 100$$

- reflects the aim to find a balance between supporting and operating personnel;
- 'ideal' for a branch is 1/4;
- 'ideal' for a country or a region is 1/3.

Field Services vs. Home Base Services

$$\frac{Sales\ from\ services\ in\ the\ field}{Sales\ from\ services\ from\ the\ home\ base} * 100$$

- reflects the aim to find a balance between operations in the fixed base unit location (the sale of replacement parts, components, modernizations, etc.) and operations in the field (contract base services, on-call services, etc. executed at the premises of customers);
- 'ideal' 70%/30%.

Pricing Ratio

$$\frac{Sales\ of\ SP21,\ SP22\ and\ SP23\ at\ (pre)fixed\ prices}{Total\ sales\ of\ SP21,\ SP22\ and\ SP23} * 100$$

- SP21 refers to contract based inspection and maintenance work; SP22 to small planned repair work and field modernizations; SP23 to on-call repair work (see Table 9.2);

Table 9.2 Cumulative deliveries of CSF in 1996 (€ thousands)*

	Period 12	Cumul. 12	Budg. 12	Variance	Var.–%	Budg./year	Order base 97
SP20+21 Inspection and long-term service contracts	252	4,334	4,278	57	1.3	4,278	4,047 (agreement base)
SP22R Smaller planned repairs	346	3,346	3,047	300	9.8	3,047	
SP22M Field modernizations	517	4,183	3,501	682	19.5	3,501	586
SP23 On-call service	106	1,082	1,155	–74	–6.4	1,155	
SP24 Spare parts on shelf	64	868	795	73	9.1	795	
SP25 Manufactured spare parts	81	1,291	1,678	–388	–23.1	1,678	280
SP28 In-house fab. & repair	62	739	714	24	3.4	714	31
SP29 Consulting	73	109	66	43	66.2	66	
SP31 Internal sales/field	284	2,228	839	1,390	165.7	839	115
Total	1,783	18,179	16,072	2,107	13.1	16,072	1,012 (only order base)

* The figures in the table have been *moderately* disguised. All the different row items have been modified using the same procedure in order to maintain an unchanged ranking order.

- measures how much (%) of total sales from the field are quoted and sold at fixed prices instead of 'time and material' based prices;
- is meant to be an improved version of the Pricing Ratio currently in use;
- target ratio ≥ 85%.

CMII %

- CMII[12] refers to contribution after a profit centre's variable operating costs (before profit centre's fixed operating costs, depreciation and interests);[13]
- has been used for a long time at KCI;
- a certain minimum target level has been set; 1% annual improvement is pursued.

Days Sales Outstanding (DSO)

$$365: \frac{Sales\ from\ last\ three\ months * 4}{Accounts/receivables\ (3\ months\ average)}$$

- measures the number of days sales are outstanding;
- target around 45;[14]
- DSO is today typically around 60 at KCI, which is regarded as unacceptable by the CFO.

Contract Renewal Rate

$$\frac{Number\ of\ renewed\ service\ contracts}{Number\ of\ existing\ service\ contracts} * 100$$

- measures the number of renewed service contracts divided by all existing contracts, the renewal of which becomes considered during the period;
- core idea: 'Better keep the customer base you have';
- meant to be a more 'optimistic' version of the Lost Contract Ratio used currently;
- target values: 100% for key customers and 90% for others.

According to CFO Rintamäki's plans, these (partly) new benchmark measures will replace, in the course of time, the currently used three non-financial measures, described above. At the moment they are not yet formally used in a systematic manner, with the exception of the traditionally used CMII%. However, the CFO has the impression that they may be used on an ad hoc basis in some units of the Maintenance Services business.

The profit centre perspective

> It was rather surprising . . . when the reliability concept was imported here it was only banderoles on the walls, and official notices stating that we have decided that this is our model of operation. Though I do believe in it, and most of our customers believe in it . . . (Mr Haapanen, the Head of CSF)

Leadership style and management control at CSF

Engineer Rauno Haapanen, the leader of CSF, has come a long way to obtain his present position. He can argue he knows the business and the needs of its customers. His 35-year experience in the field includes major transformations in the business. During the last 10 years, especially the Maintenance Services business has developed rapidly. While in the mid-1980s, servicemen walked into – mainly Finnish – factories to commonly undertake a specific repair task, today the global maintenance business is of a totally different nature. The procedure has developed into selling total service packages, including comprehensive and carefully planned preventive maintenance programmes for each individual customer. Rather than running around after emergency calls, CSF sells availability, which means that the crane will reliably work whenever the customer wants it to work. The idea of preventive maintenance is the core of the business today.

Mr Haapanen's leadership style relies heavily on his long experience in the field. He has a thorough knowledge of the work of the regular servicemen as well as close contact with customers. Mr Haapanen pursues management control largely using hands-on principles. He values the financial reports as management tools, but not without reservations. He considers non-financial measures useful, especially those they have been applying for a long time. These include a set of traditional 'factory-measures', making the production efficiency especially visible.

The role of non-financial measures at Crane Services Finland

Mr Haapanen has been involved with the initial non-financial measurement project led by CFO Rintamäki in terms of commenting on the measures during their development phase. While Mr Haapanen has considered the efforts to develop the measurement system a valuable task, he has not been satisfied with the outcome:

> . . . they are not our models of operation, they are not built into our target models, they are nowhere. You cannot see them in the annual reports and nobody follows them. We can, though, discuss them quickly informally, but what we really concentrate upon is the report on financial results . . . (Mr Haapanen)

The CSF Controller, Mr Jari Virtanen, employed by KCI for 5 years, calculates and reports every month the Lost Contract Ratio, the Service Hit Ratio and the Pricing Ratio to the CFO at Headquarters. His concern with these measures is limited to the fact that they have to be calculated and reported. He does not know exactly for what purposes Headquarters is using these measures, nor who in addition to the CFO is looking at these figures.[15] In his view, the calculation and reporting is just another job to be done, since there exist detailed orders from Headquarters, and computational instructions are provided. The instructions are clear to Mr Virtanen, but in his view, the underlying strategic motives for calculating these figures remain ambiguous in the formal 'manual'.

The attitude of CSF management towards the non-financial measures is somewhat mixed. Whereas there is scepticism of the need for 'official' measures calculated for further reporting, the role of non-financial measures in general is considered very important. Their role in explaining the background to financial data is considered valuable.

> . . . the financial data are carefully followed. Every month, we go through the reports line by line . . . but when we reach the question of why it is like it is, then we start to miss measures on what has occured behind the financial figures. When we go deeper, the non-financial measures tell us of the reasons for the realised financial performance. (Mr Virtanen)

In addition to the 'officially' reported financial and non-financial measures, CSF has traditionally undertaken productivity measurements of its own, offering insights into the background of financial figures, as referred to by Mr Virtanen above. Such measures as maintenance services hours spent per crane, the proportion of sold service hours per total hours paid, sales in monetary units per hour, contribution in monetary units per hour, and sales per crane, are being applied locally at CSF. Sometimes also productivity figures, like added value per wages and salaries, and added value per capita, are calculated.

Views on the currently reported non-financial measures

In Controller Virtanen's view, the Lost Contract Ratio 'doesn't say anything in practice'.[16] He sees also some technical problems with the Lost Contract Ratio, for instance its focus on the absolute number of contracts.

> What if we lost one agreement worth of 1 000 and gained three agreements worth of 1 000, or gained three agreements worth 1 000 and lost one of 100 000. The measure shows excellent performance in both cases, even though we received only 2 000 in the first case, and, in the latter case, made a loss of 97 000 . . .[17]

In addition, the strategic motives for calculating the Service hit ratio are ambiguous to Mr Virtanen. He comments on the ratio and its monthly-based calculation as follows:

> . . . we may offer in this month for 500 000 and get 5000 in new agreements. Then we have 5/500. Next month, we may offer only 50 000, but get 500 000, and the value is 500/50. If we really want to see how we 'hit', it should be calculated in 3, 6 or 12 month averages . . .

Controller Virtanen knows that there are two versions of the Pricing Ratio – the one currently in use and the forthcoming benchmark version – and that a change is probably going to take place in the items included in the Pricing Ratio in the near future. In the older version, the numerator consisted of SP22M, while in the new version the numerator includes SP21 and SP22M (see Appendix 1 and Table 9.2).

Correspondingly, the denominator will change from the sum of SP22 and SP23 to include all items going from SP21 to SP23.[18]

In Controller Virtanen's view, what the Headquarters is seeking with the Pricing Ratio is the proportion of their work which they have been able to define or sell in advance. The remaining sales include much more uncertainty. In sum, the more KCI has sales in fixed price bids, the more systematic the operation would be. However, Mr Virtanen finds the Pricing Ratio complicated in the sense that time and material based sales are often a profitable business for CSF (see Table 9.3).[19]

Mr Virtanen has understood that the performance targets provided by Headquarters imply something which can be pursued on a voluntary basis. He views them as long-term objectives, which cannot be affected in a shorter perspective than half a year. The target levels for the non-financial measures basically appear appropriate to Mr Virtanen, with the exception of the target for the Pricing Ratio, which does not gain full support from him. He is very sceptical about the objective of 85%, or more, related to the forthcoming benchmark version of the formula: he does not believe it is realistic for any kind of operation within the Field Services business, regardless of where the operation is geographically located, or in which growth phase a unit is.

In general, with the exception of the Pricing Ratio, Mr Virtanen does not consider he is well informed as far as the forthcoming six benchmark measures, currently under development by the CFO, are concerned. He is roughly aware of their calculation bases, but has only a vague picture of their rationales. In sum: 'I know they are being developed and, perhaps soon, even being implemented at the profit centre level'.

Remarks on the style of introducing and implementing the non-financial measures

In both Mr Haapanen's and Mr Virtanen's view the development of non-financial measures is a 'nice effort' at the level of ideas, but the implementation leaves a lot to be desired. Also, they both share the view that these measures should not, in any case, be taken to lower levels of the organization than the profit centre level.

It has not occurred to Mr Haapanen that the non-financial measures could relate to changes in strategy or the business concept in general. For him, they more or less represent just a new way of playing with numbers, implemented by the accounting people at Headquarters. In his view, a good management information system includes plenty of information on one 'simple' issue – the customer. Actually, at CSF, they try to create customer reports including various items on the customers' characteristics and their relationship to KCI. People at CSF hoped that Headquarters could provide them with information about customer issues: they know that Headquarters deals directly with many of the larger customers. Still, Mr

Table 9.3 1996 CMII report of CSF (€ thousands)*

CSF	1995 Total Vol.	1995 Total CMII%	1996 Total Vol.	1996 Total CMII%	1996 Total CMII	Budget for this year Vol.	Budget for this year CMII%	Budget for this year CMII	Forecast Vol.	Forecast CMII%	Forecast CMII	Unsold/Forecast Vol.	Unsold/Forecast CMII%	Unsold/Forecast CMII
SP20	224	13.4	217	13.0	28	289	12.9	37	221	12.8	28	4	8.6	0.3
SP21	3,830	35.4	4,117	37.4	1,538	3,988	30.3	1,210	4,102	32.6	1,336	−15	1,333.3	−202
SP22R	3,024	38.3	3,346	40.0	1,337	3,047	34.5	1,051	3,258	39.4	1,285	−88	59.8	−52
SP22M	3,214	32.0	4,183	30.9	1,294	3,501	30.0	1,051	4,371	30.4	1,330	188	19.4	36
SP23	1,147	40.1	1,082	42.1	455	1,155	37.7	436	1,051	38.9	409	−30	153.3	−46
SP24	821	40.6	868	42.4	368	795	39.0	310	862	40.7	351	−6	283.3	−17
SP25	1,814	36.6	1,291	38.5	496	1,678	36.4	612	1,381	37.3	515	91	20.0	18
SP28	778	32.9	739	26.6	197	714	33.8	241	733	26.0	191	−6	116.9	−7
SP29	64	59.0	109	65.7	72	66	50.8	33	92	64.8	60	−17	70.6	−12
SP31	1,217	6.8	2,228	14.5	323	839	19.7	165	2,208	12.2	270	−20	260.0	−52
Total	16,134	33.5	18,179	33.6	6,108	16,071	32.0	5,146	18,278	31.6	5,774	99	−336.8	−335

* The figures in the table have been *moderately* disguised. All the different row items have been modified using the same procedure in order to maintain an unchanged ranking order.

Haapanen's formal, personal performance objectives – which also serve as a basis of a bonus incentive scheme – relate only to financial figures, primarily to the operating result, ROA, and fixed cost items. All CSF employees are under bonus incentive schemes, tailored for everyone in accordance with their job contents. None of the three non-financial measures now in use in the Maintenance Services business affect directly any of those schemes.

Mr Haapanen and Mr Virtanen are dissatisfied with the way in which new things are being introduced in the KCI organization in general. They both demand more open communication and more consideration for the 'opinions in the field'. They both believe in management by financial and non-financial measures, but they observe that the measures should be rolled out into their organization in a different way:

> . . . more bottom-up . . . in this form I don't believe in it, since nobody else but accounting is doing it here. (Mr Haapanen)

> . . . you have to ask the field whether the measures are helping them. If you want the measures to be used, you should ask for several opinions from different places . . . the measures should be constructed in co-operation. You also have to realise that these are not new issues as such. This is just a new way of bringing these issues forth. (Mr Virtanen)

It is worth noting that CSF management in principle does not feel uneasy with the criticisms of the ideas launched by the CFO. Rather, for one reason or another, there seems to exist a certain lack of enthusiasm among the CSF management to participate in the improvement of the measures: '. . . it has just been left undone somehow' (Mr Virtanen).

CSF vis-à-vis other Maintenance Services units

Both Mr Haapanen and Mr Virtanen have a feeling that in Maintenance Services units of some other countries the non-financial measures – which at CSF are calculated only for Headquarters' use – might be more actively applied in managing unit operations. The explanation for this is clear-cut to them: they see a relation between the business position a unit has been able to achieve and its style of management control.

As far as they know, CSF is often used as a benchmark for other Maintenance Services units within KCI: it is a well-established unit having shown exemplary performance, located in the same area as the Headquarters of KCI. In comparison, the US profit centre, for instance, is a fast growing, but much less established unit, and moreover, is located geographically far away from the Headquarters. As a result, the need to measure at arms length the different dimensions of its performance is likely to be more prominent.

Endnotes

1 We would like to thank Teuvo Rintamäki, Rauno Haapanen and Jari Virtanen from KCI Konecranes for making this teaching case possible. The helpful comments of Tom Groot, Marko Järvenpää, Vesa Partanen, Hanno Roberts and Tero-Seppo Tuomela are gratefully acknowledged.

2 The data concerning the case company are updated to June 1997. Any changes thereafter are not considered in this text.

3 The FIM values are changed to the Euro currency with the official exchange rate (1 January 1999) of 1 Euro = 5.94573 FIM.

4 Including internal sales.

5 Before group costs and consolidated items.

6 The number of orders does not include the value of renewed annual maintenance contracts.

7 However, as far as the Maintenance Services business is concerned, this matrix organization does not exist. Accordingly, there is no global director of Maintenance Services at KCI.

8 At that time, the business that now constitutes KCI Konecranes was not yet an independent company, but part of a larger international corporation, Kone Oy. In 1994, Kone Oy undertook a major reshaping of its activities, and its crane business was bought by a consortium led by Industri Kapital Limited Partnership. For the purpose of this case, no distinction will be made between the former crane business area of Kone Oy and KCI Konecranes as an independent company, since operationally there is no difference between the two.

9 Rintamäki states that a profit-centre manual for Crane Services Finland from the 1980s was one of the major sources of ideas for his development work.

10 According to Rintamäki, Lost Contract Ratio values tend to be close, or even more than 100% in mature Maintenance Service business units, while in growing business units they should be less than 100%.

11 See the Appendix for details.

12 Read 'CM two'.

13 CMII is thus a variable costing based gross margin. In KCI's financial reporting there is currently no such concept in use as CMI (read 'CM one'), but a margin equalling the value added (contribution after materials, semifinished products, subcontracting, internal purchases, freight, provisions, and change in WIP).

14 KCI's customers' options typically are: in-house services, which cause payrolls with a cycle time < 30 days, and local small competitors, which require payment in < 45 days in order to survive.

15 These three non-financial measures are not part of the routine monthly reporting of CSF.

16 Even though Mr Virtanen has very limited knowledge of the Contract renewal rate – one of the forthcoming Benchmark measures, meant to replace the Lost contract ratio over the course of time – he has yet formed an idea that it represents an improvement as compared to the Lost contract ratio: 'This new one focuses on the importance of keeping the existing customers and agreements, a new idea compared to the old one . . .'.

17 For reference, in 1996 CSF had about 1,400 agreements (about 10 cranes per one agreement) and the value of an annual agreement amounted to around 3,000 Euro on average (figures moderately disguised).

[18] For further consideration of these measures, note that SP23 is merely time and material based sales; SP22R is mainly time and material based, but may include a small amount of fixed price sales; and SP22M is mainly fixed priced, but may include a small amount of time and material based sales. In practice, the fixed price sales and the time and material based sales within these two latter mentioned revenue items are not distinguished from each other in routine reporting.

[19] However, CFO Rintamäki argues that the high margin time and material based sales of CSF come particularly from sales to KCI's long-term customers, from which CSF gets sales registered primarily in items of SP21 or SP22M.

STUDENT ASSIGNMENTS

1. Discuss the competitive environment of KCI Konecranes and the recent changes in its strategy.

2. Describe the main characteristics of the Crane Services Finland (CSF) unit.

3. Evaluate the way the development and implementation of non-financial measures was organized at KCI. What could have been the alternatives for the selected organization?

4. How do the three non-financial measures developed support the strategy of the Field Services segment of the Maintenance Business at KCI? How about the six forthcoming ones, i.e. the so-called Benchmark measures of performance? Do you think it is a good idea that the currently applied three non-financial measures will probably be soon replaced by the benchmark measures?

5. In your view, what other non-financial measures could have been considered as useful for the Field Services segment of the Maintenance business at KCI?

6. Using the data in Table 9.3, calculate both versions of the Pricing Ratio (the currently used and the forthcoming Benchmark version of it) of CSF in 1996. Evaluate the differences from a strategic perspective.

7. Consider the balance between financial and non-financial measures at KCI. How would you comment on the fact that Controller Virtanen finds 'the Pricing Ratio a bit complicated in the sense that the time and material based sales is often indeed a good business for CSF' (quote from the case text)?

8. What might explain the fact that CSF's monthly Lost Contract Ratio values in 1996 are often more than 100%, whereas the monthly Lost Contract Ratios of the US Field Services profit centre tend to be below 100% (Figures 9.4 and 9.5)? In addition, compare the Pricing Ratio figures of CSF and those of the US profit-centre in Figures 9.4 and 9.5. Explain the differences.

9. Provide reasons for the limited application of the non-financial measures, developed by CFO Rintamäki, at CSF.

Appendix: A quote from KCI reporting instructions

The non-financial measures for the Maintenance Services business – a quotation from KCI reporting instructions:

Lost contract ratio

$$\frac{Number\ of\ lost\ service\ contracts}{Number\ of\ new\ service\ contracts} * 100$$

Service contracts (SP21) here mean maintenance contracts as defined in the Rush Steering report. A contract is lost when a customer either cancels it or refuses to renew it. This might be due to loss to a competitor or an internal maintenance department. Sometimes a customer's preferred solution is to stop maintenance altogether. Losses due to such reasons as insolvency, bankruptcy or shutdown of a plant do not count. Losses initiated by ourselves are not counted. Renewals are not counted as new contracts. A 100% ratio means that we have lost (number-wise) as many old contracts as we have been able to win new ones during the period. Lost contract ratio is reported on ROW N915 (RUSH Steering) and measures performance during that particular month or period.

Service hit ratio

$$\frac{Total\ orders\ received}{Total\ quotations} * 100$$

If we are winning orders then it is assumed that our maintenance services are well perceived by customers. If the hit ratio is very low then obviously we have not been found attractive or sufficiently competitive. On the other hand a very high hit ratio may indicate that the growth potential is not fully utilized. The service hit ratio should be interpreted together with volume and CMII development. This ratio is reported on ROW N916 (RUSH Steering) and it measures performance during that particular month or period.

Pricing ratio

$$\frac{Sales\ or\ orders\ quoted\ at\ (pre)fixed\ prices}{Total\ sales\ or\ orders} * 100$$

This ratio measures how much (%) of total repair works and on-call services (SP22 and SP23) are quoted and sold at fixed prices instead of 'time and material' based prices. This figure is reported on ROW N917 (RUSH Steering) and it measures performance during that particular month or period.

CASE TEN

—

Management control in the Credito Italiano Bank during passage from a protected to a competitive market

Angelo Riccaboni
Antonio Barretta

Introduction

Credito Italiano was founded in 1870 under the name Banca di Genova. It conserved this name for more than twenty years, during which it operated primarily on a regional level. In 1895 it adopted the title Credito Italiano and began to expand its operations beyond the confines of the region of Liguria. In that same year the main Milanese branch was opened. From that point on the bank underwent considerable growth and became the first Italian credit institute to open a branch in London, in 1911.

The recession of the 1930s represented a moment of economic crisis, both in Italy and internationally, and its repercussions were equally felt in the credit sector. Credit institutes which had become closely linked to industry (mixed banks), as was the case of Credito Italiano, were particularly hard hit. The Italian government was forced to take over the industrial portfolios and share capital of those major banks in difficulty,[1] including Credito Italiano, which became a bank of national interest in 1933. [2]

The most noteworthy event in recent years was the privatization of Credito Italiano, which took place in 1993. Prior to this transformation, 65% of its share capital was publicly owned. At present the bank is a public limited company in which no single investor may control more than 3% of the share capital with his voting rights.[3]

Table 10.1 reports some significant data taken from Credit's 1997 annual accounts and compares them with those of other important Italian banks.

In recent years Credito Italiano has had to adapt to not only a significant change in the scenario, which has made the banking sector much more competitive, but also a revision of the corporate framework which has greatly influenced the way the bank runs its business. These upheavals have required the corporate organism

Table 10.1   Accounting and extra-accounting data for Credito Italiano Bank, 1997

Characteristics	Data	Position in the classification of Italian Banks[4]
Average number of employees	14,129	6
Number of branches	665	7
Interest margin (€)	1,151,182,000	6
Earning margin (€)	1,955,822,000	7
Operating profit (€)	211,230,000	4
ROE	6.18%	25
Accounts receivable (€)	26,366,157,000	U
Doubtful debts (€)	608,386,000	12
Frozen assets (€)	7,157,576,000	U
Total assets (€)	53,243,091,000	7
Bond engagements (€)	14,199,465,000	U
Due to clients (€)	18,854,808,000	U
Net assets (€)	3,626,560,000	5
Securities administered/in custody (€)	67,596,605,000	U

U = data unavailable

to be modified in various ways: organizationally, strategically, commercially, etc., not to mention management control techniques.

In particular our attention will be focused on the recent evolution that the managerial incentive system has undergone, recognizing this aspect as part of the vaster realm of management control instruments.

The evolution of management control from the 1970s to the end of the 1980s

The 1970s

Banking activity in Italy had long been rigidly regulated as a result of the importance it had assumed in developing and maintaining the macro-economic balance of economic systems. This importance may be explained in two ways:

- Banks play the role of indispensable financial intermediaries in the process of accumulation.
- Banks are capable of producing money and therefore of influencing the overall liquidity of the economic system and consequently its monetary stability.

The banking law issued in Italy in 1936 served as the legislative point of reference for the Italian banking industry for 50 years. It appeared during a historical period which was profoundly affected by the banking crisis of the 1920s and 1930s resulting from intertwined bank and industrial ownership. It is therefore understandable that the main goal of the legislator was to ensure the stability of the banking system in order to avoid similar crises in the future.

From the outset the credit authorities[5] and the Bank of Italy in particular perceived their goal of stability and competition as being mutually exclusive. They therefore provided for a rigid segmentation of the banking markets,[6] forcing intermediaries to become highly specialized. The objective of stability was also sought by strictly limiting opportunities to enter the sector and open new branches, supposedly in the 'overriding interest of the market'. In reality this policy allowed the supervising authority to use its discretionary power to authorize the establishment of new subsidiaries and to cover up the true motivations behind certain decisions taken to determine economic policy.[7]

The banks, Credito Italiano being no exception, grew and developed in this protected environment for half a century, unaffected by external competition, and thus proved to be only scarcely efficient in their operations and allotment. What is more, Credit's single shareholder, the Istituto per la Ricostruzione Industriale (Institute for Industrial Reconstruction – IRI),[8] appeared to be satisfied with the bank's progress and made no demands for higher dividends.

At the beginning of the 1970s, the organization of Credit was essentially authoritative, lacked accountability at all levels and was centrally focused (Figure 10.1). All functional areas with a segmented organizational structure were to report to the two managing directors, as had been typical of Italian banks throughout the 1960s. Peripheral organization was based on the classification of branches into

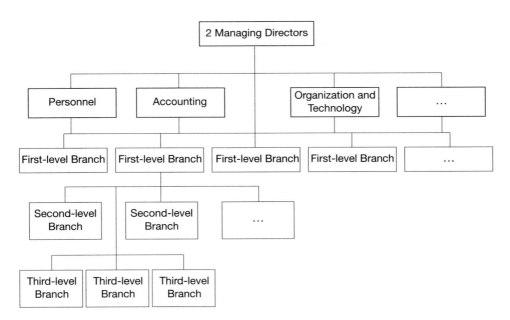

Figure 10.1 Diagram of the organization of Credito Italiano during the 1970s

three categories (first, second and third) according to the decreasing level of decision-taking autonomy attributed to their directors. A first-level branch director answered directly to the top management and was responsible for holding each area manager (for personnel, accounting, organization and technology, financing, international operations and market relations) to perform his assigned duties. Second and third-level branches answered to a first-level branch.

In theory, each branch office was free to perfect its services and there existed as many back-offices as branches, each with its own administrative framework authority over personnel.

At that time Credito Italiano operated with a considerable spread (approximately 9–10%) which allowed it to make up for its inefficiencies and conduct its risk management within the bureaucratic procedures imposed by the supervisory authority.

The entire reporting system was based on an accounting procedure carried out at the branch level which had been designed during the 1940s to deliver information to the supervisory authority, not to bank managers. It failed to consider the internal fund transfer rate[9] and only allowed an evaluation of the global results achieved by the bank as a whole.

The first-level branch directors were considered in light of their achievements, by measuring the overall amounts of deposits and loans, but without comparing their results to pre-defined goals. In any case such evaluation carried little weight because it was not tied to any short or long-term incentive programme. No monetary bonuses were foreseen, and careers often evolved according to criteria which took no account of individual merit, while sometimes rewarding seniority.

The crisis which affected the raw material, labour and money markets in the 1970s revealed the excessive rigidity of the Italian banking system and its inability to efficiently allocate credit within a turbulent scenario.

The supervisory authorities decided that introducing the stimulus of competition into the banking system would have encouraged intermediaries to seek greater working efficiency and would have thus made them more involved in the process of economic development.

Several foreign banks opened Italian branches, introducing their innovative financial products into the country. Competition within the banking sector grew in intensity and profit margins began to narrow. These developments forced Italian banks to set their prices according to their production costs, consequently encouraging them to formulate ways of measuring the costs of their products and services.

The top management of Credito Italiano foresaw the changes at hand and took steps to meet them. It understood that in a competitive market, banks would be bound to give rise to their own new culture, to ways of attaining greater precision and detail in collecting data for management use and to a greater focus on goal achievement. These principles have underlied the initiatives of the bank's top management throughout its evolution which began in the mid-1970s.

In 1974 Credit enacted a system of budgets for its branch offices. Although branch office budgets were not unknown to Italian banking at the time, the system adopted by Credito Italiano was probably the first to be implemented and perfected in the country.

The branch budget system implemented included a total of approximately forty accounting and non-accounting goals set both in terms of volume and margins. Top management was given the task of assigning the goals to the first-level branch management which in turn divided them between the second and third-level branches that reported to them. The extent of goal attainment was evaluated twice per year, every six months. The possibility of revising the budget and the set goals during the course of the year was provided for. Such revisions generally took place at six-month intervals and only rarely more frequently.

During the same period a project was under way which was to place Credito Italiano among the foremost Italian banks involved in researching management accounting systems. A special group was formed within the data compilation unit whose job was to determine the relative costs of various portfolios and processes. The first products to undergo such cost analysis were cheques. In the end 600 different products were identified, but this concerted effort failed to lead to a new system of management accounting, hampered by an approach which was overly complex and detailed.

The developments enacted during the 1970s represented the debut of a management control system based on results rather than on methods. As such they demonstrate the understanding that the bank's top management had of the changing scenario and the factors which had become critical for success in it.

The 1980s until 1988

The end of the 1970s marked a yet greater opening of the market by the supervisory bodies. From 1978 to 1990 it again became possible to grant authorization for the opening of new banks, following the freeze imposed in 1966 to ensure the stability of the market. The supervisory authority formulated a 'branch office plan' to be revised every four years in order to regulate access to the credit business. However, the Bank of Italy continued to wield considerable discretionary power in granting authorization.

In 1983 the creation of the first OICVMs (*Organismi di Investimento Collettivo in Valori Mobiliari*), commonly known as investment funds, marked the end of the banks' monopoly of brokerage. At the same time the government had begun to issue short-term bonds at relatively high interest rates, soon to be followed by the first parabanking brokers (leasing and factoring firms). Finally, the supervisory authorities began to do away with the various types of specialized categories previously introduced[10] in order to open the market to individual intermediaries and encourage competition within the banking system.

The second half of the 1980s was marked by a profound legislative renovation as a result of the first European Community banking directive (77/780) enacted by DPR (Presidential Decree) 85/350. This directive stated that access to the credit business was to be contingent on objective characteristics such as a minimum starting capital and the honourable and professional reputation of the administrators and managers in question, rather than being regulated by discretionary criteria. Although the branch office plan remained in effect until 1990, access to the market was essentially opened in 1986.

That same year the supervisory authorities took a second step towards precautionary rather than structural surveillance by introducing minimum legal asset coefficients.[11] As a result, advisory bodies no longer were required to oversee each single operation performed by intermediaries, but began to grant increasing management freedom, making operative and strategic decision-taking contingent on the possession of an adequate capital supply.

The government made use of its legislative powers to change the rules of the game and practically forced banks to evolve. The greater entrepreneurial freedom that banks were granted was to be reflected in similar decision-taking freedom which they were forced to grant to their subsidiaries. Increasing competition and the growing complexity of banking products and customer requirements made it necessary for banks to become more active in the market. Credit's top management took this step in two phases: at the beginning of the 1980s and in 1988.

An amendment was made at the beginning of the 1980s which increased the level of autonomy enjoyed by the first-level branches, each of which was to govern a group of branches answering to the director of the leading branch (Figure 10.2). The number of such 'leading' branches was set at 45; these were geographically concentrated in the areas with the greatest potential wealth. The group leader branches (previously first-level) performed credit activities in the same way as the hierarchically inferior branch offices, but with respect to the latter enjoyed involvement in co-ordination and planning.

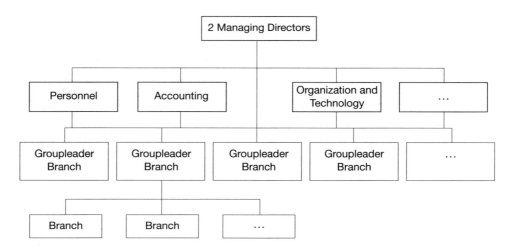

Figure 10.2 Diagram of the organization of Credito Italiano at the beginning of the 1980s

Organizationally, the structure remained essentially unchanged but was distinguished by the appearance of a new figure, the groupleader branch director, who substituted the first-level branch director and was invested with greater decisional authority, although this did not attribute specific additional responsibilities.

This sort of organization allowed the bank to draw attention to the procedural requirements imposed by the supervisory body and afforded the necessary flexibility for a relatively stable market.

This was also the period when a bonus system for the general managers and the 45 groupleader branch directors was introduced. Bonuses were awarded according to discretionary criteria and therefore totally unassociated with preset objectives.

The new and more influential developments which affected the banking industry during the second half of the 1980s[12] made it necessary to create a more flexible structure. The authoritative component of the decision-making process was reduced and greater freedom and responsibility were attributed to middle management. Thus, when the changes in the scenario began to be acutely felt, Credit's top management implemented new structures and processes within this same framework. In fact, the organization as it was structured permitted only the group leader branch directors to have an overview of the activities of the groups of branches.

At a time when the scenario was witnessing growing competitive pressure and a gradual transformation of the conception of the business itself,[13] the top management of Credito Italiano undertook a second phase of development. It identified two priorities:

1. Finding a way to assign goals to lower and middle management and incentives to top management in order to create greater involvement in corporate management and increase accountability in decision taking.
2. Promoting a new management culture for all managers to replace that which had taken shape when the market was still organized as a directed oligopoly.

1988 marked a significant turnover at the head of the firm: 4 out of the 15 executive directors and department heads retired or simply left. The top management took advantage of this turnover to introduce new instruments and management techniques.

1988 was a year of vital importance. It became evident that the network of branches would have to be more actively co-ordinated to become more competitive over a large territory. This might also serve to bridge the gap which had developed between the branches and the general management in addition to ensuring that the latter's policy was uniformly applied throughout the network and adapted, where necessary, to special needs.

Thus in 1988 the 45 groups of branches were organized into five (Italian market) geographical areas, each headed by a director who answered to a Mercato Italia[14] representative (Figure 10.3).

The continuing liberalization of the banking market led to the substitution of a strategy aimed at maintaining a competitive position with one aimed at market penetration and development.[15] This meant that those individuals in the banking

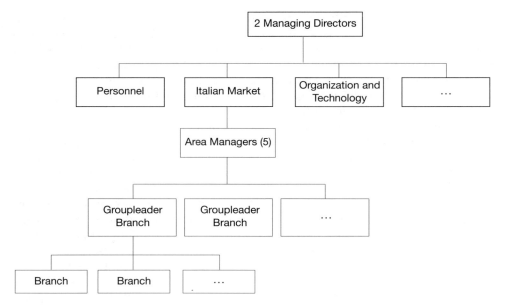

Figure 10.3   Diagram of the organization of Credito Italiano in 1988

structure with decision-making power had to become more used to achieving results in terms of objectives set by the top management rather than in terms of procedures.

In 1988 management roles were redefined at all levels. In order to focus the managers' attention on their results, the members of the general management, the 45 groupleader branch directors and other executives were included in an evaluation system (PAS: Performance Assessment System) which considered the achievements of each manager with respect to budget goals and other qualitative objectives, including the management of human resources.

No salary increases were directly linked to positive evaluations. The PAS was only used to determine career prospects over the long term.

A bonus system was also introduced in an attempt to link remuneration to goal attainment in some way.

The new bonus system introduced in 1988 was based on performance and was structurally similar to systems of management by objectives (MBO) used in Italian manufacturing firms. The project had two essential characteristics:

- risks were primarily borne by the groupleader branch directors;
- the value of the bonuses was set according to predetermined rules at the foundation of the system.

The groupleader branch directors were assigned five or six quantitative goals set in terms of margins or volumes which were to remain stable throughout the year.

The MBO system did not foresee the eventuality of revising set goals and thus the groupleader branch directors bore full responsibility in the eventuality of negative performance, regardless of whether this was brought on by their conduct or external factors linked to the scenario which were beyond their control. In turn, each area manager was responsible for all the goals assigned to all the group-leader branch directors under his command. Also area managers, who were under the direct command of the managing director, were assigned performance goals, including not financial targets associated with administrative changes or promotional campaigns.

The area managers were charged with communicating the five or six budget objectives to the 45 groupleader branch directors by letter. These objectives were the same for all 45 and included a series of key accounting figures (gross operating profit, total deposits, total credit, total outstanding credit). The only variations regarded the relative importance of each objective and the time spans allotted for successfully attaining these goals. No objectives were to be changed during the course of the year; any eventual risk of unforeseeable events or scenario modification was the responsibility of the groupleader branch directors. Ironically, when these latter were fortunate and able to reach their goals easily, they might have received a monetary bonus but a negative PAS rating and therefore possibly penalized their career possibilities.

The lowest performance level awarded with a bonus was usually higher than the budget objective and measured as 80–120 possible points. If an executive reached 80–120 points he was to receive a monetary bonus totalling 5–12% of his annual salary. The average bonus of 8% was awarded to 60–70% of those eligible.

No incentives based on the attainment of performance goals were awarded below the level of groupleader branch director. However, some bonuses were awarded discretionally for particularly outstanding performance in terms of attitude and contribution to reaching the group branch budget goals. At the end of the year each groupleader branch director received a certain quantity of funds to be distributed as awards to collaborators and which were subdivided at his discretion according to the limitations imposed by the general management for the various hierarchical positions covered by the recipients of the awards. The general management was consequently to be informed of the manner in which these funds had been distributed.

Table 10.2 illustrates the evaluation and incentive system used by Credito Italiano.

The general aim of the three levels of evaluation and incentives was to make managers concentrate on achieving goals. In order to measure achievements, the managerial accounting system had been refined to procure the information necessary for management control. The costs sustained in offering the principal products were for the first time calculated using a system of multiple internal transfer rates.[16]

The organizational changes introduced in 1988 were imposed by top management following the development of a new strategic orientation and a new organizational structure. However, these innovations were also accompanied by significant

Table 10.2   Organizational positions and their respective incentives

Organizational position	Incentive system for each organizational position
1. Members of general management 2. 45 groupleader branch directors	Performance evaluation system – influential on long-term career development Management by objectives (MBO) – greater focus on short-term performance
3. Officers below the level of groupleader branch director and general management director	Evaluation of achievements and attitude – discretionary bonuses

collaboration from lower levels, since the link between bonuses and achievements stimulated local-level managers to request greater freedom of initiative.

The adoption of the incentive system was at once both a cause and a result of the cultural developments the bank's top management intended to introduce.

The goal of such cultural change was to diversify the operations of the bank, which had traditionally focused on furnishing and managing loans to industry, to include a significant role in the commercial sector and furnishing services to private parties. The incentive system facilitated the spread of this new culture, or rather required the participation of each individual invested with responsibility, but at the same time the bank was obliged to undertake a vast training scheme to ensure that the new instrument was clearly understood by all those involved in it.

Seminars were organized to uniformly distribute this new managerial culture.

The training programme previously used at the Managerial Training Centre (established by the bank's top management in 1975) was consequently modified: the technical questions to which approximately 80% of training time had previously been dedicated came to receive the same emphasis as management questions, which had previously been considered for only 20% of the total course hours. The courses assumed vast proportions both in the number of managers involved and in the subject matter considered: 2,300 managers received training concerning the newly introduced changes, including the new strategy, structure, MBO system and a renewed emphasis on the development of human resources.

Management control and incentives in the passage from a protected to a competitive market

From 1988 to the mid-1990s Credito Italiano concentrated on absorbing the newly introduced developments and adapting the new management instruments as necessary.

The changes enacted in 1988, and in particular the performance evaluation system connected to the incentive system, brought about an increase in salaries. As time passed, however, limitations to the system became apparent. The greatest of these was that the system was composed primarily of discretionary criteria, especially at the lower levels of the corporate hierarchy. It was clearly time to update the system to take into consideration the changing needs that the market, customers and shareholders were beginning to express.

In the 1990s the Italian government, under the pressure of political changes and a vast public debt, undertook a privatization process which involved the sale of two banks of national interest.[17] Credito Italiano was privatized in 1993.

Privatization gave new vigour to the process of change and management overhaul in which the bank was involved. In fact the government, in having opted for privatization, was actually redefining the scenario and the criteria for success in banking. The transition had been made from a directed oligopoly to a competitive market.[18]

Upon privatization, the question of management salaries assumed greater importance and the entrepreneurial nature of banking activity was rediscovered. This new context directed even greater attention towards results, including those over the short term, and towards the efficiency and effectiveness of operations.

Since the shareholders, particularly those of considerable proportions, were primarily interested in financial results, it became necessary to strategically reorganize management policies in order to satisfy the altered needs of the market and align the goals of the firm with those of its various interlocutors. One manager from Credito Italiano aptly described this evolution by noting that 'before we concentrated on our clients; now we concentrate on both our clients and shareholders'.

This redefinition of the scenario made it necessary to procure and use reliable information concerning the cost of the principal products and services in order to ascertain which of these generated profits and which brought losses.

Although the new management accounting system had produced earnings reports since 1990, the system of internal reporting used until 1992 was based on entry procedures required by the supervisory body and in no way produced results for specific services or market sectors. Once the limitations of the system in use had become apparent, it became necessary to take measures to make the entire corporate structure homogeneously responsible for the procurement of revenues. The need to operate over a wider territory, to adopt more incisive policies, to perceive and when possible foresee the needs of clients made it imperative to define new initiatives to stimulate the personnel working at all points of the sales network.

In fact, from an organizational perspective, it was becoming obvious that the structures for overseeing corporate activity were excessively centralized. At the same time, having recognized how greatly the markets of reference varied according to their territorial position, organizational restructuring was becoming imminently necessary to identify the wide variety of market requirements and the ways to best react to the scenario.

Radical intervention was necessary to adapt management control systems to a changing scenario. Changes were introduced, in particular, in terms of cost accounting, accountability and incentive systems.

As to cost accounting, the 1990s marked the inauguration of a project which made it possible to generate highly analytical data concerning the composition of the costs and revenues associated with banking operations. A work group of 19 members, some enrolled from the Management Control Office and including a number of information technology experts, was formed for the occasion. In 1990, over the course of a year, this group succeeded in defining a system of cost and earnings surveying which was far more analytical than that previously used. This innovation satisfied the need to make the entire corporate structure homogeneously accountable for the firm's earnings. The project was of massive proportions and required a considerable investment of resources. It did, however, make possible preliminary and definitive calculations capable of determining the specific costs of single client products and subsequent aggregate data concerning higher levels of the corporate structure. Such extreme detail was initially possible only for revenue data. The calculation of such minute statistics was a shocking development in an environment which had previously assigned responsibilities on the basis of much more general accounting data.

The creation of this vast body of information and its inherent reliability made the peripheral branches more independent of the general management. While on one hand the discretionality with which goals had been centrally established began to diminish, on the other, bargaining power during budget drafting increased, as did the freedom of the peripheral branches in management and decision taking. In order to facilitate the comprehension and application of this new management tool by those directly involved with its use, 25,000 days of training were held within a year.

In 1993 the system was put into practice, although initially only at the branch level.

Upon conclusion of the projects inaugurated in 1993 for the first time it was possible to calculate budget results subdivided by branch, by portfolio agent, by product, by client and by client segment.

Increasing market competition had required greater autonomy for the peripheral branch offices. The top management understood that in order to become more competitive, its branches needed freedom to personalize their product line and adapt it to their specific market demands.

The need to overhaul territorial subdivisions emerged following the identification of significant differences within single markets. Five territorial blocks were in fact insufficient to divide the entire nation into homogeneous markets with a common culture and common needs to satisfy. As a result, in June 1995 the decision was taken to redefine responsibility distribution while at the same time renovating the firm's territorial organization. The original five geographical areas of branch jurisdiction became eleven, each invested with considerable authority and freedom of action (Figure 10.4). The eleven are still as follows:

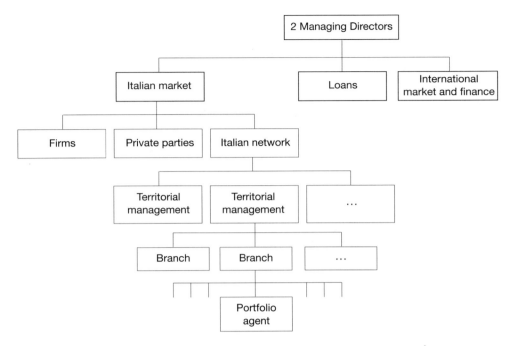

Figure 10.4 Diagram of the organization of Credito Italiano in 1995

- the provinces of Milano, Lodi, Pavia;
- other provinces in Lombardy;
- Piedmont, the Aosta Valley;
- the Triveneto region;
- Emilia Romagna and Marche;
- Tuscany;
- Liguria and Sardinia;
- Lazio and Abruzzo;
- Campania and Calabria;
- Puglia, Molise and part of Basilicata;
- Sicily.

The directors of the various territorial areas, who prior to 1995 had worked within general management, were transferred to their respective territorial bases in order to become more familiar with the areas to which they were assigned. Such close contact with each individual market made it possible for branch managers and their supervisors to communicate more fruitfully. Improved communication between the general management and the outlying working structure, in addition to the rationalization of management information flow, became the means for involving and assigning responsibility to as many positions as possible, thus encouraging delegation and choice optimization.

The position of groupleader branch director was abolished and the new territorial managers were given the authority to act 'as the general managers of a local bank'. These managers now had the resources to promote sales within their areas and were placed high enough in the corporate hierarchy to 'be globally productive while selling locally'. From the perspective of the management control system this change made it possible to define more binding budget goals. It also subjected each working unit to more stringent monitoring. As a result it became more evident which opportunities deserved more attention and which weren't worth the effort.

In order to further develop the incentive system, in 1995 it was decided that the positions below branch level should be made accountable, right down to each single portfolio agent. Although the branch manager was now in charge of the client portfolio agents, each of these was assigned a personal budget (the following section presents a table which illustrates the budget goals assigned to portfolio agents). At the same time, a system for gathering definitive data made it possible to evaluate the performance of each agent.

Budget objectives

Tables 10.3, 10.4 and 10.5 illustrate the budget objectives assigned in the corporate year 1996 to the three main organizational positions: territorial manager, branch manager and portfolio agent.

As may be witnessed from Tables 10.3–10.5, the budget objectives considered take into account the fact that the bank's general operations are divided according to two market segments: corporate and retail. The heads of these two sectors are assigned goals for the management of their particular client segment. At the territorial management level, three budgets are compiled: one general, one for the corporate segment and one for the retail segment. In the bank's organizational chart, under the authority of the territorial management there now exist a corporate head and a retail head, who are in turn in charge of the branch managers, who are in charge of the single portfolio agents.

In the same year there emerged a need to assign responsibility to those working below the level of branch manager. As a result, each client portfolio agent became accountable. Although these were under the command of their relative branch managers, each agent received his own budget connected with a personal bonus system based on a comparison of estimates and definitive data. A typical branch normally employs 20–25 client portfolio agents responsible for one client segment each (corporate, private, high-income private parties).

The number of positions made formally accountable thus rose from 45 in 1995 to 1,800 in 1996 and 2,200 in 1997.

Regarding cost calculation, up until 1997 the most detailed data were compiled at the branch office level. The present cost monitoring system remains less developed than its revenue-based counterpart for two main reasons:

Table 10.3 Budget objectives of a territorial manager

Objectives	Budget values	Definitive values
Revenues		
Gross Earning Margin[a]		
Net Contribution[b]		
Net Margin (losses detracted)[c]		
Net Revenues		
Corporate Gross Earning Margin[d]		
Retail Gross Earning Margin[e]		
Direct Provision[f]		
Investments[g]		
Indirect Provision[h]		
Managed Savings		
Deposited Securities Holdings		

[a] The Gross Earning Margin is the result of the following addition: Investment Margin + Savings Margin + Services Margin. The Investment Margin is calculated by subtracting the figurative interest paid calculated by means of the internal fund transfer rate (see note 9) from the interest receivable deriving from investments (for example, the allocation of a short-term loan). The Savings Margin represents the difference between the figurative interest receivable calculated using the internal fund transfer rate and the interest paid in connection with savings products (for example, the opening of a current account). The Services Margin is the algebraic sum of the active and passive commissions generated by the services furnished by the bank (for example, portfolio management.

[b] The Net Contribution is the difference between the Gross Earning Margin and the total expenses of the centre. By the expenses of the centre we intend those costs which may be directly attributed to organizational sub-units without eventual returns (for example, personnel costs, rent paid, energy costs, etc.).

[c] The Net Margin is calculated by subtracting all foreseen losses (or definitive, if the statistic is calculated *ex post*) from the Net Contribution.

[d] The Corporate Gross Earning Margin is the sum of the following: Investment Margin + Savings Margin + Services Margin. This total obviously includes costs and earning only for the corporate market.

[e] The Retail Gross Earning Margin is the sum of the following: Investment Margin + Savings Margin + Services Margin. This total obviously includes the costs and earnings only for the retail market. Therefore, the sum of the Corporate Gross Earning Margin and the Retail Gross Earning Margin is equal to the Gross Earning Margin.

[f] Direct Provision represents the volume of financial means collected (or foreseen to be collected) by means of deposits or the sale of bonds issued by the bank on the market.

[g] Investments measure the volume of all investment activity.

[h] Indirect Provision represents all forms of saving except for deposits and the market sale of bonds issued by the bank (for example, managed savings and deposited securities holdings).

1. Attributing costs to individuals creates considerable problems with acceptance in an environment like a bank in which considerable economic links occur.
2. While it is possible to assign revenue accountability even at the lowest levels of bank operations, the same may not be done with costs since the tools for containing them do not exist at the level of the client portfolio agents or even the branch managers, but much higher in the organizational framework.

Within the commercial realm, cost objectives are assigned in order to keep costs down and the subsequent data is used to set the prices of the services offered.

Table 10.4 Budget objectives of a branch manager

Objectives	Budget values	Definitive values
Revenues		
Gross Earning Margin		
Gross Earning Margin (losses detracted)		
Net Revenues		
Corporate Gross Earning Margin		
Retail Gross Earning Margin		
Direct Provision		
Investments		
Indirect Provision		
Managed Savings		
Deposited Securities Holdings		

Table 10.5 Budget objectives of a corporate portfolio agent

Objectives	Budget values	Definitive values
Revenues		
Gross Earning Margin (losses detracted)		
Margin from services		
Investments		
Direct Provision		
Various Products		
Number of Corporate Clients		
Medium/Long-term Loans		
Electronic Banking		

Cost limitation objectives are assigned down to the level of territorial management, where the tools for containing resource costs in fact exist. For example, the area policies for personnel hiring and salaries are defined at this level. Cost objectives are also assigned to the Purchase Office (charged with making purchases for the entire bank network) and all general management structures.

Since each member of the general management represents a cost centre in that its actions influence the bank's revenue accumulation (consider the impact that an error in procedure or human resource planning can have on the bank's revenues), a management by objectives programme for general managers was formulated which is 50% determined by the bank's profit goals.

1995 also witnessed changes in the strategic planning process. In the past it had involved only the planning staff and some of the highest management levels, but in that year it was decided to include a larger number of participants in this process.

Another important event was the elimination of the double collection of accounting data by both branch offices and central headquarters, which produced only a useless duplication of data. Therefore, since 1995 the branches have ceased to compile management data, making the Management Control Office the only source of such reliable data for branch level as well.

To limit the 'friction' which inevitably accompanies the introduction of a new incentive system, in 1996 Credito Italiano adopted a new method of evaluation which was given the name 'solidarity'.[19] Initially this method linked the incentives assigned to an individual with a certain position to the results achieved by the individual's hierarchical superiors. Since it became clear that this individual was unable to influence his superiors' achievements, the system was abandoned the following year in favour of one structured from the top down.

In 1997 the criteria underlying variable salaries were established as comprising the attainment of goals assigned to each individual and the results achieved by pertinent collaborators. For example, in addition to achieving overall positive results, a branch manager is impelled to make his colleagues attain an equally satisfying level of performance. This same method was applied to the territorial managers to encourage them to seek the growth not only of those branches located in markets with great potential, but also of those with the greatest difficulties. This approach led to a team philosophy, greater integration of the various territories and an alignment of individual goals with the global goals of the firm.

We may illustrate the solidarity aspect of this performance evaluation system in greater detail by adding that, for each position in the bank hierarchy, the awarding of bonuses attributed on the basis of individually attained results is contingent on the fulfilment of the solidarity criteria. A more detailed analysis of this mechanism is provided in the following section.

Bonus calculation procedure

The incentive system foresees three possible levels of attainment for each objective: minimum, average and maximum. A set number of points is assigned for each level: 80 points are assigned for the minimum level, 100 for the average level and 120 for the maximum level of attainment.

Table 10.6 illustrates a hypothetical attribution of points for a series of objectives and the anticipated results for each level.

Table 10.6 Attribution of points for each objective

Objective	Minimum	Points	Average	Points	Maximum	Points
Direct provision (€)	100,000	30	105,000	40	120,000	50
Revenues (€)	3,000	20	3,100	25	3,500	30
Indirect provision (€)	80,000	15	81,000	18	83,000	20
Net Revenues (€)	600	15	630	17	680	20
		80		100		120

The minimum results which must be attained in order to receive a bonus are represented by the total of 80 points, calculated by totalling the points assigned for each individual objective at its respective level of performance.

The total number of points is calculated on the basis of the results attained for each objective as follows:

- In brackets for results which satisfy or exceed the bonus criteria.
  In the example illustrated in Table 10.6, objective direct provision is assigned:
  - 30 points for results ranging from the minimum to average (from 100,000 Euro to 104,999 Euro);
  - 40 points for results ranging from average to the maximum (from 105,000 Euro to 119,999 Euro);
  - 50 points for results above the maximum (from 120,000 Euro and upwards).

- According to a continuum for results below the minimum level.
  A total below the minimum level required results in a detraction of points from the minimum level in proportion to the spread between the minimum and average levels.
  Detractions are made up to 0 points: negative points are not calculated.

Table 10.7 illustrates an example of bonus calculation in which objective indirect provision is measured using a continuum.

As regards objective indirect provision, the number of points assigned (13.5) was determined by calculating the difference between:

(a) the values of the average and minimum objectives (€ 81,000 − € 80,000) = € 1,000;

(b) the corresponding number of points (18 − 15) = 3;

(c) the difference between the minimum objective and the results achieved (€ 80,000 − € 79,500) = € 500.

The rectification coefficient is then determined as the relationship between figures (b) and (a):

(3 : € 1000) = 0.003.

Table 10.7 Bonus calculation

Results achieved	€	Points
Direct provision	100,000	30
Revenues	3,085	20
Indirect provision	79,500	13.5
Net revenues	690	20
Total		83.5

By applying this 'coefficient' to the difference between the results achieved and the minimum objective, this spread is transformed into 'negative points':

(€ 500 × 0.003) = 1.50.

The number of points taken into consideration is equal to the difference between the minimum number of points and the 'negative points':

(15 − 1.50) = 13.50.

The value of the bonus varies between the minimum (which corresponds to 80 points) and the maximum (which corresponds to 120) and is divided into two components.

In fact, only a percentage of the foreseen total bonus is initially assigned to an individual on the basis of the points he has attained. The attribution of the remaining part is contingent on the satisfaction of the conditions stipulated in the 'solidarity' clause.

Example:
Minimum bonus: € 5,000 (80 points)
Maximum bonus: € 10,000 (120 points)
Points attained: 83.50
Solidarity stipulated for the position: 30%.
First of all we must calculate the value of each point above the minimum.
Example:
(€ 10,000 − € 5,000) : (120 − 80) = € 5,000 : 40 = € 125 is the value of each point.
The bonus earned is calculated as follows:
(83.50 − 80) = 3.50 performance points above the minimum.
€ 5,000 (minimum bonus) + 3.50 × € 125 (additional bonus quota) = € 5,000 + € 437.5 = € 5,437.5 (bonus attained).
The 'solidarity' component is then calculated:
€ 5,437.5 × 70% = € 3,806.25 (bonus quota to be awarded in all cases);
€ 5,437.5 × 30% = € 1,631.25 (bonus quota to be awarded if the conditions stipulated in the 'solidarity' clause are satisfied).

Endnotes

[1] Numerous mixed banks whose destinies had become tied to those of certain manufacturing industries hit on hard times when the great depression arrived in Italy at the beginning of the 1930s. These banks, which had become veritable bank holding companies, were forced to 'burn' their financial resources in order to uphold the share prices of the industries which they had become irreversibly linked to. In the end even the most important banks (Banca Commerciale Italiana, Credito Italiano and Banco di Roma) succumbed to the crisis and the government resorted to a massive bail-out. As a result, holding activity was separated from brokerage and the banks were forced to transfer their industrial holdings to a liquidation institute in exchange for fresh financial resources.

The Institute for Industrial Reconstruction (IRI) was founded on 23 January 1933 with two distinct tasks: the Finance Office (which was able to offer financing for a twenty-year term) and the Industrial Conversion Office which was to act as administrator and unfreeze (transfer to private capital) the financial and stock holdings held by these three mixed banks. They were never to recover from the crisis, however, and in 1934 IRI took over the quotas of their share capital and transformed them into banks of national interest.

In 1937 IRI was transformed into a permanent body whose job it was to manage and direct shares which were assumed to remain public indefinitely. The Finance Office and Industrial Conversion Office were eliminated and replaced by a general structure which was to manage (and no longer unfreeze) the holdings acquired through the bail-out of the mixed banks. IRI was dismissed in the year 2000.

[2] According to article 5 of the 1936 banking law, this category included all banks of national importance founded as public limited companies with branches in at least thirty provinces and which had been recognized by presidential decree. These institutions were actually legal hybrids, belonging partly to the public and partly to the private domain, and were distinguished by: the requirement that shares be in registered form, the lack of voting rights in assembly for non-Italian citizens, administrators with Italian citizenship, the approval of statutes and modifications thereof by decree of the Exchequer, the authorization of the supervisory authority to nominate administrators and the inclusion of a member of the supervisory authority on the board of directors.

[3] The principal shareholders (the Allianz group, Franco Tosi, Commercial Union, the Maramotti group, Leonardo del Vecchio, Roberto Bertazzoni, Falk, Fidelity Investments and Ids International Inc.) control approximately 20% of the quota of capital. The remaining 80% are freely negotiated shares, one of the highest percentages in Italy.

[4] According to 'La classifica delle prime 760 banche' (a Classification of the 760 Most Important Banks), a supplement to *Il Mondo*, n. 31, July 31, 1998.

[5] The credit authorities include: il Comitato Interministeriale per il Credito ed il Risparmio (Interministerial Credit and Savings Committee – CICR), entrusted with supreme surveillance of credit affairs and the protection of savings; the Exchequer, who oversees the CICR and may substitute it in case of emergency and the Bank of Italy, which formulates the proposals to be deliberated by the CICR and actively oversees the operations of the banking system by exerting its legislative authority.

[6] The banking law of 1936 introduced a distinction between institutes holding short-term savings and those holding medium and long-term savings, denominating the former as banking concerns and the latter as credit institutes. This distinction invested the Italian system with an automatic specialization of banks according to the duration of their holdings (temporal specialization) which exerted a considerable influence over the type and duration of investment they made, further determining their general conduct.

Other types of specialization were also introduced which further segmented the banking market, if not to the extent of temporal specialization. Special credit institutes were founded to provide loans to agricultural enterprises or for the construction of vast public infrastructure projects (functional specialization). All banks were forbidden from performing any type of intermediary activity (such as with securities) beyond their credit duties (operative specialization).

[7] With reference to this last point it should be noted that the supervisory body, in exercising its power to authorize or prohibit the opening of new branch offices, was capable of influencing the total volume of available financing and subsequently the market's interest rates.

[8] For further information regarding the foundation and role of IRI, readers may consult note 1.

[9] The internal fund transfer rate is a technical accounting device which makes it possible to measure the contributions of individual branch offices (or of individual banking products) to the total earning of the bank. It is based not only on the volume of internal transfers but also on the accounting abstraction of the so-called *Pool di Tesoreria* (Treasury Pool). This is actually a hypothetical centre for the hypothetical compensation of savings capital and investment capital, which in reality never takes place. In other words, the *Pool di Tesoreria* receives figurative inflows of capital whenever a branch office engages in savings activity and discharges figurative outflows of capital whenever a branch office engages in investment activity. Its economic counterpart for the branch offices is the recognition of figurative interest receivable for all savings activity and the attribution of figurative interest paid for all investment activity. The internal fund transfer rate is the rate of return on capital adopted by the *Pool di Tesoreria*.

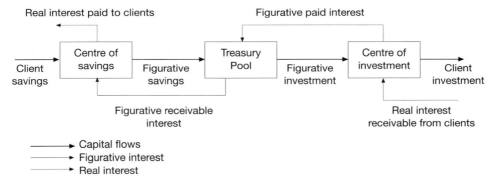

Figure 10.5 Representation of the *Pool di Tesoreria* (Treasury Pool)

Since the figurative interest (receivable and paid) is assigned to the individual branch offices for the same total but inverse value with respect to the *Pool di Tesoreria*, the ultimate effect on the bank's income statement is obviously null. In fact, the figurative interest tends to emphasize that the existence of a deposit constitutes the prerequisite for the allocation of a loan. Applying the internal fund transfer rate to savings and investments makes it possible to perceive the earnings achieved by each branch office during the course of its intermediation, allowing comparison of the results attained by branch offices engaged primarily in savings activity and those primarily engaged in allocating loans.

More specifically, the banks' management control system foresees the employment of various internal fund transfer rates through the adoption of various *Pools di Tesoreria* endowed with characteristics which reflect their various functions, which include: (a) the market, which requires a range of rates determined by typology (ordinary clientele, inter-bank activity, securities, etc.); (b) the durability of the product, which requires a range of rates determined by temporal duration (at sight, short-term, medium-long term, etc.); (c) the currency in question.

[10] For further information see note 6.

[11] These coefficients forced banks to correlate their activity, both in terms of volume and of risk level assumed, to the existence of adequate asset resources. Two separate coefficients

were introduced. The first, still in use, is linked to corporate magnitude and sets a maximum limit for loan allocation on a national level on the basis of the assets possessed by each bank. This coefficient is derived from the ratio between the loans allocated by all the branch offices throughout the nation and the net assets of the bank and must remain inferior to a limit of 22.5. The second obligatory minimum asset coefficient is no longer in use. Linked to presumed corporate risk, in its original form it strove to establish a correlation between available assets and the level of risk presented by all aspects of loans and endorsement credit, calculated for each credit institution inclusive of its entire network of national and foreign branches. The risk presented by the sum of all loans and endorsement credit allocated by all branch offices both nationally and abroad was to remain within a limit of 12.5 times the value of the bank's total assets, inclusive of the positive and negative aspects of the capital attributed to branch offices abroad.

[12] Here we refer to the changes introduced by the enactment of the first banking directive, the general process of banking deregulation and the increased competition due to the arrival of new competitors which encouraged a more sophisticated line of products.

[13] An increasingly mature clientele which began to request more and more complex products to satisfy its needs and a higher level of competition made it necessary for banks to develop a commercial culture which they had previously lacked.

[14] This denomination indicates an operative area to be co-ordinated by the branches. Over time such areas came more and more to resemble points of sale for centrally produced products.

[15] Banking operations involve high fixed costs due to the necessary infrastructure and instruments which increase less than proportionally with respect to even significant increases in brokerage volume. This allows a large bank to reduce the average unit cost of its brokerage simply by increasing its volume.

Furthermore, it should be noted that banking operations allow the creation of considerable economies of scale and goals in correspondence with significant increases in volume.

[16] See note 8 for information concerning internal transfer rates.

[17] Credito Italiano and Banca Commerciale Italiana.

[18] On this subject mention must be made of the various pertinent legislative acts: the enactment of the second EEC directive, the Amato law and the Collected Laws which set the groundwork for defining the banking sector as it now exists.

[19] In general it may be surmised that the extension of the incentive system to include almost the entire corporate structure produced the undesired effect of creating tension among the various hierarchical levels. More precisely, it may be noted that individualistic behaviour became more widespread. For example, certain branch managers concentrated their attention on those portfolio agents most likely to reach their objectives (given that, through their contributions they were able to guarantee in turn the attainment of their branch office's objectives), while neglecting those with less ability.

STUDENT ASSIGNMENTS

1. Prior to privatization, what factors moved the top management to carry out organizational reforms and transformation of the management control system?

2. How has privatization influenced the evolution of management control systems?

3. What reasons might explain the introduction of greater performance accountability at Credito Italiano?

4. What positive effects were expected from the performance-based incentive system introduced in 1995? What undesired effects arose? What efforts were made to deal with the distortions encountered?

5. Using the data presented in the two cases below, calculate the value of the bonuses earned during the month of January by a hypothetical Branch Manager, determined on the basis of only two objectives: (a) Indirect provision; and (b) Direct provision. Note that the points for the 'Indirect provision' objective are measured so that the function is flat within each of the two ranges (between minimum and average and between average and maximum), but that the points for the 'Direct provision' objective are calculated using an increasing continuum.

Goal	Minimum (€)	Points	Average (€)	Points	Maximum (€)	Points
Indirect provision	50,000	35	55,000	40	60,000	50
Direct provision	150,000	45	160,000	60	165,000	70
Total		80		100		120

Goals assigned to a Branch Manager for the month of January 1999:

- minimum bonus: € 250 (equivalent to 80 points);
- maximum bonus: € 400 (equivalent to 120 points);
- a solidarity quota of 30% is set for this position (this percentage of the bonus is to be awarded only if 70% of all portfolio agents reach their budget goals).

Hypothesis (A) Branch Manager attains the following performance results:
- Indirect provision: € 57,000;
- Direct provision: € 145,000;
- Attainment of budget goals by 80% of all portfolio agents.

Hypothesis (B) Branch Manager attains the following performance results:
- Indirect provision: € 53,000;
- Direct provision: € 166,000;
- Attainment of budget goals by 73% of all portfolio agents.

6. Recent evolutions in banking have attributed increasing importance to the sales network. How has this policy influenced the articulation of management control?

—

CSC Scandinavia: controlling and accounting for time[1]

Per Nikolaj D. Bukh
Poul Israelsen

Introduction

The Danish information technology services company CSC Danmark (CSC-DK) is a major provider of services to the public sector. The company focuses on the design, development and maintenance of IT systems and includes among its major customers Denmark's Tax and Customs offices, the Accounting Directorate, the Police and the ministries of Defence and the Interior.[2] CSC-DK (formerly Datacentralen) was acquired and named by the large US company Computer Sciences Corporation (CSC) in June 1996, and is now part of CSC's Scandinavian Division.

Besides CSC-DK the Scandinavian division consists of CSC Computer Management (CSC-CM), which is the largest facility-management company in Denmark, and a few companies of minor importance at the moment. Volume figures by business area are given in Table 11.1.

Table 11.1 Key volume and profitability figures by business area in 1997

CSC Danmark A/S		CSC Computer Management A/S	
Government outsourcing: 60%		Outsourcing, subcontracting to CSC Denmark: 62%	
Government systems integration: 25%			
Defence: 6%		Private sector outsourcing (manufacturing,	
Foreign governments (Cyprus, Russia, European Union): 5%		insurance, shipping): 38%	
Private sector: 3%			
Municipalities: 1%			
Revenue 1995:	DKK 940 million	Revenue 1995:	DKK 460 million
Revenue 1996/97:	DKK 1,200 million	Revenue 1996/97:	DKK 604 million
Net income 1995:	DKK 25 million	Net income 1995:	DKK 53 million
Net income 1996/97: DKK	−64 million	Net income 1996/97: DKK	79 million
Average number of employees: 853		Average number of employees: 252	

Note: Revenue and income figures for 1996/97 are based on a 15-month period. The 1996/97 result of CSC-DK is influenced by cost of restructuring.

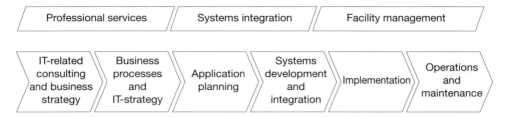

Figure 11.1 The IT value chain

CSC-DK and CSC-CM are both located in the Copenhagen metropolitan area and operate from three main facilities located at Valby, Birkerød and Høje-Taastrup.

Due to its affiliation with the CSC subsidiaries in other countries CSC Danmark is one of the few Scandinavian companies that are able to service customers in all parts of the IT value chain as shown in Figure 11.1. In its services the company uses a variety of different hardware and software platforms. Today, CSC Scandinavia operates almost exclusively in the Danish market. It is, however, the stated aim of the company to achieve strong growth in the Scandinavian market, with the goal of doubling its revenue in the year 2001.

Entering the new millennium, CSC Danmark is facing a number of obstacles, and the company still has to prove that it can attract new commercial customers for systems integration and management consulting as well as keeping its government and military customers. The competition in the Danish market is fierce, and prices, especially on facility management, are declining. Further, competition between IT companies has expanded into the labour market, making it very hard to attract and keep employees with key competencies.

Within the next couple of years, some of CSC Danmark's most important assignments in the public sector, the operation and maintenance of the comprehensive budget and accounting system used by almost all government agencies in Denmark, and the Central Personal Register (CPR) system will be put out to open tender.[3] Further, a number of CSC Computer Management largest private assignments are to be renegotiated within 1998.

The history of CSC Scandinavia

The development of the Danish welfare state has resulted in a large public sector taking care of administration, infrastructure and service. IT has enabled the expansion of centralized systems and large databases such as the Central Person Register, the tax system, the national health insurance, the value added tax system, and the automobile registration.

Based on an IBM consultancy report, CSC Danmark was established in 1959 under the name Datacentralen as a service bureau for the public sector. During the first decades of operation, Datacentralen primarily developed customized solutions to large data-handling tasks designed for large mainframes. Later when the mini-computers appeared, Datacentralen developed systems to be run on the customers' own computers and, in the 1980s, on PCs.

One of the most important assignments in the history of Datacentralen began in the middle of the 1960s when it was decided to give every citizen in Denmark a personal ID, making it possible for the government to identify and register important personal information. Since then the company has participated in the development of other systems for public offices, like tax programs, employment-agency programs, and health-care systems for hospitals and research, to name but a few.

Throughout the early years of operations Datacentralen was closely related to IBM, with IBM supplying the first managing director of Datacentralen, and until 1979 IBM was the only supplier of hardware. Further, it was not until 1965 and 1969, respectively, that Datacentralen established its own development and education departments.

In 1991 Datacentralen was converted from a government agency into a limited liability company owned by the Danish government's Ministry of Research & Information Technology.

During the 1980s and 1990s the political climate in Denmark favoured privatization. Increased efficiency and effectiveness is hoped for through private owner-ship and competition, and a privatized company is believed to have easier access to forming alliances with other partners and develop knowhow for the benefit of its current and future customers. In addition, EU regulations demand open tender-ing for all contracts over a particular level of ECU. The change of status for Datacentralen was a first step towards pursuing these benefits.

In the following years Datacentralen started to expand by establishing subsidiary companies: Dan Computer Management (now CSC Computer Management), Datacentralen Geodata (now CSC Information Systems) and buying stocks in other IT companies: Dansk Datalab ApS, and Management Application Support A/S.

The subsidiary Dan Computer Management, which was the first major facility management company to be established in Denmark, was owned 50% by Data-centralen and 50% by Maersk Data, a provider of central operating services in Denmark (Appendix 2). Since its establishment, Dan Computer Management has had a very high growth rate with only a slight increase in the number of employees.

The acquisition of Datacentralen A/S by CSC

On 1 November 1995 Søren Bansholt was appointed managing director of Datacentralen A/S and soon the Danish government started investigating the pos-sibilities of finding a strategic partner that could provide the state-owned company with new business synergy. After intense negotiations with a number of potential partners for an alliance (e.g. IBM and EDS), the large US company Computer

Sciences Corporation (CSC) acquired 75% of Datacentralen A/S in the early summer of 1996. Søren Bansholt commented on the choice of CSC:

> In the context of culture, CSC was a very decentralized structured company, i.e. a company with a lot of responsibility and therefore a lot of very good people on the front line. That situation was a very positive combo in the negotiating of the two parties.

Later the same year, CSC finalized its acquisition of Maersk Data's 50% shareholding of Dan Computer Management and appointed Finn Andersen as DCM's managing director reporting to Søren Bansholt, president of CSC Scandinavia. In addition, Søren Bansholt was appointed chairman of the board of Dan Computer Management. At the same time Dan Computer Management changed its name to CSC Computer Management (CSC-CM).

At the time of the acquisition of Datacentralen, CSC already had a significant presence in eight European countries, and Van B. Honeycutt, CSC's president and chief executive officer, explained the entry into Scandinavia in the following way:

> CSC Datacentralen will be the strategic platform from which CSC will grow its presence in Scandinavia, and it will work in partnership with the Danish State as IT plays an increasing role in Danish society

Establishing the Scandinavian Division

The acquisition of Datacentralen was the first move towards CSC's aim to be the number one IT company in Scandinavia, where the large Swedish companies in particular are attractive customers for outsourcing services. Acquiring Volvo as a customer could for example mean additional revenue of 20 billion DKK and would require about 3,000 employees. Further, the facility management services offered by CSC-CM are very competitive due to the efficient operations of CSC-CM.

In October 1997, Datacentralen changed its name to CSC Danmark and the company CSC Information Systems, which now has 90 employees, was established on the basis of Datacentralen Geodata A/S. The present ownership structure of the Scandinavian Division is shown in Figure 11.2 while the organizational structure is shown in Figure 11.3. (A/S, Aktieselskab, is the Danish legal term for Ltd., and ApS, Anpartsselskab, is the Danish term used for smaller limited liability companies.) In the same month, Søren Bansholt left CSC Danmark and Dennis Hocking from CSC's European headquarters was appointed temporary president of CSC Scandinavia. After some months Guy Hains was appointed president of CSC Scandinavia.

The market

CSC Scandinavia's approach to the market is based on a concept of total service across the entire IT value chain. This means that CSC is able to provide a service

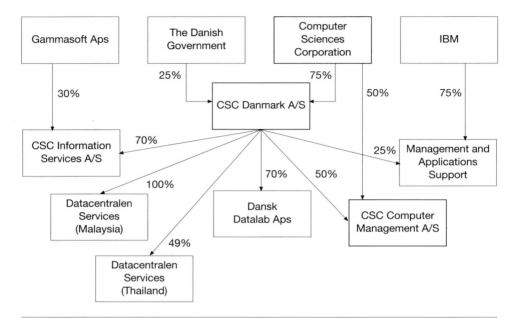

Note 1: A/S, Aktieselskab, is the Danish legal term for Ltd., and ApS, Anpartsselskab, is the Danish term used for smaller limited liability companies.

Note 2: Datacentralen Services (Thailand), 51% is owned by a Thai shareholder due to Thai law. The control of the company resides with CSC through mutual contractual arrangements.

Note 3: A brief note on the Danish Tax system. Company income tax is a flat rate of 35%. The personal income tax system has three tax brackets plus a flat gross tax. At the highest tax bracket the accumulated marginal tax rate reaches approximately 70%.

Figure 11.2 The ownership structure of CSC's Scandinavian Division

to the customer in all parts of the IT value chain. However, not all projects with customers start out at the 'professional services' end of the value chain. The aim of the company is, then, to move up or down the chain from the initial point of entry with the individual customer.

The main competitors across the IT value chain are shown in Table 11.2 (for further details of the individual competitors see Appendix 2).

Table 11.2 Main competitors

Type of work (CSC company)	Service, technology or product	Main competitors
Management consulting (CSC-DK)	IT Advisory, BPR	PA, Big Six
Systems development and Integration (CSC-DK)	Application development	IBM, KMD, Andersen, EDS
Facility Management (CSC-CM)	Service management	IBM, EDS, DM Data, LEC

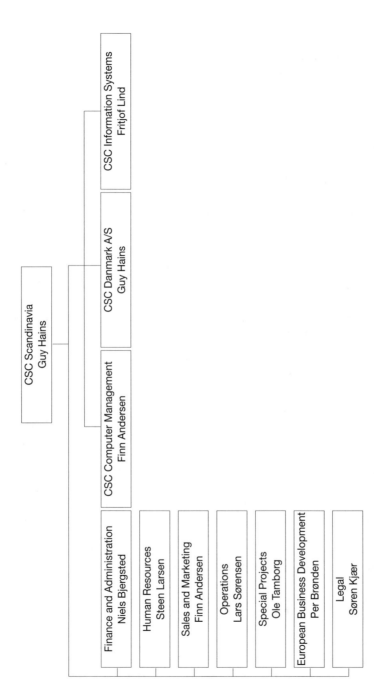

Figure 11.3 Organization chart, CSC's Scandinavian Division

The majority of CSC Denmark's large government contracts are complex contracts containing budget lines for development, maintenance operations (computer management), monitoring, etc. The operations part is carried out by CSC-CM. CSC-DK, on the other hand, carry out the back offices services (for example accounting and legal services) for CSC-CM and are paid for these services as a percentage of revenues earned on facility management services subcontracted from CSC Denmark A/S to CSC-CM.

Within CSC-DK the core competencies vis-à-vis the market are 'IT handling of public administration' and 'management of big IT projects'. The systems development and systems integration areas are characterized by increasing product complexity and shrinking technology life cycles leading to shorter product life cycles. The competition for the large public and private customers, often with high bargaining powers, is very intense and stimulated by the competing IT companies' growth desires. In addition, public sector budgets in general are under constant pressure for reduction.

Within the facility management area, the competition is driven by a decreasing contribution margin per mips (million instructions per second), and the market is expecting an annual increase in efficiency around 20%. Combined with the high fixed costs and low marginal costs the critical mass, in terms of volume of business, is increasing, and competition is further influenced by the rapid development in the communications/transmission technology.

The company

The organization of the main companies, CSC-DK and CSC-CM, are shown in Figures 11.4 and 11.5, respectively. CSC Information Systems, which was established on 1 October 1997, is owned 70% by CSC Denmark A/S and 30% by GammaSoft ApS. GammaSoft, which is situated in Aarhus, is a spin-off from R&D activities at The Aarhus School of Architecture in Aarhus and is owned by employees.

Members of the senior management team in CSC Information Systems are the CEO Fritjof Lind, who has a background as an executive in CSC-DK, and Jens V. Svendsen who is the main shareholder in GammaSoft. The board members are Jens V. Svendsen, Niels Bjergsted, the Chief Financial Officer of CSC Denmark, and Lars Sørensen, director of Operations, CSC Denmark.

Organizational structure

Before the take-over by CSC, Datacentralen was organized along four production divisions with a high degree of autonomy, each employing their own systems development staff, programmers, etc. and each with a profit & loss responsibility. As a supplement to the divisional structure a new corporate-level 'Sales and

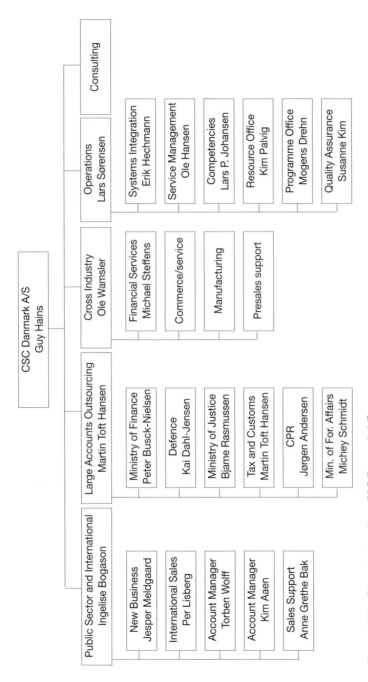

Figure 11.4 Organization chart, CSC Danmark A/S

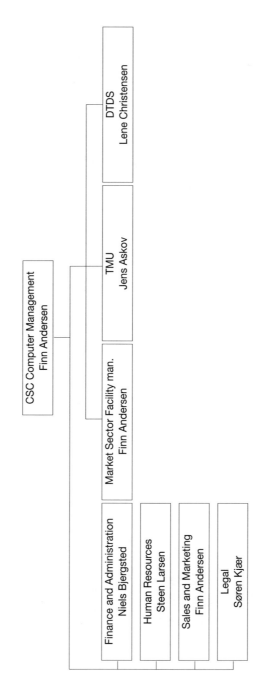

Figure 11.5 Organization chart, CSC Computer Management A/S

Marketing' department was established in 1995. The department's responsibility was to attract new clients as well as winning re-competes with existing clients. The department was assigned aggressive sales goals but no profit responsibility. The tender submissions were worked out by people temporarily borrowed from the divisions, and the actual production of orders was carried out in the divisions. While this organization structure was instrumental in focusing the organization on the demands of the customers, it proved less effective in attracting new businesses. A key explanation for the lack of success was that the company did not show 'one face to the market'. A supplementary reason was the built-in organizational conflict of where (i.e. to which projects) to deploy the most resourceful IT-people. Consequently, with CSC's take-over of Datacentralen, new ways of organizing the company were debated and it was decided to break up the divisional structure. An account organization was established in CSC-DK assigning the account/client managers profit and loss (P&L) responsibility for their current customer base as well as accountability for creating add-on sales and new contracts with existing customers. In addition, they were assigned responsibility for winning new customers/sales within their assigned market segment. The account organization has no production staff. However, the account managers are given an annual cost and expense budget to be used in their pre-contracts activities. These amounts are used to buy technological knowhow, from inside or outside the group, necessary to perform effective pre-contract activities. Similar structures are created in CSC-CM A/S and CSC-Information Systems A/S.

The Resource Office

The account managers are not allocated any production staff since all production staff members are employed by the Operations division. Co-ordination between the account management structure and Operations is handled by the Resource Office, which is a concept fostered by CSC internationally as a way of handling the allocation and reallocation of employees between projects.

Every production staff member is kept track of by the Resource Office, e.g. their 'competence profile' (see Resource planning system section below), the projects to which they are currently assigned, for how long, what the next assignment will be, etc. Key success factors of the Resource Office are related to maintaining and recruiting IT-people with the right competencies and allocating them optimally among projects. One of the means in this regard is the 'internal labour market' created by the Resource Office. In this market the individual IT-employee can apply for new forthcoming project assignments. This market is supplemented with a system in which the IT-employee can apply for the funds necessary for his or her technical skill enhancement. This feature represents a departure from the previous structure in which the budgets for skill enhancement resided with the individual systems/project managers. The management skill enhancement programme and budget stays unchanged with the personnel department. Actual staffing of projects is negotiated between the account managers and Operations and eventually brought to the CEO, Guy Hains.

The chief controller, Steen Rasmussen, comments on the implementation of the new organizational structure in CSC-DK:

> In principle, the new way of organizing is right: The Account managers are responsible for monitoring and developing our customer relationships, Operations for delivering the project and systems in the way and at the time promised, and the Resource Office in maintaining and recruiting the production staff needed. The new organizational system has been formally implemented and for the time being we are working hard to make it work; a number of management people have got new roles and therefore it will take some time. In the controller's office we are developing and installing the necessary information and control systems to support this structure

Incentive contracts

Account managers and directors have individually negotiated incentive contracts of various forms. A representative contract structure, however, will add up to 20% to the fixed salary. Typically, a section of the variable part is tied to the financial performance goals and achievements of the account manager's business unit and another section to the financial goals and achievements of the wider CSC-Scandinavia.

Planning and control systems

Five information systems form the informational core of the planning and control systems. These are the 'Sales planning system (Multimark)', the 'Resource planning system', the 'Management accounting system' and the 'Time recording system' (a sub-system to the management accounting system). The fifth system, the 'Budgeting system' is not described. The systems are interconnected through project numbers and the 'Order account code'.

Sales planning system

The sales planning system Multimark was created by Ingelise Bogason, former head of 'Sales and Marketing' and current director of the Public Sector & International Account Organization, cf. Figure 11.4. Multimark keeps track of CSC's sales order pipeline and backlog, i.e. contracts entered.

Multimark contains potential sales orders starting at the earliest possible time, preferably on receipt of the first information on a potential project, e.g. an IT-project in a Danish ministry. The main identifiable steps in the order pipeline are 'entry into pre-qualification process', 'pre-qualification obtained', 'tender material received', 'contract negotiations in progress', and 'Order/no order'. Among the entries at each step in Multimark are estimated revenue, amount and qualification of production staff required as well as the timing of the manpower needed. The transition from one stage to the next is typically much faster in the private sector segment than the public client segment.

Aggregating across all entries in Multimark, and taking into consideration the likelihood of winning the order, forms the basis of the sales budget. Probabilities of winning individual projects range from zero per cent to 90 per cent once the contract negotiation stage has been entered. Multimark is updated weekly by the account managers.

The Multimark system provides management with an overview of potential contracts in the pipeline and contracts won, and in monetary terms of the relationship between budgeted sales (based on the probabilities) and actual sales.

The system is fully implemented in Public Sector & International and planned for in the remainder of CSC-DK.

Resource planning system

This system is operated by the Resource Office to monitor IT 'knowhow' resources. A central feature of the system is the 'Competence profile code'. This code segregates the production staff into 38 competence categories, and is a more detailed description of the production staff competencies than the one used in the Order Account Code's 'Application' dimension (see below and Appendix 1, Table 11.4). For example, within the legacy products, i.e. individually in-house-developed software systems for a number of large public sector customers, the following nine categories are used:

1. Legacy system developer, programmer, COBOL/DB2/IMS
2. Legacy system developer, programmer, NATURAL/DB2/IMS
3. Legacy system developer, programmer, PL1/DB2/IMS
4. Legacy system developer, programmers, other
5. Legacy system developer, Integrated system development (planning/programming/test), COBOL/DB2/IMS
6. Legacy system developer, Integrated system development (planning/programming/test), NATURAL/DB2/IMS
7. Legacy system developer, Integrated system development (planning/programming/test), PL1/DB2/IMS
8. Legacy system developer, Integrated system development (planning/programming/test), other
9. Legacy system developer, planner (planning, test, task co-ordination), IBM mainframe.

These competence categories determine the level of detail to which the Resource Office is able to plan the allocation of employees across projects and periods. The same competence categories are used in the management accounting system, making integration possible.

Management accounting system

Time recording system and labour costing

All consultants, programmers, project managers and system managers, etc. in CSC-DK are hired by the Operations Division. The Resource Office, managed by Kim Palvig, handles this. Salary and other personnel related costs (e.g. training costs) are booked in the Resource Office Cost Centre. Time entry cards with hours booked on projects are used to transfer salary expenses from the Resource Office Cost Centre to projects (identified by project numbers). These so-called Internal Work Order (IWO) bookings are done automatically by the Time Recording System. The time entry cards identify the individual and his or her 'competence profile code'.

Also staffing of projects is co-ordinated by the Resource Office. For the year 1998 budgeting is based on 1,420 productive hours per individual derived as follows:

	Hours per year
Working days in financial year 1998	1,843
Holiday, Christmas, etc.	(222)
Education	(52)
Illness	(41)
Lunch breaks, etc.	(89)
Internal meetings	(19)
Productive hours/chargeable hours	1,420

It is the responsibility of the Resource Office to make use of all productive hours. Except managers, all employees can have overtime. Costs of overtime are booked against projects at 150% of normal pay. Furthermore, some employees are paid for being available, for instance during weekends. The cost of 'being on call' is booked at 25% of normal pay (if activated the employee transfers to overtime pay). When preparing the budget the labour rate is DKK 360 (disguised), covering the salary plus personnel-related costs.

In the actual bookings labour rates are based on the individual's actual salary plus a mark-up for personnel-related costs and administration. The actual rates vary between DKK 280 and DKK 650 (disguised) whereas the market value of some of these productive hours may run into DKK 1,500 per hour. The mark-up is calculated so that the budgeted Operating Income for the Resource Office equals zero when all chargeable hours are actually charged to projects. Any over- or under-absorption is taken to P&L.

Periodically, the actual use of labour hours is compared with budgets at the project level and discrepancies are broken down into a labour rate variance and an efficiency variance.

Accounting for projects

Basically, the customer and CSC Danmark enter into either a 'Fixed Price' contract or a 'Time & Materials' contract. About 30% of CSC Danmark's revenue stems from Fixed Price contracts with CSC providing an agreed service at a fixed price while about 70% of the revenue is from Time & Materials contracts where CSC charge the customers according to the use of time, materials, etc. Very often fixed price contracts will last several years making it very complicated to take into account the actual characteristics of the projects as well as the technological possibilities.

For all sales projects profitability is calculated including all revenue and direct costs. The consumption of costs not specifically related to individual projects (e.g. headquarters, or IT infrastructure) are allocated using various statistical key figures (e.g. number of productive hours, number of employees, etc.). The purpose of this procedure is to be able to calculate an Operating Income per project after all over-head expenses have been allocated. The budgeted Operating Income for the overhead cost centres after allocation equals zero. No under- or overabsorption is encountered in the allocation of costs from overhead cost centres.

Each month the expenses booked at the business unit cost centres and overhead cost centres are allocated to projects and an operating income per project is reported. As an example, consider the March 1998 report on a specific project:

Project 1112101-66 / March 1998 – accumulated

	DKK
Revenue	1,000,000
Subcontractors	(10,000)
Cost of materials	(10,000)
Internal Work Orders[1]	(700,000)
Operation income pre-allocations	280,000
Account management	(4,000)
Sector overheads	(1,000)
Common IT infrastructure	(20,000)
Sales & Marketing	(10,500)
Headquarters	(30,000)
Operating income	214,500

Note (1): This number can be decomposed into a rate and efficiency variance

Tying this report structure to the organization chart Figure 11.6 illustrates the economic accountability structure of the account organization, here 'Large Account Outsourcing'. At the project level revenues and project direct costs are recorded. Summation across all projects in an account area (e.g. Tax and Customs, Figure 11.6 and 11.4) less costs that are indirect to the individual projects but direct to the account area (recorded in the 'cost centre') brings a 'profit centre' result for which the account manager is accountable. Summation across all 'profit centres' in the

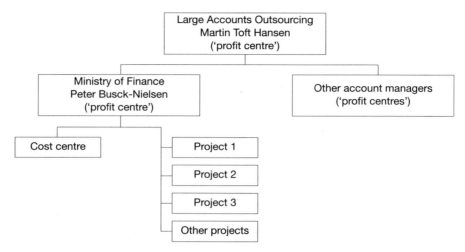

Figure 11.6   Economic accountability structure – illustration of Large Account Outsourcing

'Large Account Outsourcing' area brings the higher-level 'profit centre' result for which the Large Account Manager, i.e. Martin Toft Hansen, is accountable. This procedure is performed with and without allocations as illustrated by project 1112101-66.

Order account code of the management accounting system

Project numbers (like example 1112101-66 above) identifies all external orders, i.e. 'production' of projects for paying customers. These project numbers are used in the invoicing system and the time recording and labour costing system. On top of this all external orders are assigned attributes as described in Appendix 1, Table 11.4. Using the coding system of Table 11.4 every production order [Function/(order type) 10] is coded in terms of Application, Market, Safety and 'Operations Code'. The latter is a reference to the supply organization, i.e. the specific Operations managers in charge.

Internal orders, i.e. orders with no directly paying customers, are also assigned attributes. These internal orders are described in Table 11.4's Function/(orders type) 11 to 50. The amount of attributes assigned varies among the internal order types as described in the Table's 'notice' section. This information is used in allocating overheads (indirect costs).

Chief controller, Steen Rasmussen, comments on the planning and control systems:

> Once the systems have been tuned we expect to gain a number of benefits from them. At the operational level we should be able to do away with the 'number discussions' at internal project meetings. Quite often too much time is spent during these meetings debating the adequacy of the numbers. Part of this was due to discrepancies between

central and local systems. Also, due to our contract structure with customers, reliable account entries are essential.

At the tactical level the combined information contained in Multimark and the Resource planning system makes it easier to monitor the development in our customer base and the competencies needed to serve them. In addition the history contained in the Management accounting system should be able to bring signals about which type of projects to put in more effort in the planning stages of resource consumption.

Critical success factors

As part of the monthly reporting to senior management, a summary report of critical success factors (Table 11.3) is prepared by the management accounting department.

Table 11.3 Critical success factors in CSC Scandinavia

Key area	Critical success factors	Measures
Financial	Budgeting performance	Budget targets and variances
	Revenue on orders	Gross margin
	Fixed-price contracts	Gross margin and completion rate
	Corporate relations	Income in subsidiaries and associated companies
	Free cash flow	Balance and liquidity
	Productivity	Key ratios, e.g. invoiced hours and 'billability'
Growth, market positioning and customer relationships	Business development plans	Actions taken in business and applications areas
	Penetration of new markets	Actions taken on market areas
	Stock of orders	Safety in revenue and bit-won ratio
Product and competence development	Progress in investments	Cost/revenue and completion rate
	Specialist education	Actions taken
	Scarcity of specialists	Actions taken in relation to staffing plans and recruitments
Human resource	Employees	Target number, variances
	Wages	Wage trends
	Employee turnover	IT-people entries and exits
	Social targets	Health, flexible hours, etc.

In addition we provide information for senior management concerning project milestones and their achievement and also information on quality of performance. This is done at the project level. We find no use for aggregated measures on delivery time and quality of performance across projects.

Project progress and quality of performance in the eyes of the customer are monitored closely by the account organization and taken up at scheduled meetings with clients.

Where necessary quality of performance evaluation is informed by questionnaire surveys. Our performance in these areas is essential in all projects, not least the public sector projects where the ultimate customer is the same, the Danish government. (Chief controller, Steen Rasmussen)

Endnotes

[1] The authors would like to thank Steen Rasmussen at CSC Danmark for making the writing of the case possible and for commenting on the case. Also thanks to Tom Groot, Peter Bjørn Jensen, Kari Lukka, Hanne Nørreklit and Peter Skærbæk for comments on an earlier version of the case.

[2] The data concerning the case company is, unless otherwise stated, updated as at June 1998. Any changes that may have occurred thereafter have not been considered in this text. Some of the numbers are disguised in order to preserve confidentiality.

[3] CPR is comparable to other countries' Social Security Numbers but more all embracing since it is used in all interfaces between the individual Danish citizen and all public offices, i.e. local, county or state.

STUDENT ASSIGNMENTS

1. Why did the Danish government want to sell the majority of its shares in Datacentralen A/S to the private sector?

2. Why was the CSC chosen as the partner and not, for instance, IBM?

3. Which parts of the total IT value chain does CSC Danmark provide, and which are the successful ones?

4. What are the principal competitive forces within the two main segments of the market, i.e. 'System Development and System Integration' and 'Facility Management'?

5. Why was the organizational set-up of Datacentralen changed from a divisionalized structure to a structure using 'Account managers', 'Operations' and a 'Resource Office'? What are the advantages and drawbacks of this structure?

6. How does the management control system in general and the management accounting system in particular support this structure?

7. Which performance measures are calculated regularly and which are the strategically important ones? How do these measures fit with the management incentive contracts?

8. CSC Danmark's share of the IT market in the private sector is very modest. Part of the solution to this problem was the creation of an account management structure. Is the current account management structure likely to increase the turnover in the private sector? Why?

9. CSC-CM's payment for back-office services provided by CSC-DK is handled rather simply. Why might this be?

10. Is the Resource Office likely to be able to solve its task in terms of allocating the right people to the right type of project with the current system of internal transfer prices?

Appendix 1   Coding the orders in the accounting information system

Every activity (e.g. production, education, marketing and management) is regarded as an 'order'. These orders are used for the coding of external invoices as well as for allocating overhead costs. The same coding is used for registering time used by all employees except at upper management levels.

When using the coding system shown below every order is coded in three dimensions: Application, Market and Function. Further, the sales/production orders are coded according to Contract form/Safety.

Table 11.4   Coding of the orders in the accounting information system

Field name	Project code	SAP code	Text
Application (Competencies)	11	111	Legacy systems
	12	112	Oracle, etc.
	13	113	HPS
	15	115	PowerBuilder
	32	232	Microsoft etc.
	34	234	Workflow/EDI etc.
	35	235	Professional Services
	37	237	Solutions for the insurance sector
	38	238	Solutions for the banking sector
	60	360	SAP
	64	364	Business Intelligence (SAS/EIS)
	71	471	Products for State Data Net (SDN)
	79	479	Network Services (Consultancy)
	82	582	Facility Management, centralized
	86	586	Facility Management, decentralized
	97	997	Secondary activities (rental fees, etc.)
	99	999	Sundries
Market (Customer types)	11	11	Tax and Customs offices
	12	12	Ministry of the Interior (Central Person Register)
	13	13	Police
	14	14	Defence
	15	15	Accounting Directorate
	16	16	State departments, other
	21	21	Municipalities
	22	22	Ministry of Foreign Affairs
	29	29	Private sector, service

Table 11.4 Continued

Field name	Project code	SAP code	Text
	30	30	Private sector, service and financial sector/DK
	31	31	Private sector, services and financial sector/FSG
	32	32	Private sector, manufacturing
	34	34	Private sector, trade
	35	35	Oil & Gas
	36	36	Health Care
	41	41	International and EU
	51	51	Large state-owned companies
	blank	98	Unspecified (only allowed for order type 20, 30 or 40)
	99	99	Other or cross functional (e.g. R&D)
Function (order type)	10	10	Production
	11	11	Education
	20	20	Sales & Marketing and Pre-sale activities
	30	30	Management & Administration
	40	40	Maintenance, Systems and Equipment
	50	50	Product and competence development

Notice: 10: APPLICATION, MARKET, SAFETY and "Operations Code" (only CSC-DK) are mandatory
11: APPLICATION is mandatory, ONLY indirect costs
20: APPLICATION and MARKET is mandatory; ONLY indirect costs
30: No mandatory identification/coding requirements; ONLY indirect costs
40: No mandatory identification/coding requirements; ONLY indirect costs
50: APPLICATION is mandatory; ONLY indirect costs

Field name	Project code	SAP code	Text
Safety (Contract form) only order type	1	1	Fixed price
	2	2	Invoiced as used (Time & Materials)
	3	3	Cost plus
	4	4	Other
	9	9	Inter-company, Intra-company or Intra-group
Individual field 1			Can be used individually, Numerical
Individual field 2			Can be used individually, Numerical
Individual field 3			Can be used individually, Numerical

Notes
PowerBuilder is an object-oriented general systems development milieu supporting Microsoft client/server platforms, Solaris as well as MacIntosh platforms. PowerBuilder is used for the construction of IT systems but not the analysis and design.
HPS (High Productivity Systems) is a development milieu used in the development of large, complex applications with an expected long lifetime. HPS can be used in all phases of the systems development including analysis and documentation when the actual construction is done with the use of other software tools.

Appendix 2   The main competitors of CSC's Scandinavian division

IBM Denmark A/S (IBM)

IBM Denmark A/S is a part of the global company IBM. With a number of Danish subsidiaries, IBM as a whole employs 4,600 people in Denmark and is considered a leading company in information products, solutions and services. With a business idea focusing on network solutions, system integration and services and consulting, IBM is capable of delivering total solutions using IBM products and technology. IBM offers facility management services through its subsidiary, Responsor.

Electronic Data Systems (EDS)

Electronic Data Systems (EDS) is the largest supplier of information technology services in the world. EDS offers a portfolio of IT-based services comparable to CSC, i.e. ranging from management consulting through systems development, integration and management, outsourcing to process management.

LEC

LEC was founded in 1962 as a service bureau for the agricultural sector, but has now expanded into other markets. Among them are the Danish slaughterhouses and dairies, industrial companies, the financial sector, the state and other public institutions in Denmark. LEC has 700 employees and a yearly turnover of DKK 795 million. The products range from consulting, system developing, operations, and delivery of hardware, network and software solutions for PC, client/server solutions and mainframe environments.

DMdata

DMdata is a facility-management company jointly owned by Den Danske Bank A/S and Maersk Data A/S. As well as running the systems of Den Danske Bank and Maersk, DMdata also offers commercial facility management services. The company, with its 100 employees, manages central IT operations for private as well as public customers. DMdata is the largest facility management company in the Nordic countries with a capacity of 3,000 MIPS.

Danske Data A/S

Danske Data was a spin off, formed in July 1996 with 700 staff, from the largest Danish bank, Den Danske Bank. This was done in order to make the bank's systems operations more cost conscious and to start selling some of its systems on a commercial basis. In another split in March 1997 around 60 of Danske Data's staff joined DMdata, a facilities management joint venture set up by Den Danske Bank and Maersk Data.

Maersk Data A/S

Maersk Data, which is part of the global A.P. Moller Group, is a large supplier of client/server, mainframe and network-based solutions to large companies and organizations in Denmark and abroad. Maersk Data A/S offers consulting, systems development, systems integration business process analyses as well as systems development and integration, data communications and a broad range of facility management services. Maersk Data has been operating for more than 25 years and its main office is located in Copenhagen. A total of 690 people are employed in the Maersk Data Group and associated companies in the United States, Japan, India, England and Denmark.

Kommunedata I/S (KMD)

Kommunedata (KMD) was established in 1972 as the result of a merger of the three largest IT-centres in Denmark. Since then, KMD has grown to its present position as Denmark's largest systems operation and software house. The company delivers a broad range of services such as computer systems operation, software development, consulting services and facilities management. The customers are mostly in the public sector – local authorities, counties and the central government. KMD have 2,200 employees and nine systems operation and development centres in Denmark.

Among other things, KMD ensures that every month the salaries of almost one million Danes are transferred to their bank accounts, and that all Danes receive their tax deduction cards. The Danish National Association of Local Authorities (60%) and the Danish National Association of County Councils (40%) own the company. KMD has an annual turnover of DKK 1.65 billion.

—

Intellectual capital at Den norske Bank Group (DnB): the customer account manager's support system (CASS)[1]

Hanno Roberts

CASS is intended to provide an integrated systems solution that increases the effectiveness of working with small and medium-sized enterprises, which are the commercial banking division's market.

It is not just the account manager (to which the name of the system refers) who is to benefit from this system, it is equally beneficial as a sales support, case processing and information system for all those that are involved in customer-oriented work; managers, customer service, compliance, product salesmen etc.

An overarching goal with the new version has been to contribute to improved effectiveness and production flow.

CASS is to receive and provide full information on customers and customer relationships, the planning and implementation of activities, document processing and retrieval, analyses, customer profitability etc, both on existing customer and on prospective customers. CASS is to provide the fundament for cross-functional work – in customer teams – to promote sales of the full product width of the bank.

(CASS User Manual, 8 August 1998)

Introduction

The business strategy of the Commercial Banking Division of DnB for the two-year period 1997–1999 established as a key goal the increase of non-interest sources of revenue. Given its banking competences and wide range of products, DnB identified two major instruments to accomplish this goal – customer relationship building and cross-selling of the bank's products. The role of sales and, especially, of the existing customer account manager was defined as crucial; the change in sales strategy could only be effected when the customer account manager accepted and implemented this new strategy. This individual could make or break the entire strategy.

However, the wide range of bank products meant that one account manager simply could not handle the entire sales process of all products; the manager's role needed to be redefined and his/her position reasserted.

The manager's primary task was therefore refocused on relationship building, credit management, identification of customer needs and supervising the product line managers and the customer team. The pure sales function would be the prime task of the product line managers and the product salesmen. Thus, the goal of the CASS project was born – supporting the sales process by simultaneously providing all relevant information while redefining the role of the customer account manager. CASS was to support and alleviate the co-operation between a reinvented customer account manager and his sales team of product line managers and product salesmen.

DnB

Den norske Bank (DnB) is Norway's largest financial service firm with approximately one million private customers (retail banking) and thirty thousand business customers, the latter accounting for around 25% of the total business customer market (commercial banking). Moreover, DnB is the main banking partner for more than half of Norway's 300 largest firms.

The main product areas are investment banking, asset management, life and pension insurance and payment transfer and trade finance services. The main divisions within DnB are retail banking, commercial banking, corporate banking, and shipping and international offshore oil production. Its product range is comprehensive and comprises loans, credits, asset management, payment transfer and trade finance services, financial consulting and advice, currency and capital market products, and life and pension insurance.

DnB's corporate strategy is to be a leading financial services firm in the Scandinavian countries (Norway, Sweden, and Denmark) and the biggest provider of financial services in Norway itself. Its target is to provide unique solutions for the customer in all its market segments. Simultaneously, DnB is to be the most attractive workplace in Norwegian financial business.

At 31 December 1998, the DnB Group had total assets of 245 billion Norwegian kroner (NOK)[2] and 5,978 full-time employees. Its pre-tax operating profit before losses and loans, guarantees and long-term securities was 2,580 million NOK for 1998 and 2,667 million NOK for 1997. Net profits for 1998 and 1997 were 1,314 million NOK and 2,590 million NOK respectively. Earnings per share decreased from 4.04 in 1997 to 2.05 in 1998, while dividends per share decreased from 1.75 in 1997 to 1.35 in 1998, all in NOK. The Group had a Return On Equity (ROE) of 17.4% for 1997 and an 8.4% ROE for 1998. The pre-tax operating profits of the four divisions indicate a negative income pattern across divisions, with the shipping

Table 12.1   Extracts from profit and loss accounts (amounts in NOK million)

	Retail Banking Division		Commercial Banking Division		Corporate Banking Division		Shipping Division	
	1998	*1997*	*1998*	*1997*	*1998*	*1997*	*1998*	*1997*
Net interest income	1,616	1,715	1,391	1,438	539	468	397	431
Other operating income	1,117	1,003	876	832	801	744	184	217
Operating expenses	2,292	2,003	1,339	1,331	789	696	292	292
Pre-tax operating profit before losses	441	716	927	938	552	516	289	356
Net losses/(reversals) on loans etc.	13	(56)	(62)	(241)	121	(107)	852	143
Cost allocations	185	161	83	107	42	56	12	24
Pre-tax operating profit/(loss)	242	611	906	1,073	389	567	(575)	189

Source: 1998 Annual Report DnB group

division reporting a significant loss. The latter is due to a one-off restructuring charge in the Greek office. In a press release, the Group stated that

> . . . The DnB Group achieved acceptable operating profits before losses in 1998, with a positive trend in net interest income . . . However, group performance reflects the turbulence in financial markets as well as heavy losses of an unusual nature . . .

The DnB Group is organized in a matrix structure, with four customer divisions – Retail, Commercial, and Corporate Banking, and Shipping – and five product divisions – *Vital* insurance company, investment banking, asset management, life and pension insurance, and payment transfer services. This corporate matrix is mirrored by each of its ten banking regions in Norway. Every product area has product salesmen (PS) and a customer account manager (CA) who are represented in every region, thus creating regional customer/product matrixes also (Figure 12.1).

However, not all product competences are located in every region; in some regions, demands for certain banking competences are quite different. For example, along the northern coastline, the export-intensive fishery industry has a special demand for trade financing and payment transfer services, while on the south-western coast, the capital-intensive shipping and offshore construction industries require a totally different mix of capital asset and project financing services. As a result, some offices offer the full DnB product line while other offices offer only selected product lines. In the latter case, regional centres exist that concentrate special competence, for example on cash management or foreign exchange, on which local branch offices can draw when a special customer request comes in.

Customers in the commercial banking division (CBD) are small to medium-sized companies, categorized into three customer groups according to their size and

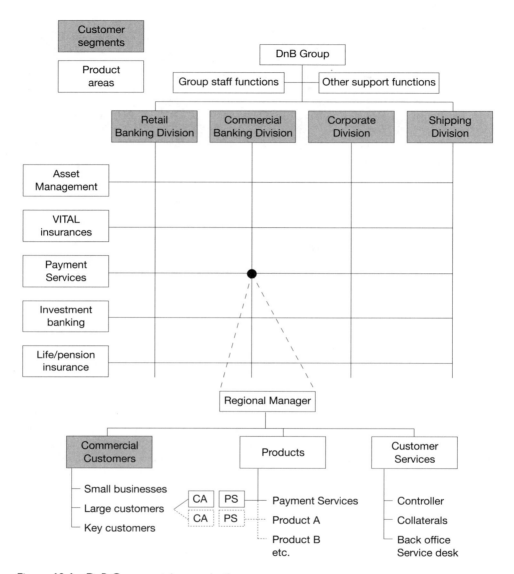

Figure 12.1 DnB Group matrix organization structure

needs: small commercial customers (SCs), medium-sized commercial customers (MCs), and key commercial customers (KCs).

A small customer (SC) typically has less than two million NOK worth of business with DnB and SCs contributes around 10% to the division's results. The SC group constitutes 9% of average gross lending volume in the division, which amounted to 55.2 billion NOK in December 1998.

Medium-sized customers (MC) accounted for 44% of average gross lending volume while key customers (KC) accounted for the remaining 47%. The MC group contains around 5,000–6,000 firms and contributes about 40% of the results. The key customer group contains about 1,000 firms and provides approximately 50% of the division's results. Key customers (KC) are defined as up-scale medium-sized businesses and are the most profitable.

In each customer group, a number of customer account managers (CAs) operate, each of which has a different account portfolio. For example, the account manager for small commercial customers has about 200–250 customers in his portfolio, while the account manager for medium-sized or key customers has between 10 and 40 customers in his portfolio. Each customer portfolio offers a number of product sales opportunities, to be indicated by the account manager but to be sold by the product salesman. The co-operation between account managers (CAs) and product salesmen (PSs) thus is crucial in identifying sales opportunities, following up prospects, and finalizing and servicing the sale. This co-operation takes place in all ten regional districts (see Figures 12.2 and 12.3).

The account manager and the product salesman

The co-operation between the CA and the PS is not only the result of the organization structure; it has also developed under pressure from external market developments. Many actors are entering the Norwegian banking market, either full service banks selling a comprehensive range of products or niche banks selling a limited set of products. As a result, sales prices and margins are falling and an increasing number of customers are willing to change their banking partner. With falling margins, the need to increase sales volume across the entire product range is evident. To allow for that, the sales organization itself needs to be reconsidered in terms of increasing its effectiveness and efficiency.

Sales managers

Various sales channels are presently used in the commercial banking division. The account manager is the main sales channel; he sells all products while the product salesman only sells products from his product areas. To realize cross-sales of a larger number of products, the account manager will become the key person. Cross-sales via many individual product salesmen, each with their single-product competence, is an unrealistic option. Cross-sales will have to involve the CA for that reason alone.

In addition, the relationship between the account manager and his customers is one of the bank's most important assets, and that asset has to be maintained. The account manager *is* the bank in the eyes of the customer.

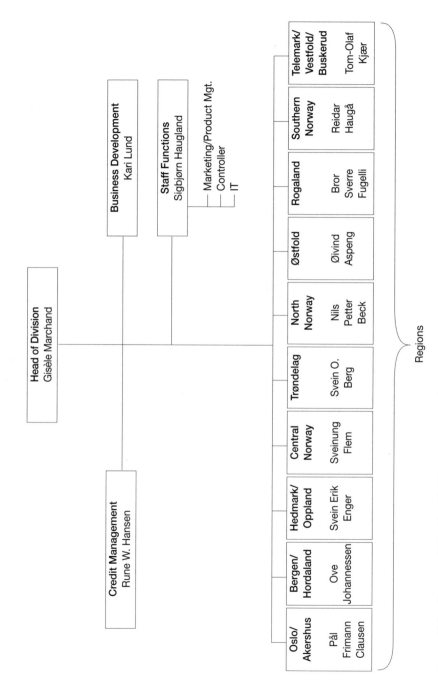

Figure 12.2 Commercial Banking Division organization chart

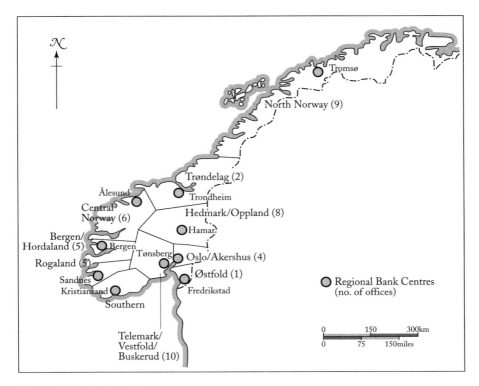

Figure 12.3 Regional bank centres

Table 12.2 DnB commercial banking division

Business Profile	• Serving around 30,000 small and medium-sized companies • DnB is the leading bank in this segment • 25% of companies in this segment use DnB as their main banking partner • 10 regional centres with special competence within cash management, foreign exchange, interest rate and securities products • Lower risk profile than the national average for this customer segment
Strategic Focus	• To increase cross-sales • More effective credit process (credit scoring) and service concept for small companies • Upgrading professional skills

Source: 1998 Annual Report DnB Group

Given this competence and reputation, the sales responsibility is unclear: Who is responsible changes with almost every sales situation. Is it the account manager, who can cross-sell many products and has a long-standing bank relationship with the customer, but lacks the product competence of the product salesman? Or is it the product salesman, whose competence allows him to customize the product to the specific needs of the customer, thus creating both a good profit margin and customer satisfaction, but who is unable to achieve high sales volume other than in his own field of competence?

As a result of the unclear responsibilities, the roles of both CA and PS were re-defined in terms of their overall sales responsibilities and their position in the sales process – who does what when? Role redefinition occurred vis-à-vis the two major customer groups in commercial banking – small customers, and medium-sized and key customers. Redefinition of roles took place during the first three months of 1997 (see Figure 12.5).

Responsibility structures in sales

The roles of the account manager and the product sales man vis-à-vis the various customer groups are shown in Table 12.3.

The clearer definition of the roles allowed clearly delineates responsibilities. It provides agreement on when the CA and the PS should co-operate and on the moments when they have individual responsibilities. For example, the CA is not required to participate in the actual sales activities; he/she has to delegate, rely on and trust the PS in these matters.

Roles and responsibilities were identified by means of a sales process mapping. The map provided the basis for assigning sales activities to the account manager and the product salesman and provided the linkages between different stages of the sales process (Figure 12.4).

The sales process map fed into the credit process map, which again featured the account manager but now in connection with other internal banking functions.

Communication

Communication between the account manager and the product salesman is now firmly grounded in their specific tasks and responsibilities. The Customer Accountmanagement Support System (CASS) takes over much of the formal com-munication between them, providing both with real-time and on-line status reports on activities, customers, and persons responsible.

Competences

As a consequence of the clear role definitions of the CA and the PS, the com-petences required for the two task sets became clear. Large portions of the actual sales work transferred from the account managers to the product sales force, which had to reorganize themselves via the product lines. For example, the product line

Table 12.3 Sales roles

Customer type	Customer Account manager (CA)	Product salesmen (PS) and the product line
Small customers (SC)	<ul><li>Overall customer responsibility</li><li>Credit handling</li><li>Planning sales process:<ul><li>Mapping customer/portfolio potential</li><li>Setting sales goals</li><li>Establishing activities and time schedules</li></ul></li><li>Implementing sales activities:<ul><li>Direct marketing</li><li>Campaigns</li><li>'Team sales'</li></ul></li><li>Follow-up of the sales process</li><li>CA is responsible for sales of all products offered in this segment</li><li>Relationship management</li></ul>	<ul><li>Support the CA in planning the sales process:<ul><li>Mapping portfolio/segment potential</li><li>Setting sales goals</li><li>Establishing activities and time schedules</li></ul></li><li>Support the CA in implementing sales activities:<ul><li>Direct marketing</li><li>Campaigns</li><li>'Team sales'</li></ul></li><li>Support the CA in the follow-up of the sales process</li><li>Training</li><li>Towards the product areas: take care of product delivery</li></ul>
Medium-sized (MC) and Key customers (KC)	<ul><li>Overall customer responsibility</li><li>Relationship management</li><li>Credit handling</li><li>Covering the demand, leading the planning of the sales process</li><li>Planning the sales process:<ul><li>Mapping customer/portfolio potential</li><li>Setting sales goals</li><li>Establishing activities, time schedules, responsibilities</li></ul></li><li>Introducing the PS to the customer</li><li>The CA does not necessarily participate in the sales activities</li><li>Follow-up of the sales process and of the PS</li><li>Administrate the customer team (KC)</li><li>The CA is responsible for the sales of loan and deposit products</li></ul>	<ul><li>Sales responsible for his products</li><li>Participate in the customer team (KC)</li><li>Support the CA in planning the sales process:<ul><li>Mapping customer/portfolio potential</li><li>Setting sales goals</li></ul></li><li>Establishing activities, time schedules, responsibilities</li><li>Responsible for the implementation of sales activities</li><li>Responsible for reporting the achieved results relative to the established sales activity goals</li><li>Co-operate with the CA in the follow-up of the sales process</li><li>Towards the product areas: take care of product delivery</li></ul>

areas appointed regional contact persons while the regions in turn appointed product co-ordinators, thus creating a vertical chain of competence and expertise from the product area to the PS in the regions and regional branch offices.

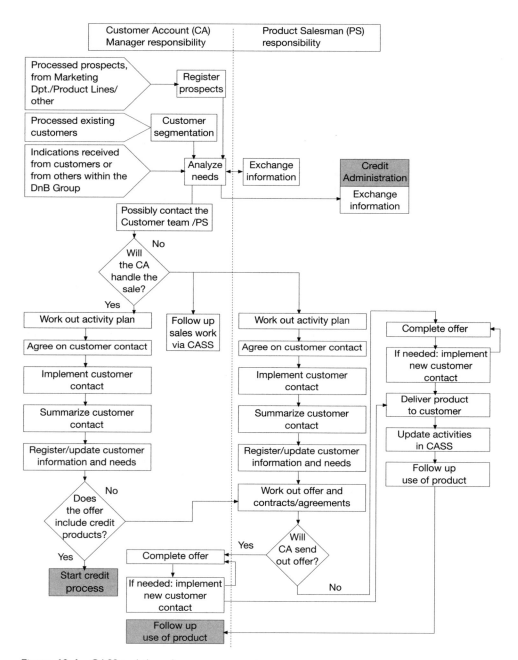

Figure 12.4   CASS and the sales process mapping

The CA, on the other hand, was allowed to continue sales activities and set aside time for it. For medium-sized and key customers, the CA has direct sales responsibility for so-called balance sheet products (e.g. loans, credits and deposits). For all other products, the CA had to have sufficient product knowledge to make a first presentation to the customer as well as to look after specific customer needs and build a relationship. For the small customers, the CA had to have competence in all products offered to this customer group.

The separation in roles and responsibilities indicated that individual skills and competences also were involved. Notably, competences in sales, sales management, team and project co-operation, and relationship building were focal areas. These touched upon general issues of human resource management. On average, the personnel buildup at DnB is skewed; a majority of staff is 45 years or older and this is felt to have consequences for introducing significant changes in work patterns and in implementing IT-based co-operation modes, such as CASS. However, the issues of human resource management and human competence building were delayed until the CASS system has settled in and a more accurate picture could be made of what precisely was involved.

Lessons learned from the CASS predecessor

A sales support predecessor of CASS, called SalesMaker, was launched some years before but performed unsatisfactory because of low functionality and limited user friendliness. In an internal evaluation of its IT systems in 1996/1997, DnB also evaluated SalesMaker. It came to the conclusion that SalesMaker did not fit the bank's existing data models and had insufficient interfaces with the bank's existing standard applications. The results were unacceptable long processing times between the various databases, high risk of failures and errors because of the many and complex interfaces that were needed, and a strong dependence on the supplier of the database in the case of failures. The early computer technology on which SalesMaker was based did not help either, and it was decided to replace SalesMaker with a self-developed sales support model that would become an integral part of the CASS concept.

The early lessons learned helped to formulate the goals for the further development of the CASS system, which were identified as:

- an integral concept, combining CASS and production flow;
- a single common database in which data needed to be entered only once;
- high user friendliness;
- a limited number of interfaces and standardization with the bank's MS-Windows applications;
- improved and secure data quality.

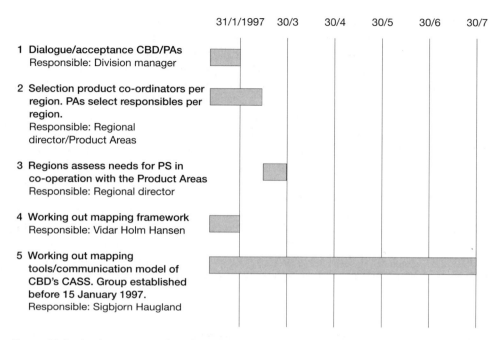

Figure 12.5 Implementation plan of the new role of the account manager

CASS concept development and implementation

The development of the concept of the new role of the account manager started and was completed during 1997 (see Figure 12.5).

The involvement of the regional branches and the regional product co-ordinators and product salesmen was accomplished in four steps (Figure 12.6). During the period from 1 January to 31 December 1997, normal sales activities continued.

The implementation was labelled the establishment of the new role of the account manager, not as the rollout of an IT-system. The reason was that the change focus was to be on the work behaviour of the account managers: the fact that it was a computerized sales support system that would change their work was only instrumental and not an end in itself.

The implementation per region followed a standard format (Figure 12.7). A so-called Day Zero (day 0) was set for each region on which the transfer to the new system took place – a regional 'big bang'. Every region had a different Day Zero, with the smallest (business) regions first and the biggest two regions (those around the cities of Oslo and Bergen) last. This allowed for learning experiences to have accumulated by the time transfer was required at the two biggest and most complex business regions. Learning took the form of the creation of a pool of so-called 'super

1.1   31.12

1 **Meet all Product Areas and product co-ordinators per region. Prepare implementation plan/priorities.**
Responsible: Product co-ordinator and Product Areas

2 **Mapping of products, customers etc. per region. Priorities.**
Responsible: Product co-ordinator and Product Areas

3 **Work out the goals, activities, responsibilities, implementation.**
Responsible: All regions and Product Areas

4 **Sales:**
  • **Report to Management Board 30.6 and 31.12**
  • **Report per region per quarter**
  Responsible: Product Areas and CBD line management

Figure 12.6 Planning of implementation follow-up

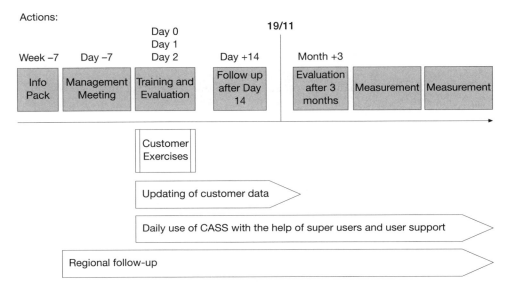

Actions:

                        Day 0
                        Day 1   **19/11**
                        Day 2
Week −7   Day −7   Day 2   Day +14   Month +3

| Info Pack | Management Meeting | Training and Evaluation | Follow up after Day 14 | Evaluation after 3 months | Measurement | Measurement |

Customer Exercises

Updating of customer data

Daily use of CASS with the help of super users and user support

Regional follow-up

Figure 12.7 Status overview per region on 19 November 1997

users' per region, i.e. additionally trained users able to educate their colleagues within each region.

Seven days before Day Zero, all management was assembled in a general meeting and the implementation team once again explained the purpose and details of the new role for the account managers. Additionally, a follow-up team per region was created during that general meeting, and maintained after the system was formally implemented.

On Day Zero, the technical conversion took place and the entire region switched over to CASS. All other systems that CASS replaced were shut down completely; no shadow or back-up systems were permitted.

On days one and two, everybody received training on how to handle CASS; training was on the job and used employee's own PCs. A mobile team of twelve instructors took care of training, equipped with various, screen icon-based manuals and a preset training approach. The ratio was one instructor per two employees. After day two, preliminary evaluation and feedback from employees was organized ('what did you learn?') and a one-page guideline was left behind to bridge the 14 days till the next (formal) evaluation (see Appendix 1).

Having completed the training after day two, handling customer requests and other daily use of CASS began. Continued user assistance was provided by the regional 'super users' and other on-line user services.

Fourteen days after Day Zero, a local follow-up took place, based on a short and uniform checklist to be filled in by the user (see Appendix 2). This follow-up evaluation took place with the 'super-users'. Three months after Day Zero, another regional evaluation of CASS took place.

To complete the process, regular measurements every three months on whether CASS is actually being used, are established. Measurement criteria for assessing actual use focus on the account manager. Criteria include the following:

- an activity measure of twelve customer meetings per month minimum while using CASS to plan these meetings;
- the systematic versus backlogged use of CASS to register customer needs; and
- the registration of all basic data in CASS, e.g. contact persons at the customer.

The latter implicitly reviews whether account management is handled as a team process. Every team member, either account manager or product salesman, can contact the customer, but every contact should be either planned or real-time logged into the system. Furthermore, use of the credit process module of CASS is mandatory for all credit decisions, no alternatives are allowed. Consequently, a drop in the average number of credit decisions would signal actual usage or not.

Implementation assessment

At this moment, 3 December 1998, and the last week of the full rollout, it is too early to establish whether sales work routines have indeed been changed as a result of CASS. However, during the implementation process, an important lesson was learned. It was noticed how important leadership and managerial attitude was. The ingrained culture of DnB was one very much oriented towards customer satisfaction and credit decisions of a financial technical nature; issues of effective and efficient work processes are not (yet) that prominent.

The rollout of CASS to the 700 people in the various offices and regions was assessed as successful. The main factors considered to account for the successful rollout were the lessons learned from the previous Salesmaker system implementation: to succeed, one needs a cross-functional address of all the users, developers and managers involved, combined with a technical trajectory of pilot testing at four sites with a full set of specification criteria.

The Customer Account manager's Support System (CASS)

The CASS supports the redesigned role of the customer account manager, the CA. CASS is linked to the various document, customer and internal mail databases of the bank. The main link is with the customer database, called DnB-Port. Every update or entry of information in CASS will automatically lead to a change in the Port database, and vice versa. Data from CASS can be entered into Excel, a spreadsheet software package, MS-Outlook, an agenda and time schedule software package, and into MS-Word, a word processing software package. Data can also be uploaded to CASS from these packages.

To access CASS, the user has to be authorized as a user of Port as well as a user on the main server. To gain access to the customer data in CASS, the user has to be either a customer account manager (CA) or a member of a customer team. Product salesmen have predefined roles in the system and gain access to specified system functions tied to these roles. Other users can access customer data if they belong to the CA's department or if they have additional authorization to access Port. The CA is intended to be the prime user of CASS.

After accessing CASS, the first screen is a search screen, providing six search buttons and a Search and Cancel button. Searches are possible on bank account number, bank employee number, authorization code, customer code, customer name and a list of own customers.

Once the latter is selected, the main screen opens in a Windows-format, containing a clickable toolbar, an opened window of Own Customers and a floating panel with a set of twelve icon-based buttons. These buttons are the keys to the various functions of CASS, each of which opens in a clickable window format, displaying various data entry and retrieval options. Working with CASS comes down to using these windows for daily information and communication exchange and storage. The buttons and subsequent windows are explained in Figure 12.8. An example of an individual screen of customer information in CASS is provided in Figure 12.9.

Each button also fulfils the function of a responsibility indicator. For each button, a specific task in the sales process is called upon and the person responsible

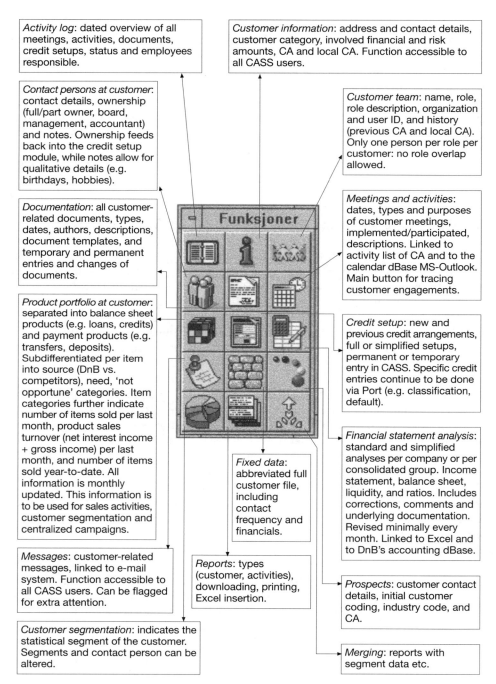

Activity log: dated overview of all meetings, activities, documents, credit setups, status and employees responsible.

Customer information: address and contact details, customer category, involved financial and risk amounts, CA and local CA. Function accessible to all CASS users.

Contact persons at customer: contact details, ownership (full/part owner, board, management, accountant) and notes. Ownership feeds back into the credit setup module, while notes allow for qualitative details (e.g. birthdays, hobbies).

Customer team: name, role, role description, organization and user ID, and history (previous CA and local CA). Only one person per role per customer: no role overlap allowed.

Documentation: all customer-related documents, types, dates, authors, descriptions, document templates, and temporary and permanent entries and changes of documents.

Meetings and activities: dates, types and purposes of customer meetings, implemented/participated, descriptions. Linked to activity list of CA and to the calendar dBase MS-Outlook. Main button for tracing customer engagements.

Product portfolio at customer: separated into balance sheet products (e.g. loans, credits) and payment products (e.g. transfers, deposits). Subdifferentiated per item into source (DnB vs. competitors), need, 'not opportune' categories. Item categories further indicate number of items sold per last month, product sales turnover (net interest income + gross income) per last month, and number of items sold year-to-date. All information is monthly updated. This information is to be used for sales activities, customer segmentation and centralized campaigns.

Credit setup: new and previous credit arrangements, full or simplified setups, permanent or temporary entry in CASS. Specific credit entries continue to be done via Port (e.g. classification, default).

Fixed data: abbreviated full customer file, including contact frequency and financials.

Financial statement analysis: standard and simplified analyses per company or per consolidated group. Income statement, balance sheet, liquidity, and ratios. Includes corrections, comments and underlying documentation. Revised minimally every month. Linked to Excel and to DnB's accounting dBase.

Messages: customer-related messages, linked to e-mail system. Function accessible to all CASS users. Can be flagged for extra attention.

Reports: types (customer, activities), downloading, printing, Excel insertion.

Prospects: customer contact details, initial customer coding, industry code, and CA.

Customer segmentation: indicates the statistical segment of the customer. Segments and contact person can be altered.

Merging: reports with segment data etc.

Figure 12.8   The CASS system (functions)

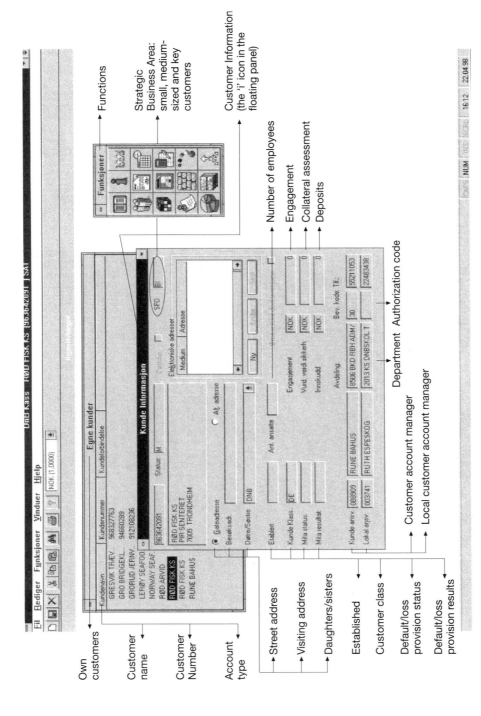

Figure 12.9 Customer information screen in CASS

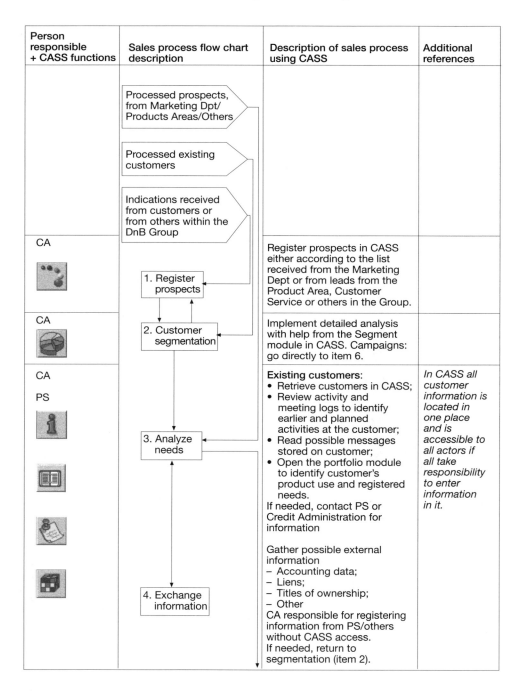

Person responsible + CASS functions	Sales process flow chart description	Description of sales process using CASS	Additional references
	Processed prospects, from Marketing Dpt/ Products Areas/Others		
	Processed existing customers		
	Indications received from customers or from others within the DnB Group		
CA	1. Register prospects	Register prospects in CASS either according to the list received from the Marketing Dept or from leads from the Product Area, Customer Service or others in the Group.	
CA	2. Customer segmentation	Implement detailed analysis with help from the Segment module in CASS. Campaigns: go directly to item 6.	
CA PS	3. Analyze needs	**Existing customers:** • Retrieve customers in CASS; • Review activity and meeting logs to identify earlier and planned activities at the customer; • Read possible messages stored on customer; • Open the portfolio module to identify customer's product use and registered needs. If needed, contact PS or Credit Administration for information	*In CASS all customer information is located in one place and is accessible to all actors if all take responsibility to enter information in it.*
	4. Exchange information	Gather possible external information – Accounting data; – Liens; – Titles of ownership; – Other CA responsible for registering information from PS/others without CASS access. If needed, return to segmentation (item 2).	

Figure 12.10 Intregration of responsibilities, tasks and CASS

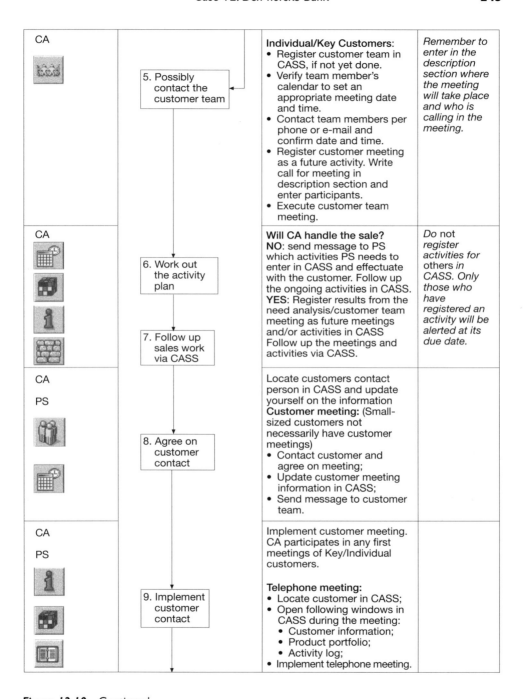

CA	5. Possibly contact the customer team	**Individual/Key Customers:** • Register customer team in CASS, if not yet done. • Verify team member's calendar to set an appropriate meeting date and time. • Contact team members per phone or e-mail and confirm date and time. • Register customer meeting as a future activity. Write call for meeting in description section and enter participants. • Execute customer team meeting.	*Remember to enter in the description section where the meeting will take place and who is calling in the meeting.*
CA	6. Work out the activity plan 7. Follow up sales work via CASS	**Will CA handle the sale?** **NO:** send message to PS which activities PS needs to enter in CASS and effectuate with the customer. Follow up the ongoing activities in CASS. **YES:** Register results from the need analysis/customer team meeting as future meetings and/or activities in CASS. Follow up the meetings and activities via CASS.	*Do not register activities for others in CASS. Only those who have registered an activity will be alerted at its due date.*
CA PS	8. Agree on customer contact	Locate customers contact person in CASS and update yourself on the information **Customer meeting:** (Small-sized customers not necessarily have customer meetings) • Contact customer and agree on meeting; • Update customer meeting information in CASS; • Send message to customer team.	

CA
 	
PS
	9. Implement customer contact	Implement customer meeting. CA participates in any first meetings of Key/Individual customers.
		
		Telephone meeting:
		• Locate customer in CASS;
		• Open following windows in CASS during the meeting:
		  • Customer information;
		  • Product portfolio;
		  • Activity log;
		• Implement telephone meeting.	

Figure 12.10   Continued

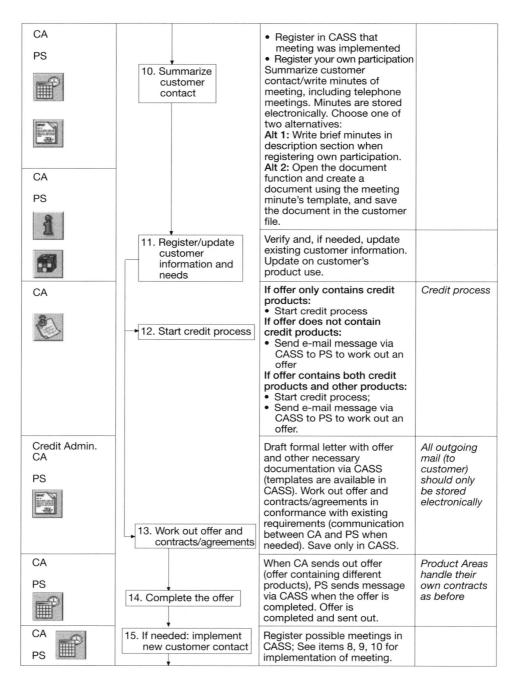

CA PS	10. Summarize customer contact	• Register in CASS that meeting was implemented • Register your own participation Summarize customer contact/write minutes of meeting, including telephone meetings. Minutes are stored electronically. Choose one of two alternatives: **Alt 1:** Write brief minutes in description section when registering own participation. **Alt 2:** Open the document function and create a document using the meeting minute's template, and save the document in the customer file.	
CA PS			
	11. Register/update customer information and needs	Verify and, if needed, update existing customer information. Update on customer's product use.	
CA	12. Start credit process	**If offer only contains credit products:** • Start credit process **If offer does not contain credit products:** • Send e-mail message via CASS to PS to work out an offer **If offer contains both credit products and other products:** • Start credit process; • Send e-mail message via CASS to PS to work out an offer.	*Credit process*
Credit Admin. CA PS	13. Work out offer and contracts/agreements	Draft formal letter with offer and other necessary documentation via CASS (templates are available in CASS). Work out offer and contracts/agreements in conformance with existing requirements (communication between CA and PS when needed). Save only in CASS.	*All outgoing mail (to customer) should only be stored electronically*
CA PS	14. Complete the offer	When CA sends out offer (offer containing different products), PS sends message via CASS when the offer is completed. Offer is completed and sent out.	*Product Areas handle their own contracts as before*
CA PS	15. If needed: implement new customer contact	Register possible meetings in CASS; See items 8, 9, 10 for implementation of meeting.	

Figure 12.10 Continued

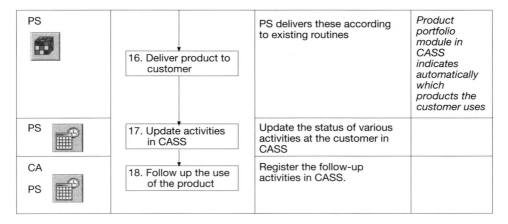

Figure 12.10 Continued

for that task is designated. In addition, the abbreviated sales task description as well as the person responsible is matched to the button in CASS. See Figure 12.10 for an example of this integration.

Performance measurement

One of the methods to affirm and strengthen the use of CASS within the sales organization of the Commercial Banking Division is the linkage with the existing performance measurement system. Notably, the performance measurement of the account manager is keyed to the regionally decentralized and broken down set of corporate performance measures.

DnB uses a Balanced Scorecard system, containing both financial and non-financial indicators. The indicators are grouped into four categories:

- Customers
- Quality
- Employees
- Profitability

These four categories are maintained throughout, both at regional and national level. Some of these measures are also used for external purposes, explicitly disclosing these in the annual and quarterly reports of the DnB Group.

The following measures are included in the four categories:

- Customers
  - Customer satisfaction index
  - Number of customer meetings
  - Market share lending (externally disclosed as well)

- Quality
  - Lending portfolio quality
- Employees
  - Employee satisfaction survey – total score
  - Employee satisfaction survey – feedback
  - Employee satisfaction survey – development
- Profitability
  - Result before actual losses (externally disclosed as well)
  - Result after actual losses (externally disclosed as well)
  - Result before losses/lending ratio (both numerator and denominator are separately disclosed as well)
  - Cost/income ratio (ratio externally disclosed as well)
  - Net other operating income income/total income ratio (both numerator and denominator are separately disclosed as well)
  - Total lending (externally disclosed as well)
  - Total deposits (externally disclosed as well)

The lending ratio is calculated as the percentage ratio of *Deposits from customers* to *Net lending to customers*, while the cost/income ratio is calculated as the sum of *Net Interest Income* and *Net Other Operating Income*, divided by *Operating Expenses*.

The lending portfolio quality indicator (PRI) is a credit risk measure, proprietary to DnB. It is computed by weighing a figure related to the risk classification of each company to the amount of exposure to each company.

Each account manager is held accountable each month, using six performance measures, each of which is derived from the regional Balanced Scorecard set of indicators. These six are:

- number of customer meetings (flat count, originating from DnB Port);
- lending portfolio quality (portfolio risk indicator – PRI; a ratio);
- net interest income (total financial amount in millions of kronor);
- net other operating income (total financial amount in millions of kronor);
- total lending (total financial amount in millions of kronor);
- total deposits (total financial amount in millions of kronor).

The latter four individual performance measures are also externally disclosed at an aggregate, group level.

Reporting

Each month, the Commercial Banking Division's manager is presented with a report on the performance of all account managers in all ten regions making up the Norwegian market (see Table 12.4). For each region, the total financial amounts (numerator) are individualized for the account manager headcount (denominator) thus creating an average score per account manager per region.

Table 12.4 Performance measurement, customer account managers

Market report March 1998 Region	Customer meetings (DnB Port)*	PRI	Loans (mill.kr)**	Results Pr.Account Manager		
				Deposits (mill.kr)**	Net interest income (thousand kr)**	Other operating income (thousand kr)**
Region A	15.3	9.36	94	137	1,288	773
Region B	12.6	8.02	168	126	1,261	630
Region C	16.7	7.03	138	119	791	395
Region D	17.5	8.74	194	166	1,108	554
Region E	17.3	9.86	145	103	930	620
Region F	17.0	10.31	161	129	1,290	645
Region G	16.5	8.62	231	173	1,349	771
Region H	10.3	9.22	184	143	1,429	816
Region I	18.8	6.98	278	167	1,111	1,111
Region J	13.8	11.26	171	109	932	311
Total CBD	15.2	9.14	149	132	1,171	661

All numbers and regions are disguised for confidentiality reasons

* Measured by: (customer meetings + tlf. meetings)/(number of account managers SC + MC + KC (excl. mgt))

** Measured by: (operational account [month or year-to-date])/(number of account managers KC, SC and Specially assigned staff (incl. mgt))

Table 12.4 Continued

March	Customer meetings	Net loans	Total deposits	Accounting Net interest income Year-to-date	Total operating income Year-to-date	Staff CAs in KC+ SC+MC (excl. Mgt./CorBD and SBD)	CAs in KC+ SC+MC (excl. CorBD/SBD, incl. Mgt.)	Specially assigned staff	Total	Regions
	1,200	11,000	16,000	150,000	90,000	78.4	97.2	19.3	116.5	A
	450	8,000	6,000	60,000	30,000	35.78	43.55	4.05	47.6	B
	350	3,500	3,000	20,000	10,000	21	23.3	2	25.3	C
	250	3,500	3,000	20,000	10,000	14.3	15.8	2.25	18.05	D
	550	7,000	5,000	45,000	30,000	31.8	39.3	9.1	48.4	E
	200	2,500	2,000	20,000	10,000	11.75	13	2.5	15.5	F
	350	6,000	4,500	35,000	20,000	21.2	24.2	1.75	25.95	G
	200	4,500	3,500	35,000	20,000	19.5	22.5	2	24.5	H
	150	2,500	1,500	10,000	10,000	8	8	1	9	I
	350	5,500	3,500	30,000	10,000	25.3	30.6	1.6	32.3	J
	4,050	54,000	48,000	425,000	240,000	267.03	317.45	45.55	363	Total

CBD = Commercial Banking Division
CorBD = Corporate Banking Division
SBD = Shipping Banking Division
CA = Customer Account manager
KC = Key Customer
SC = Small-sized Customer
MC = Medium-sized Customer
Mgt. = Management

The total number of account managers is the sum of all CAs for small, medium-sized and key customers in the Commercial Banking Division region, including regional management and specially assigned employees. This total number of account managers is also reported excluding management and specially assigned employees, and leaving only 'pure CAs' as a reference point.

A similar use of full staff capacity is employed in creating all the average financial performance measures. Only the non-financial customer meeting measure uses the 'pure CAs' as denominator. Customer meetings include both meetings in person and meetings by telephone.

The lending portfolio quality or PRI ratio is inserted from outside CASS. It provides a reference point in considering whether the meeting activity of the account manager is focused. For example, a high PRI in a certain region would justify an increased customer meeting activity to correct for the increased credit risk exposure.

The PRI ratio is related to the risk-adjusted performance measurement ratio disclosed by DnB. This corporate level ratio calculates risk-adjusted return on risk-adjusted capital (RARORAC) for the DnB Group. The calculation is based on annual profits from the Group, which are normalized with respect to accounting principles used in the managerial accounts, non-recurring items, calculations of expected losses and normal tax charges. Normalized profits are then measured relative to a capital requirement based on (management information on) actual risk exposure. The DnB Group has set the minimum RARORAC at the long-term risk-free interest rate plus a risk premium of 6%. The Board of Directors, depending on the level of operations and the market situation, may change the latter. The RARORAC for 1998 has been established at 12%.

Having completed a successful rollout of CASS and on the brink of seeing the collaboration between CA, PS and CASS materializing, the head of the CASS project is reflecting. The redesigned tasks and responsibilities of the account manager are well thought out and carefully designed into the organization's systems, building on lessons learned the hard way. But how can these successes be made to last?

Endnotes

[1] Professor Hanno Roberts prepared this case as the basis for class discussion rather than to illustrate either effective or ineffective handling of an administrative situation. Sigbjorn Haugland and Einar Offer-Ohlsen of Den norske Bank Group's Commercial Banking Division provided invaluable assistance.

[2] One Norwegian kronor (NOK) is equivalent to 0.1129 Euro at 1 January 1999. One Euro is equivalent to 8.8575 NOK at 1 January 1999.

| **STUDENT ASSIGNMENTS** |

1. Explain the relationship between CASS and the intellectual capital of DnB's Commercial Banking Division.

2. What has the role of the account manager to do with DnB's Commercial Banking Division's intellectual capital?

3. Why is DnB so careful with the implementation and rollout of CASS?

4. Comment on the design of the Balanced ScoreCard (BSC) for a financial service organization such as the DnB Group. What characteristics of their strategy and business are reflected in the BSC?

5. DnB is using a Balanced ScoreCard (BSC) throughout the organization. Would you consider their use of the BSC as supporting the intellectual capital of DnB's Commercial Banking Division? Or as supporting the use of CASS?

6. DnB can be considered a knowledge-based service organization that is undergoing structural changes as a result of changes in its competitive environment and the strategies it subsequently adopts. How can the success of CASS be made to last other than by improving the performance measurement system?

Appendix 1   Implementation guidelines for the first 14 days after CASS training

Now you have completed your training in CASS, you will be using CASS for customer support in your daily work. This memo provides you with guidelines on how the CASS-project expects the first 14 days after the CASS training to be implemented.

1. Implementation of the first 14 days

It is important you use these first 14 days to familiarize yourself with the new CASS, and to get used to working with it in the new work setting. Here is some good advice on how to get by in the next 14 days:

- Use CASS actively in your daily work. This implies that you use all possible reasons in your daily activities to 'key into' CASS and get to know the system. Use the materials distributed during the CASS training (user manual etc.) as help when you get stuck or are wondering about something. Please discuss with others too!
- Read through the process descriptions of the sales and credit processes distributed during the training, and consider what is new in respect to the previous situation. Use the process descriptions to teach yourself the new way of doing your work, by actively using the process descriptions together with CASS in your daily work.

- Use the checklist distributed during the training to see whether you have been through as many work tasks as possible in these 14 days.
- Don't despair if it takes some time at the start! A bit of extra time spent in the beginning will result in timesavings when you soon have the new processes and the new system 'at your fingertips'.

2. Help tools

Below, several help tools are listed which you can use during these 14 days. Use these tools actively to find out about things on CASS and the new work setting!

- Process descriptions of the sales and credit processes
- User manual
- Practical guidance in the use of CASS
- Help-function within CASS
- Checklist to follow up on customer tasks in the first 14 days
- List of 'super users'
- List of central user support
- List of Roles and to which functions several groups have access

3. Follow-up after 14 days

After the first 14 days of practical use of the new work setting and the new CASS, a local manager will arrange a follow-up meeting to exchange experiences. The main points for such a meeting are indicated below:

- Purpose is that the customer team/possibly the CA, the credit administration/ product salesman and other people involved can exchange experiences with the use of the work setting and CASS after the first 14-day period.
- You will have to prepare the meeting by writing down what you have done relative to your customers in this 14-day period. Use a couple of selected customers as examples.
- The distributed checklists and process descriptions will be used as the basis for a discussion of the 14-day period. Fill out the checklist and bring it with you to the meeting.
- The local manager will indicate the specific time and place for the follow-up meeting.

Success in your work with the new CASS and the new work setting!

Appendix 2   Checklist for the follow-up of customer tasks in CASS after the first 14 days

In order for you to decide whether the customer tasks have given you new insight in your new work setting in relation to the new CASS, we kindly ask you to fill out this checklist after the first 14 days of your training. Take it with you to the follow-up meeting.

Role (CA, Credit Administration, customer service, PS etc.): ——————————
Region: ——————————

Cross off in the below table what you did or did not do during the course of your work time. When one/several of these items are not relevant for your role, or when the situation described has not occurred, cross the column 'Not relevant' left of the irrelevant item. When you answer 'No' to some of the items, write a short comment/reason in the column 'Why not'.

Part A: the sales process

Not relevant	In my work time I have:	Yes	No	Why not
	1. Registered prospects in CASS			
	2. Segmented customers in CASS			
	3 Used CASS as an effective tool in analysing customer needs			
	4. Communicated effectively with the customer team/PS and other functional specialists with the help of CASS			
	5. Worked out an activity plan in CASS in connection with sales preparations			
	6. Followed up sales tasks effectively via CASS			
	7. Updated information in CASS on agreed customer meetings			
	8. Used CASS effectively as work tool when simultaneously talking to a customer on the phone			
	9. Written meeting minutes and updated meeting information in CASS after a completed customer meeting			
	10. Entered and updated customer information and product needs after a completed customer meeting			
	11. Ticked off 'done' or 'participated' in CASS when meetings are completed			
	12. Worked effectively together with the PS via CASS in cases when customer offers contained more than just credits products			

Not relevant	In my work time I have:	Yes	No	Why not
	13. Worked out offer documentation and/or contracts/agreements in CASS			
	14. Checked in CASS whether an offered product has been put into use			
	15. Send and received reports to/from a PS, and updated and registered necessary activities in CASS			
	16. Entered information in CASS as a consequence of mail from a PS without CASS access			

Part B: the credit process

Not relevant	In my work time I have:	Yes	No	Why not
	1. Worked out decision arguments in CASS based on a credit setup and a financial statement analysis			
	2. Sent messages in CASS to Credit Administration to assess risk or other customer items			
	3. Received answer from Credit Administration/ Customer service via a message in CASS			
	4. Written a refusal letter and saved it in CASS			
	5. Worked out and saved an offer, based on a template in CASS			
	6. Registered not accepted offers in the 'customer account file' in CASS			
	7. Followed up the status/progress of a credit application with the help of CASS			
	8. Established that credit products are used by customers based on the *Product use* in CASS			

Part C: general

Not relevant		In my work time I have:	Yes	No	Why not
	1.	Been flagged by customers, went in and considered new information			
	2.	Used CASS actively to exchange information between CA, Credit Administration, PS, Customer service etc. in sales and credit tasks			
	3.	Experienced advantages of a centralized electronic database in CASS			
	4.	Made use of customer information others in DnB have entered			
	5.	Avoided filing outgoing customer mail in the physical customer file, while rather filing the documents electronically in CASS			
	6.	Received messages on customers, entered by Credit Administration, PS or others			
	7.	Established that management and others have used CASS to send out documents in preparation of a meeting (i.e., they avoided making hard copies)			

CASE THIRTEEN

—

Scandlines Ltd – Privatization and accounting stability in a political environment

Peter Skærbæk
Preben Melander

Introduction

This case deals with a large Danish Ferry Company, Scandlines Ltd., which in 6 years has changed from a governmental monopoly – owned by Danish Rail, DSB – to a privatized market-run enterprise that will be offered to private stockholders. Over the course of 3 years, the company's customer platform has been reduced by 70% due to the replacement of the ferry routes between Zealand and Fyen and between Denmark and Sweden by new bridges. These routes were the company's most important routes. Thus, the company's level of activity dropped to one-third of its previous rate, and the company's permanent staff had to be reduced correspondingly. Driven by these dramatic circumstances the company's top management was replaced and the entire organization restructured. First, the old Government Services Management was replaced by a new and professional administration, which divided the company into profit centres. Then, a dynamic and commercial business-oriented management head-hunted from the private shipping industry replaced this administration and carried through an entirely new 'sustainable' matrix organization with strong central strategic managerial functions.

In the Case, the company's development through the 6 years is illustrated by, for example, managers, who have worked in the company since the Government Services days. At the time we join the company, its new commercial business management has implemented the new organizational structure and is now working on enhancing the company's efficiency in order to facilitate the sale of the government's share of the company to the highest bidding private stockholders. However, this 'enterprising' and 'privatizing' of the company is not easily achieved, especially as the political owners of the company, namely government officials, interfere with the business dispositions. The company finds itself caught in a field of tension between politics and the market.

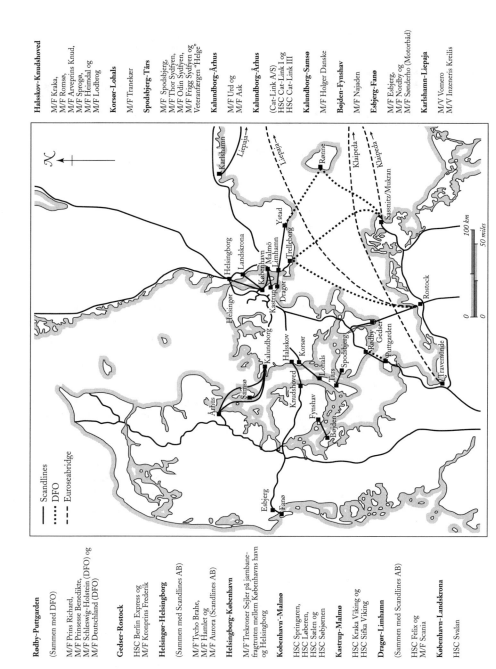

Figure 13.1 Denmark and Scandlines' routes

With the company's market dynamics, political ownership and managerial development as a background, we gain an impression of the company's administrative processes and managerial competence. We see how the management control system is designed, and we wonder how it is possible to run a company on such simple accounting principles and such rigid management information systems. Apparently, the rules of the game that dominate the company differ from those that govern rational economic logic. The fact is that the company is a politically governed company; the employees belong to different cultures and the customers have other demands than mere transportation.

Background and history

For geographical reasons navigation has always played a vital part in Denmark. In 1872, the postal service organized all navigation between the different parts of the country. When the railways were constructed the first train ferry route opened at the end of the nineteenth century. Later, this route was taken over by the state railways DSB. The 1950s saw a heavy increase in transport by road, and car ferries became a more and more important part of the business. Many new ferry routes were established, both within the country and internationally. The international ferry routes were mostly operated as a 50% joint venture with other government-owned ferry operations. Each company would have its own service and price policy, but ferry berths, timetable and ticket systems were shared. In the mid-1950s the domestic motor (cars and trucks) and train traffic between the provinces were separated by Scandlines. Investments were made in new large ferry ports and landing facilities. From being primarily a train ferry operator the company changed into one of the largest car ferry operators in the North of Europe. Until 1995 Scandlines was a division of DSB. DSB and its subdivision Scandlines were owned totally by the state. The Ministry of Transport represents the state.

A general feature of the Ferry Company has always been its emphasis on operations combined with its status as a government department. The focus on operations has meant a reliable ferry service, while the status as a government department has maintained strong bureaucratic rules and traditions such as permanent public servant status, certain careers, tenured positions, etc. In other words, there was more focus on operations and departmental culture than on market and customer development.

Moreover, DSB has always regarded the ferry division (later on Scandlines) as a necessary element in the development of train technology on a domestic level. Developing the technology to drive both passenger and freight trains directly on board ferries was crucial to an expansion of the railway service and its importance. Even on an international level the technology developed by the company rates as unique. At the same time as transport by road increased dramatically in the 1960s, the company's car ferries became an important cash cow for DSB, which was able to obtain large subsidies for carrying cargo and passengers by train on these routes.

In the 1980s discussions about Marketing Management increased in DSB leading to a divisionalization of DSB with Scandlines as a profit centre. Another result of market management, which in general prevailed throughout the 1980s, was an increased emphasis on customer relations, including various customer concepts such as catering (based on customer needs and requests), booking (easier access to booking), punctuality (no delays) and local responsibility (employees should react whenever something was wrong). An important part of the service concept consisted of catering, which in Scandlines traditionally has been organized by private enterprise as far back as 1891. For many years several independent catering enterprises were involved, but at the beginning of the 1980s all these catering operations were replaced by one single proprietor, who was granted a concession covering all Scandlines activities. The rationality behind this private organization was to gain greater business flexibility by being independent of regulations applying to government operations. However, this form of organization created ambiguity in the chain of command and made it more difficult to optimize the overall business concept on the ferries. It was a problem that there were two firms on the ferry. The crew always suspected the catering staff of cashing in on any services provided to them by the crew, although the contract with the catering business implied that the Ferry Company received almost 100% of the profit in rental. The result was suspicion and lack of co-operation regarding efficient operation and customer service. In 1996 Scandlines bought 75% of the shares in the catering company in order to create a more consistent and effective business concept. However, the acquisition did not result in a cancellation of the concession agreement, which to a large extent is still functioning. However, the importance of catering might decrease when the speed of the ferries is increased.

As a parallel to this development in the 1980s, strong efforts were made by government to establish fixed bridge and tunnel links between different parts of the country and neighbouring countries. Figure 13.1 shows a map of Denmark and the various routes Scandlines operated. Since 1991 it has been clear that the most important routes have been made superfluous by fixed links. What should happen to Scandlines began to be discussed. After hard pressure from the unions it was decided by the ministry in 1991 that Scandlines should take advantage of the knowledge and competence it had accumulated through the previous 125 years to develop the company's key areas. The vision was not to cut down on services but rather to develop the company to survive future market conditions.

However, the CEO of Scandlines and the ministry assessed that it would only be feasible to follow a development and business strategy if the company was allowed the necessary financial latitude and given the necessary freedom to act on commercial terms. After a long period with many political discussions about whether to establish an independent company, it was finally decided in 1995 to convert Scandlines into a public limited company. At first, DSB owned the shares, but in 1996 they were transferred to the Ministry of Transport. The board of directors refers directly to the Ministry of Transport, which stresses the great societal and political importance placed on developing the Ferry Company. As such the intention of privatization was just to enable Scandlines to survive. The political solution was chosen primarily because of pressure from the unions, who argued that it was a matter of saving jobs. While converting the company into a limited company the old CEO was discharged in 1995. Afterwards a new CEO and a new vice-CEO were employeed. The new CEO had a background as a shipbuilding engineer and had been CEO of two Danish shipyards. The new vice-CEO had a background in shipping companies and a company that invests in ships. His interest is much more in how to charter out or in new ferries. He is working closely with the CEO.

It was always going to be a difficult task because the fixed links had already begun to make some inroads into the profit-yielding activities of Scandlines. In the period mid-1997 to 2000, the result was expected to be a substantial cut in profits. It is further expected that in the year 2000 the activities and number of employees will be reduced to one-quarter of the figures in 1996.

In 1996 when Scandlines became a limited company there was political pressure on the company to pay the state 1.3 billion Danish Kr.[1] as payment for taking over the infrastructure (ferry berths, goodwill, etc.). The Treasury, the Ministry of Transport and Scandlines were involved in debate on the size of the amount. The interest of the Treasury was to maximize the amount in order to minimize the deficit of the state budget. However, Scandlines tried to minimize the amount in order to secure survival. The Ministry of Transport was mediating. The 1.3 billion Danish Kr. was, after enormous pressure from the Ministry of Transport, paid by Scandlines to the Treasury in late December 1996. However, in 1997 some 400 million Kr. was paid back as the state paid a greater amount of the costs related to the sacking of staff than was originally agreed upon.

As Scandlines became a limited company at the beginning of 1996 the Ministry of Transport put a new top management group in charge. The new top management group mainly consisted of people trained in shipping and with practical experience from other shipping companies. They took a no-nonsense, commercial and action-oriented approach to management, based on intuition, network contacts, fast orders, successive adjustments, etc. They were quick to take crucial decisions based on intuition. This group were especially interested in tonnage and focused on in-chartering and out-chartering of old and new ferries, including the newest ferry technology. They had minor interest in calculations and accounting issues in general. They played a big role in setting the agenda for the more important decisions of the company, such as acquiring and closing down routes, purchasing and selling ferries, including the necessary phasing out of ferries and laying-off of personnel in connection with the opening of the new fixed links. The accounting department was considered a bookkeeping and banking department.

Main tasks (mid-1990s view)

On a domestic and international level, Scandlines operates approximately 20 ferry routes. As a result of the bridge and tunnel links, the transfer of trains on board ferries has been drastically reduced, and only a few ferry routes remain committed to the transport of trains. The motor and passenger transport has also declined, but not at the same rate as the rail traffic. The company's customer segments consist mainly of passenger cars and trucks, which in the following will be termed business segments for passengers and cargo, respectively.

Most ferry routes are operated on normal commercial terms. However, within Denmark Scandlines renders services to a number of regions, which are not self-supporting: this is why such routes must be subsidized by the government. These routes are regulated by concession agreements granted through public invitation to tender.

In addition, the company has entered into new and alternative activities, one of which is operating as a tourist and travel agency. The idea is to combine letting out holiday homes with the booking of ferry tickets.

Service activities

Service activities form an important part of the overall marketing concept. The services are related to the different phases of the customers' path through the system. 1. Advance booking, 2. Approach lane, 3. Ticket sales, 4. Waiting time, 5. Driving on board, 6. Crossing and stay on ferry (including consumption, resting period and purchases).

Concerning the first phase, Scandlines wishes to provide easy access to the ferries for the customers. Therefore, new initiatives are often taken to facilitate reservation, e.g. by means of computer technology, allowing one to make bookings from a home computer, etc. One of the new ideas is to offer executive cards, which ensure customers a space on the ferry, even without reservation. Concerning the sale of tickets it is possible to pay with various international credit cards. In addition, a ticket covering 10 crossings can be bought at a discount.

During a crossing a number of services are offered to customers, such as selling newspapers and convenience goods. In addition, there are cafeterias, restaurants, bars, etc. as well as such facilities as telephones, cabins, and various gambling machines, etc. International routes offer duty-free sales of such items as wine, tobacco, perfume, chocolate, etc. The profit from duty-free shopping is very important to the overall earnings of the company, but such sales are expected to cease in mid-1999. However, this will probably lead to new negotiations within the EU resulting in a compromise allowing some duty-free shopping.

Another service relates to the number of departures and the time of crossing. The company tries to emphasize punctuality, i.e. the ferries must, as far as possible, depart on time, but the size of the ferries and the frequency of departures must also correspond to the demand. Customers also demand increased safety, and in both national and international maritime regulations safety requirements are constantly being tightened. This trend is especially clear after the tragic loss of Estonia in 1994, where approximately 1,000 people lost their lives. This development also makes heavy demands on the company's investment in safety measures and materials, etc. In sum, it is important to provide good customer service.

Information to customers about cancellations, delays, etc. plays a very important role. However, in practice there is a difference between the declared service policy and customer experiences. Ferries still work as technical production units with only slight knowledge of market issues.

Production

In production the focus is first and foremost on stability of operations. The company runs, on average, 545 daily trips with, on average, two daily cancellations. The ferries must depart on time. In order to meet this objective a range of tasks have to be carried out on land and at sea. On land, service staff handle the sale of tickets and reservations, including information to customers and marketing activities. At ferry terminals, sailors take care of mooring the ship, emptying tanks of various waste products and filling up tanks with oil and water.

At sea, ship's officers handle navigation, check up on passenger lists and maintain contact with land. In the engine room the staff operate and maintain the engine. On each ship navigators and engine room staff make special agreements on the distribution of work and maintenance duties (cleaning, rust chipping and painting) and other operational activities. This distribution of work is defined in relation to a zone division of the ship that excludes the bridge and engine room. To ensure a safe crossing it is vital that officers and engine room staff co-ordinate their work. For example, departure and calling at a port require extensive co-ordination just as periodic and extraordinary shipyard visits do, where the two groups have different needs.

Ferry manning is regulated by crew plans and duty rosters for all personnel groups, creating a pattern of routine. By means of personnel plans, sailing schedules, shipyard plans, maintenance plans, contingency plans, rescue plans, etc. all activities are organized within a fixed framework. A captain of a ship comments on these efforts:

> Each ferry is a self-governed unit. Each of us is doing exactly the same things. Unfortunately, we do not co-ordinate our efforts at all (Captain of ship X).

In mid-1995, when Scandlines became a public limited company, it began to replace the old ferry technology by new, modern ferries that were able to sail faster than the old ferries thus reducing the crossing times and increasing the frequency. On special routes Scandlines invested in fast ferries able to reduce crossing times by one half on long distances, which makes them more competitive in relation to fixed links and alternative ferry services. In future, the company will operate with signed-on crews; i.e. staff will work on board several days at a time instead of the usual 10–12-hour shifts. This will allow Scandlines to economize operations, and staff will learn teamwork. As a result, the number of sickness days should be reduced.

In production, civil service educated officials and selected navigation officers with extensive operational experience, loyalty and strong ties to their organization are a dominating group. Often their view of management is pragmatic, production-oriented and based on improvization, compromises, dialogue and close relationships. This group of staff has been drastically reduced (1997), but although it is barely represented in the new functional management, and the influence of the unions has decreased, the group still has sufficient influence in the many manning and safety regulations to ensure a fairly high degree of stability. As representatives from other group's remark:

> The navigation officers have always had and still have a large influence on operations. It is very difficult to make them take a business view of the company. (Route manager)

Markets

The following matrix describes the markets of the company:

	Private	*Business*
Passengers	Tourists/commuters	Business people
Cars	Passenger car/caravans, etc.	Trucks/passenger cars

Tourists: Tourists are passengers who arrive at the ferries by train, bus or car, and who walk on board. One group is en route to a holiday destination, while another group are day tourists, wishing to do some duty-free shopping or just enjoy the trip. Some of these tourists go ashore and return later the same day with another ferry. Others remain on board. Finally, there is a group of commuters.

Business people: This segment covers one group of business people who arrive at the ferry by train, bus or car, and who often are en route to a third destination. They differ from the typical tourist in their comfort needs.

Passenger cars/caravans, etc.: This segment covers primarily tourists en route to a holiday destination and persons on their way to pay a visit somewhere.

Business: trucks/passenger cars: This group of business people wants to bring their car on board. As the first group of business people they demand special comfort on board. This segment also covers the voluminous transport of goods by truck. This group also has special requirements of the service on board. In Scandlines these markets are defined as cargo and passenger markets and organized into separate departments.

To some extent the different segments have different action parameters. Price, punctuality, and speed play an important role for cargo operations. For passengers, price is more important than punctuality and speed. The company has been in a position to base the price of tickets on the monopoly it has on several routes. Since

1996, the company has been involved in several EU cases, where it has been charged with exploiting its monopoly. In a couple of these cases the EU has imposed a settlement that allows other ferry companies access to some of the routes. However, so far the increased competition has not had serious consequences. In 1995, when the company was transformed into a public limited company, it advertised in the large Danish newspapers announcing it would now operate as a private shipping company. The objective was to break the ingrained image of the company as a bureaucratic and monopolistic government-owned operation. A motto in the advertising campaign was 'Full speed ahead'.

Organization

The company is organized according to functions. Typical functions are all placed at the headquarters: marketing, operational technology, personnel, and development accounting and purchasing. All these departments co-operate with the individual routes. The central departments have local representatives at the ferry stations, but in practice the communication distance between headquarters and the ferry stations is long and inconvenient. Top management and CEO operates at headquarters, and they have been recruited from other businesses than shipping. The catering department, which is very extensive, is an independent company – in which Scandlines owns 75% of the shares and an option to buy the rest at a fixed price. Many actors in Scandlines point out:

> That catering is a state within the state, in which nobody has any real influence. A sin of the past which still raises its head. (Financial Controller)

Similar to headquarters, the local ferry offices are often organized according to functions. Ranking below the route manager there are the personnel, accounting, technology and purchasing departments, etc. The route manager has a local co-ordinating responsibility for functions, reporting directly to the central functions at headquarters. At the ships the operation is organized according to functions and the shift work patterns. Continuous operation of the ship involves two or three complete shifts of officers, engine room staff and service staff. There have been strong disagreements between headquarters and local managers about the distribution of responsibilities and the chains of command on the ships. Top management prefers a business-oriented management structure comprising all three work shifts. However, as the captain always is the undisputed leader of a ship according to maritime law, the navigators' organization claimed that you could not simultaneously have a chief captain and a captain. In the end, the discussions led to the appointment of a co-ordinating captain who should co-ordinate all production and financial activities together with the co-ordinating chief engineer and co-ordinating catering manager. Together, these three co-ordinating persons constitute the ship's troika management. This business-oriented management structure was established in 1992. Formally, the structure is functioning, but in reality not on all routes. A

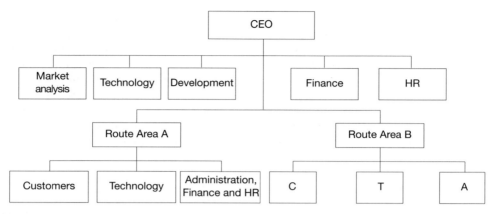

Figure 13.2   Scandlines Ltd 1990–1997

co-ordinating captain describes the troika management as a result of the academic influence on Scandlines' development.

At the beginning of 1997, the new management introduced the new matrix organization. A significant breakthrough was the creation of two new departments: one for passengers and one for cargo. This is also part of the centralization. Each department has a manager and a number of salesmen who look up customers. Figure 13.2 shows the company organizational chart for 1990–1997 and Figure 13.3 shows the management hierarchy for 1997 onwards. The CEO gives the following explanations for the new matrix organization:

> The idea is to have two budget holders in each production unit, e.g. the operation of route X. The local route manager must ensure that the operation functions without problems, and that the plans and the budgets are respected. The functional manager at headquarters is responsible for strategy and budget conditions. As financial units, individual, functional units on a route (traffic, technique, and finances) are also subjected to central functional managers. The route manager, e.g. is responsible for the budget on route X and has to co-ordinate operations with the local traffic manager. In case of disagreements the problems must be taken to a higher level, i.e. at the executive board. Such a procedure ensures that disagreements come out in the open air and allows management to intervene in time. In such a case of disagreements the combatants are called into the headquarters. Each part will be asked to argue and then vice CEO and I we will judge. (CEO in 1997)

	Passengers	Cargo	Operational technology	Personnel	Finance	Purchasing
Route 1						
Route 2						
⋮						
Route 20						

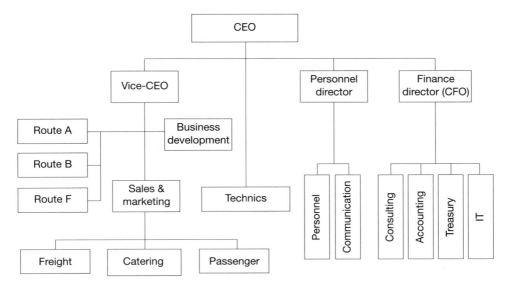

Figure 13.3 Management hierarchy of Scandlines Ltd

Evaluating the new organization, actors find that the functions at headquarters have been strengthened at the expense of the responsibilities of the route managers. A remark by an actor is very telling:

> The route manager has been reduced to a caretaker or watchdog, who is only allowed to bark when something goes wrong. (Route manager)

Top management's response to this interpretation is that:

> Management must keep an eye on whether trouble is brewing somewhere. In the event that insoluble problems occur or the collaboration between the managers in the matrix is not functioning, the umpires must interfere. And as everyone knows the umpire is always right. Things have to work. (CEO)

Others are critical, saying that CEO has no detailed implementation plan:

> It is like they expect things to happen by themselves. Nobody seems to take action. We are very dissatisfied with this. (Sales manager)

On three of the most important routes Scandlines have formed business alliances with other government-operated companies in two neighbouring countries. It is an important principle in these business alliances that both partners must agree on changes in tonnage, pricing and timetables, etc. As a consequence decision making is very inflexible.

Management/administration/accounting

The company's finance department comprises in total approximately 40 employees, with half of them placed at local ferry stations. At headquarters there is a chief finance director (CFO) who is part of the board of management. The controlling manager, the accounting manager, the treasury manager and the IT-manager are reporting to him. In practice, the centrally placed debtor and creditor functions in the accounting section imply that headquarters handles all payments. The local routes are dissatisfied with this arrangement, as such a payments system is more time consuming and makes it more difficult to follow up on specific payments.

The procedure for financial reporting involves the following steps. The finance department sends monthly and quarterly accounts to be commented on by the local financial managers at the various routes. The local managers prepare one or two pages of comments, explaining any budget deviations, general prospects, etc. On this basis the central finance department prepares an overall quarterly report for the whole company. The reports primarily focus on revenues in addition to a range of figures and statistics on traffic, i.e. large figures. The comments prepared by the local accounting departments refer primarily to revenues.

When employees in the company are asked what the results of these routines are, the typical answer is that they do not know. A route manager says:

> I don't use the monthly and quarterly reports for anything at all, I don't even read them. I believe, they are only for the benefits of headquarters.

Similarly, the local financial managers do not know what effects their comments and accounts have. They think that the possibility of them exercising any influence locally is very limited, especially on the ferries. A manager from one of the central areas at headquarters states:

> The accounting department makes a song and dance about rearranging old and useless figures.

The accounting data used for control purposes is shown in Tables 13.1–13.3. The data primarily consolidate the total number of activities (route areas and ferries to company level). Table 13.4 shows traffic statistics, indicating the control orientations of the company. Table 13.5 highlights some financial information from the annual report from 1997.

The IT-department refers to the CFO and comprises 15 employees. The department focuses on operations without having much influence on which initiatives or action areas should be given priority in the long run. It is a major problem for the department that it has to service many different part-systems, including different accounting systems that lack coherence and cause consolidation problems. Also the accounting department employs many resources for consolidation. Other duties of the IT-department are to service the various booking systems, e-mail systems, schedule systems, duty roster systems, etc. The IT-department is characterized by 'emergency solutions' and 'rush jobs'. IT plays an important part in the company's market policy, but there are no plans to co-ordinate market development and IT-development.

The Scandlines management group consists of graduates in economy and technology with a market economy and analytically more administrative approach to management. This group is primarily placed in the financial and administrative functions (management accounting, IT and market analysis). They are skilled in analysing complex relationships and producing knowledge and information. This personnel category has little influence on decisions taken by top management, and among others a market analyst has been discharged.

Market relations

The individual routes focus on operational problems and punctuality. Various co-operation agreements provide a relatively fixed framework for price policy and tonnage. However, ticket prices and tonnage are determined once or twice a year in negotiations between the co-operative partners. Market communication is handled through advertisements, where the duty-free sales are highlighted. At present, efforts are being made to implement a new ticket system providing the routes with more information about customers. The system is supplemented by extensive customer interviews made while customers are waiting for the ferry.

Relations with government owners

In Scandlines there are many discussions about what privatization has meant. The CEO thinks that privatization is total:

> From the time that Scandlines became a limited company the politicians were out. (CEO)

As such, the new management is not prepared to submit to the government in all matters without criticism. As the CEO points out:

> If we are going to operate on business terms, we cannot accept that the government interferes with bureaucracy causing action paralysis. If we are going to survive it is mandatory that we do not have to consult anybody, but are free to act while we have the opportunity. Otherwise, they might as well run the operations. (CEO)

However, the head of department at the Ministry of Transport is in total opposition to his view: he says:

> Political uncertainty is an important factor that is overlooked, played down and under-rated in the internal debate in Scandlines. As long as Scandlines is going to handle domestic transport tasks (the small, local and often uneconomic routes linking islands with the mainland) and be part of the domestic infrastructure, the company will depend on political backing and public support. They just do not see this! This is why we have many problems with Scandlines.

Table 13.1 Scandlines Ltd: an economic outline

Account, Scandlines Ltd.	Month X			Year to date			The Year		
	Realized t kr./pbe	Budget t kr./pbe	Variance t kr./pbe	Realized t kr./pbe	Budget t kr./pbe	Variance t kr./pbe	Estimate t kr./pbe	Budget t kr./pbe	Variance t kr./pbe
Income, traffic	114,581	107,448	7,133	464,583	450,286	14,298	–	1,201,431	–1,201,431
Transferral of trains, etc.	44,312	54,134	–9,822	223,169	231,764	–8,595	–	583,597	–538,597
Governmental Grants	27,064	27,024	40	135,322	135,121	201	–	324,291	–324,291
Other Turnover	22,588	18,407	4,180	94,238	90,232	4,006	–	222,940	–222,940
Turnover	208,544	207,013	1,531	917,312	907,402	9,910	–	2,287,259	–2,287,259
Other Operating Income, excl. catering	3,702	3,526	176	21,994	20,596	1,398	–	92,890	–92,890
Wages and Personnel Expenses	60,154	47,783	12,371	261,254	239,395	21,859	–	574,936	–574,936
Oil	12,195	9,518	2,678	48,429	47,369	1,060	–	113,599	–113,599
Ship on Charter	4,199	9,450	–5,250	21,934	47,248	–25,314	–	113,395	–113,395
Other Ferry Services	29,047	19,029	10,017	159,985	168,486	–8,501	–	368,215	–368,215
Total Ferry Service	105,595	85,779	19,816	491,602	502,498	–10,896	–	1,170,145	–1,170,145
Technical Functions	3,029	2,994	35	11,616	14,969	–3,353	–	35,923	–35,923
Places	1,532	1,497	35	7,472	7,483	–11	–	17,959	–17,959
Harbours	10,263	9,356	906	45,683	46,719	–1,035	–	114,121	–114,121
Operating Cost of Stocks	1,022	259	763	2,231	1,294	937	–	3,106	–3,106
Depreciations	26,729	17,202	9,527	98,716	86,010	12,706	–	206,423	–206,423
Production Cost	148,169	117,086	31,082	657,320	658,973	–1,652	–	1,547,678	–1,547,678
Gross Profit	64,078	93,453	–29,374	281,986	269,026	12,960	–	832,471	–832,471

Market Function	5,682	5,347	335	22,927	26,173	-3,246	—	62,925	-62,925
Sales and Services	4,896	4,658	238	21,133	23,352	-2,219	—	55,954	-55,954
Depreciations	—	—	0	—	—	0	—	—	0
Sales and Distribution Cost	10,578	10,005	573	44,060	49,525	-5,465	—	118,879	-118,879
Joint	15,486	11,577	3,909	50,404	53,901	-3,497	—	143,800	-143,800
Financial Department	2,732	3,434	-702	14,336	16,370	-2,034	—	39,809	-39,809
Personnel Department	1,156	939	217	4,961	4,694	266	—	11,267	-11,267
Depreciations	774	249	525	3,666	1,244	2,423	—	3,334	-3,334
Depreciations, goodwill	3,968	11,905	-7,936	59,524	59,524	0	—	142,857	-142,857
Administrative Expenses	24,116	28,104	-3,988	132,891	135,732	-2,842	—	341,067	-341,067
Income, catering	14,843	16,770	-1,927	33,627	39,906	-6,279	—	162,513	-162,513
Primary Result	44,227	72,114	-27,887	138,663	123,674	14,988	—	535,038	-535,038
Income, interest on capital	4,336	8,827	-4,491	-15,729	-12,181	-3,548	—	13,800	-13,800
Net Interest	-2,124	-6,452	4,327	-13,891	-28,109	14,217	—	-60,821	60,821
Exceptional Items	-128		-128	-128		-128	—	—	0
Profit before Taxes	46,310	74,488	-28,178	108,914	83,385	25,530	—	488,017	-488,017
Company tax (Main Office)	-15,413	-15,413	0	-77,067	-77,067	0	—	-184,960	184,960
Result of the period	30,897	59,075	-28,178	31,848	6,318	25,530	—	303,057	-303,057
Account, Scandlines Ltd.									
Turnover	110,116	124,011	-13,895	459,813	514,472	-54,660	1,360,788	1,412,045	-51,257
Used stock	46,667	55,217	-8,549	204,990	228,325	-23,335	618,578	636,600	-18,022
Expenses	46,226	48,412	-2,186	212,613	231,677	-19,064	550,421	572,390	-21,968
EFC Operating Result	17,222	20,382	-3,160	42,210	54,470	-12,261	191,788	203,055	-11,267

Table 13.2 Specification of route areas and Scandlines restaurants

	Month X			Year to date			The Year		
	Realized t kr.	Budget t kr.	Variance t kr.	Realized t kr.	Budget t kr.	Variance t kr	Estimate t kr.	Budget t kr.	Variance t kr.
Main Office									
Turnover	3,403	0	3,403	3,772	0	3,772	0	0	0
Production Cost	3,663	–941	4,604	–21,464	–4,705	–16,759	0	–11,293	11,293
Sales and Distribution Cost	992	1,094	–102	4,680	5,470	–790	0	13,128	–13,128
Administrative Expenses	5,929	16,551	–10,622	65,052	82,755	–17,703	0	198,612	–198,612
Catering incl. Subsidiary	14,843	16,770	–1,927	33,627	39,906	–6,279	0	162,513	–162,513
Result of the Period	–5,648	–12,364	6,716	–117,860	–162,079	44,219	0	–279,216	279,216
Scandlines Restaurants and Operating Result 3	0	0	0	0	0	0	0	0	0
Profit incl. Scandlines Restaurants	–5,648	–12,364	6,716	–117,860	–162,079	44,219	0	–279,216	279,216
Route A									
Turnover	0	473	–473	0	1,318	–1,318	0	5,528	–5,528
Production Cost	464	2,076	–1,613	8,455	14,373	–5,918	0	27,967	–27,967
Sales and Distribution Cost	0	0	0	0	0	0	0	0	0
Administrative Expenses	26	580	–554	124	2,067	–1,942	0	6,061	–6,061
Catering incl. Subsidiary	0	0	0	0	0	0	0	0	0
Result of the Period	–489	–2,172	1,683	–8,579	–15,090	6,511	0	–28,393	28,393
Scandlines Restaurants and Operating Result 3	0	0	0	0	0	0	0	0	0
Profit incl. Scandlines Restaurants	–489	–2,172	1,683	–8,579	–15,090	6,511	0	–28,393	28,393
Route B									
Turnover	24,541	23,760	780	117,603	116,997	606	0	287,679	–287,679
Production Cost	17,311	18,505	–1,195	107,220	109,351	–2,131	0	247,358	–247,358
Sales and Distribution Cost	0	0	0	0	0	0	0	0	0
Administrative Expenses	5,477	2,119	3,359	10,677	7,434	3,243	0	18,241	–18,241
Catering incl. Subsidiary	0	0	0	0	0	0	0	0	0
Result of the Period	1,949	3,228	–1,279	951	670	281	0	65,709	–65,709

	1	2	3	4	5	6	7	8	9
Scandlines Restaurants and Operating Result 3	3,777	3,205	572	10,078	9,307	771	35,542	34,771	771
Profit incl. Scandlines Restaurants	5,726	6,433	-707	11,029	9,977	1,051	35,542	100,480	-64,939
Route C									
Turnover	36,761	39,090	-2,329	166,013	176,879	-10,866	0	476,452	-476,452
Production Cost	34,483	22,219	12,264	156,770	136,455	20,315	0	336,213	-336,213
Sales and Distribution Cost	4,442	2,729	1,713	15,013	13,646	1,368	0	32,742	-32,742
Administrative Expenses	2,906	1,987	918	14,477	9,136	5,341	0	22,447	-22,447
Catering incl. Subsidiary	0	0	0	0	0	0	0	0	0
Result of the Period	-1,293	14,890	-16,184	-1,368	34,311	-35,679	0	125,950	-125,950
Scandlines Restaurants and Operating Result 3	18,744	19,001	-257	70,249	74,585	-4,336	207,320	211,656	-4,336
Profit incl. Scandlines Restaurants	17,451	33,891	-16,441	68,881	108,896	-40,015	207,320	337,606	-130,286
Route D									
Turnover	29,657	38,483	-8,826	146,379	155,203	-8,824	0	359,463	-359,463
Production Cost	38,219	29,120	9,099	147,386	154,437	-7,051	0	352,792	-352,792
Sales and Distribution Cost	0	0	0	0	0	0	0	0	0
Administrative Expenses	1,894	1,745	149	8,475	8,725	-250	0	20,940	-20,940
Catering incl. Subsidiary	0	0	0	0	0	0	0	0	0
Result of the Period	-10,401	7,701	-18,102	-9,409	-7,542	-1,866	0	-13,268	13,268
Scandlines Restaurants and Operating Result 3	-464	318	-782	-1,913	-732	-1,181	138	1,319	-1,181
Profit incl. Scandlines Restaurants	-10,865	8,019	-18,884	-11,321	-8,274	-3,047	138	-11,949	12,088
Route E									
Turnover	87,030	78,183	8,847	348,227	321,884	26,343	0	833,846	-833,846
Production Cost	28,216	25,489	2,727	141,930	139,461	2,469	0	334,087	-334,087
Sales and Distribution Cost	4,870	5,500	-630	23,047	26,998	-3,952	0	64,822	-64,822
Administrative Expenses	3,992	907	3,085	14,731	4,542	10,189	0	24,188	-24,188
Catering incl. Subsidiary	0	0	0	0	0	0	0	0	0
Result of the Period	49,841	46,299	3,542	168,877	155,096	13,781	0	427,503	-427,503
Scandlines Restaurants and Operating Result 3	-641	-237	-404	-6,193	-5,966	-227	-8,468	-8,241	-227
Profit incl. Scandlines Restaurants	49,200	46,062	3,138	162,684	149,130	13,554	-8,468	419,262	-427,730

Table 13.2 Continued

	Month X			Year to date			The Year		
	Realized t kr.	Budget t kr.	Variance t kr.	Realized t kr.	Budget t kr.	Variance t kr.	Estimate t kr.	Budget t kr.	Variance t kr.
Route F									
Turnover	27,153	27,024	129	135,318	135,121	197	0	324,291	−324,291
Production Cost	25,814	20,617	5,196	117,023	109,600	7,423	0	260,554	−260,554
Sales and Distribution Cost	273	682	−409	1,321	3,411	−2,091	0	8,187	−8,187
Administrative Expenses	3,892	4,215	−323	19,354	21,074	−1,720	0	50,578	−50,578
Catering incl. Subsidiary	0	0	0	0	0	0	0	0	0
Result of the Period	−3,062	1,493	−4,556	−765	952	−1,717	0	4,772	−4,772
Scandlines Restaurants and Operating Result 3	−425	−299	−126	−2,860	−2,537	−323	−4,923	−4,600	−323
Profit incl. Scandlines Restaurants	−3,487	1,194	−4,682	−3,625	−1,585	−2,040	−4,923	172	−5,096
Sum									
Turnover	208,544	207,013	1,531	917,312	907,402	9,910	0	2,287,259	−2,287,259
Production Cost	148,169	117,086	31,082	657,320	658,973	−1,652	0	1,547,678	−1,547,678
Sales and Distribution Cost	10,578	10,005	573	44,060	49,525	−5,465	0	118,879	−118,879
Administrative Expenses	24,116	28,104	−3,988	132,891	135,732	−2,842	0	341,067	−341,067
Catering incl. Subsidiary	14,843	16,770	−1,927	33,627	39,906	−6,279	0	162,513	−162,513
Result of the Period	30,897	59,075	−28,178	31,848	6,318	25,530	0	303,057	−303,057
Scandlines Restaurants and Operating Result 3									
Turnover	110,116	124,011	−13,895	459,813	514,472	−54,660	1,360,788	1,412,045	−51,257
Used Stock	46,667	55,217	−8,549	204,990	228,325	−23,335	618,578	636,600	−18,022
Expenses	46,226	48,412	−2,186	212,613	231,677	−19,064	550,421	572,390	−21,968
Operating Result	17,222	20,382	−3,160	42,210	54,470	−12,261	191,788	203,055	−11,267

Other matters are still to be discussed with the government, such as who shall pay pensions for the many public servants made redundant, how much shall the company pay to the Treasury in cash, and how much does Scandlines have to pay for the ferry berths. Furthermore, the company might encounter another EU monopoly case.

Statements and opinions about Scandlines' mission and its transition into a public limited company

Head of Department at the Ministry of Transport

The railway Ferry Company has never earned money on rail traffic. It was not until motoring increased dramatically in the 1970s that the company yielded a profit. The new bridges will be a serious threat to the Ferry Company.

When the shipping company was separated from the railway operations in 1991, the intention of the new management was 'development' not 'liquidation'. This was of course understandable, but in terms of politics it was difficult, and strategically it was unrealistic. Scandlines was not an independent organization controlled by the market, but a politically controlled dependent company that in the long run would lose political importance. At this stage, it was essential to be set free from the problems in the Ferry Company. A government owned operation is not suited to run risks and to operate on market terms. This was why the idea of a public limited company was developed. In addition, it was a natural way of organizing a 'public service activity'.

In future, Scandlines must be able to function on the free market if it is to survive as a place of work. This is only possible if the company becomes politically more independent within the next few years. In 1994, there was no longer any reason to maintain the company as a part of the state railways, and by turning Scandlines into a public limited company its marketability would increase. Obviously, nobody would buy a government owned shipping operation. It is the political goal that Scandlines shall provide society with the cheapest transport infrastructure during the period of transition. Therefore, a market model is appropriate. But share trading will not be possible until the phasing out of personnel made redundant by the fixed links has been completed. As long as the Ferry Company yields a profit, and as long as there are no problems with the staff, Scandlines and its management can count on political support. The politicians cannot accept if the large ferry routes are closed down due to strikes. On this issue we are confident that the new management is able to secure the transition, maintain order in the workplace and increase the marketability of the company. In realizing this huge societal project it does not matter whether it costs a hundred million Kr. more or less. In my opinion, Scandlines' many new investments in routes, ferries and technology are somehow exaggerated in relation to the demand of the market. However, the ferries can be sold again in case of excess capacity, although the purpose of the company is not to buy and sell ferries.

Table 13.3 An economic outline: Ferry Denmark

	Month X			Year to date			The Year		
	Realized t kr./pbe	Budget t kr./pbe	Variance t kr./pbe	Realized t kr./pbe	Budget t kr./pbe	Variance t kr./pbe	Estimate t kr./pbe	Budget t kr./pbe	Variance t kr./pbe
Transferred Traffic									
Passengers, landing	45,877	0	45,877	281,683	0	281,683	0	0	0
Passengers, car/train	142,751	0	142,751	418,576	0	418,576	0	0	0
Cars	36,972	0	36,972	97,453	0	97,453	0	0	0
Trucks	10,776	0	10,776	85,816	0	85,816	0	0	0
	4,368	0	4,368	15,912	0	15,912	0	0	0
Passenger Waggon	154	0	154	4,103	0	4,103	0	0	0
Goods Waggon	12,240	0	12,240	100,770	0	100,770	0	0	0
Account, Scandlines									
Purpose of Income	17	6	12	35	41	–6	53	70	–17
Drive	2,604	2,548	56	17,358	17,555	–197	29,858	29,161	697
Running Costs	1,056	705	351	5,207	4,937	270	8,207	8,464	–257
General Average	14	83	–70	–426	583	–1,009	60	1,000	–940
Off-hire	129	0	129	3,165	0	3,165	3,255	3,990	–735
Shipyard	0	0	0	368	0	368	368	0	368
Other Expenses	1,740	1,200	540	9,796	8,406	1,390	13,601	14,406	–805
Result of the period	–5,525	–4,531	–994	–35,433	–31,440	–3,993	–55,295	–56,951	1,656

Account, Scandlines Restaurant									
Turnover	3,826	5,247	-1,421	16,188	19,921	-3,733	26,895	32,041	-5,146
Gross Profit	2,559	3,445	-886	10,213	13,089	-2,876	17,284	21,091	-3,807
Expenses	19	205	-186	369	1,193	-824	914	2,038	-1,124
Operating result II	2,540	3,240	-700	9,844	11,896	-2,052	16,370	19,053	-2,683
Account, Scandlines Tax-free									
Turnover	27,770	28,826	-1,056	123,156	121,456	1,700	202,600	205,340	-2,740
Gross Profit	13,604	12,995	609	56,040	54,752	1,288	93,539	92,570	969
Expenses	1,458	2,339	-881	8,131	12,549	-4,418	15,850	22,543	-6,693
Operating result II	12,146	10,656	1,490	47,909	42,203	5,706	77,689	70,027	7,662
Account, Scandlines Shops									
Turnover	0	0	0	0	0	0	0	0	0
Gross Profit	0	0	0	0	0	0	0	0	0
Expenses	0	0	0	0	0	0	0	0	0
Operating result II	0	0	0	0	0	0	0	0	0
Account, Scandlines Exchange Service									
Turnover	0	0	0	0	0	0	0	0	0
Gross Profit	0	0	0	0	0	0	0	0	0
Expenses	0	0	0	0	0	0	0	0	0
Operating result II	0	0	0	0	0	0	0	0	0
Total operating result II	14,927	14,199	728	58,528	55,035	3,493	95,401	90,583	4,818
Account, Scandlines Company and Restaurants	9,401	9,668	-266	23,095	23,595	-500	40,106	33,632	6,474

Table 13.4 Scandlines' traffic statistics 1996

Route no.	Route	Passengers	Cars	Buses	Trucks
1	Halsskov-Knudshoved	5,361,568	2,243,202	15,817	264,227
2	Helsingør-Helsingborg	10,216,840	1,426,462	42,925	279,281
3	Rødby-Puttgarden	6,181,761	984,888	34,953	233,242
4	Århus-Kalundborg (Cat-Link)	1,140,238	410,254	0	0
5	Kalundborg-Århus	374,547	180,960	403	78,435
6	Gedser-Rostock	1,402,343	183,790	12,526	36,571
7	Rostock-Trelleborg	151,681	39,092	561	28,819
8	Trelleborg-Sassnitz	772,962	112,907	3,694	21,443
9	Dragør-Limhamn	2,223,997	255,099	22,711	36,994
10	Korsør-Nyborg	4,273,163	5,024	0	51
11	Spodsbjerg-Tårs	770,556	248,445	9,035	43,241
12	Esbjerg-Fanø	1,716,998	258,025	323	11,402
13	København-Malmø^c	1,379,651	0	0	0
14	København-Landskrona (Direkten)	160,370	0	0	0
15	Frihavnen-Helsingborg (Danlink)^a	0	0	0	0
16	Bøjden-Fynshav	250,133	74,179	310	2,630
17	Kalundborg-Kolby Kås	131,185	29,117	149	1,816
18	Korsør-Lohals	70,792	17,991	46	46
19	Rønne-Sassnitz	112,775	29,262	329	1,601
20	Karlshamn-Liepaja (Amber Line)^d	0	0	0	0
21	Malmø-Kastrup	391,592	0	0	0
22	Sassnitz-Swinoujsce	61,180	0	0	0
In total		37,144,332	6,498,697	143,582	1,039,799

[a] Goods trains only
[b] Figures include former operator Europa-Linien A/S
[c] Shoppinglinien included
[d] Trailers only
[e] From 1997 freight only

The political logic in Scandlines is important, i.e. to ensure that a politically controlled, technically dominated railway/ferry operation, which plays a crucial role in the domestic infrastructure, is gradually and harmoniously converted into a market controlled, strategically managed, international ferry company with an international and dynamic mission.

The new CEO of Scandlines

During the next two years Scandlines has to be fundamentally restructured. Scandlines must be changed from a production-oriented state monopoly limited by governmental appropriation rules into a market-based service organization limited only by the market prospects.

Table 13.5 Financial highlights, key ratios and some statistics

	1995	1995	1997
Turnover (Danish Kr.)	2,685.1	4,593.2	4,404.5
Profit on ordinary activities (Danish Kr.)	533.5	554.3	356.5
Operating profit margin %	22.7	13.2	8.9
Return on assets %	19.2	15.5	8.7
Return on equity %	73.4	45.7	15.0
Liquidity ratio	0.7	0.9	1.0
Equity ratio	15.6	37.4	41.6
Average number of employees	3,022	5,273	4,549

Definition of ratios

Operating profit margin %	(Operating profit * 100)/turnover
Return on assets %	(Operating profit * 100)/Assets
Return on equity %	(Profit before extraordinary items * 100)/Average shareholders equity
Liquidity ratio %	Current assets/current liabilities
Equity ratio %	(Shareholders equity * 100)/Total Assets

The restructuring must be carried out very fast. We have to adapt expenses and staff to a level of activity corresponding to 25% of the existing level. In addition, we have to ensure continued profits in order to avoid any political interference during the transition. Once our decisions are affected by politics, we have already lost the battle. It is a race against time.

We have now established a modern accounts system from which it is possible to read earnings and expenses, the amount of assets and the normal depreciation. It was quite a job, as the Ministry and the National Auditors wanted to control our expenses in detail as usual.

Now we have to teach the remaining old leaders and employees that consumption of resources must be legitimized by specific earning prospects. So far it has been possible to spend the appropriations without any considerations for the results and the whole. It is all a question of discipline and control.

The cost consciousness will develop gradually as the market forces catch on. Already in February 1997 we have gained control of the costs development. The revenues will be more difficult to control, because market trends, competitors' marketing policy and the opening of competing routes determine them. If the revenues decrease we will have to reduce the costs accordingly as quickly as possible, which will be difficult, partly because the costs are fixed or tied up in equipment, and partly because of labour agreements, contracts, security rules, transport plans, etc. We cannot just reduce the service and safety. If we do so we will lose the confidence of the customers, while politicians, the public and the media are still keeping a keen eye on our service level and pricing policy. The media hunt will probably disappear as outsourcing and market forces begin to have an effect. At present the press is against Scandlines.

Retiring Market Manager

Scandlines is not a market controlled organization. The new management does not rely on managing information as a basis for decisions. They are entrepreneurs and merchants, and their decisions are based on intuition and informal contacts. For example, a second-hand ferry was bought from another company. In less than 5 days the ferry was operating on a Scandlines route. When new routes are established, similar actions are taken.

Since 1990 we have tried to establish a market function that can prepare market analyses on a professional basis as well as other external analyses and comparisons. The function was established and supported by the former manager, but since 1995 the function has obviously wilted for lack of resources. In the new organization the analytical department has been completely eliminated.

Basically, the company is operation and production-oriented, and that presents another problem for Scandlines. The ferry operation is one of the most routine-based operated productions in existence, affecting the whole organization. Scandlines has never succeeded in making the individual members of personnel market-oriented, so that market aspects would always be included in his considerations and actions. Therefore, we have not been put in a strategically leading position. The worst thing is that at present we have no development plan for turning the company into a customer-oriented and market conscious operation. We tried last year – with the support of external consultants – to establish a strategic development plan, which would ensure that market information was systematized, and introduce a range of transverse co-ordinating activities. It was to be ensured, for example, that computer purchases would follow the strategic development, but also this project ended in the desert.

New Passenger Manager

In effect, Scandlines is a completely new company which must create a new market position. The problem is that there are a number of skeletons in the cupboard that must be removed first. And, unfortunately, we have to act fast. There is no time to make extensive strategic analyses and plans.

Our biggest strategic problem is our great dependence on our co-operators. We are not free to put our ideas into effect. Any proposal has to go through the heavy bureaucracy in the other government controlled shipping operations.

In the passenger department we have not had time to wait for the structure to be implemented. In the passenger department we have made our own strategic plan 2005, indicating our aims for our main routes concerning marketing, target sales, passenger service, etc. An important element in our plan is the introduction of the new exclusive-cards – a small magnetic-stripe card with which the customer is able to book a trip and order his ticket at the ferry station. In this way we keep in contact with the customer, meet his preferences and ensure his loyalty in addition to granting him a discount according to his transport needs.

It is important to us to compete on the service and the price and to ensure a stable and rising sale. The costs are not the main issue. The costs can only be reduced by choosing new types of ferries and by investing in new technology.

Management accounting is something completely unknown to us. We receive too little management information. The present financial reports consist of sorted prints of obsolete data. As for example what we were told by the accounting reports were that the passenger earnings on route Y in April declined 3% in relation to last year. We already know that. Our local transport staff told us that long ago. No, what we need is information about how much more we will earn from increasing the number of departures or by improving the service. But the accounting department cannot tell us that, as they have no information about the market and production.

Local Accounting Officer

I have the financial responsibility for route X. It consists of making the registration of the ferries' expenses function and ensuring that the expenses are paid on time. I get all the vouchers from the ferries. I check them and make sure that they are entered correctly. Previously, the ferry personnel made the registration. However, the procedure proved too uncertain and too expensive.

I make a financial report each month for each route comprising information about revenues (revenues on passengers, cars, trucks, catering, super market, etc.) and expenses (salaries, wages, oil, maintenance, etc.). A provisional report is sent to headquarters, which comments on the figures before we send it to managers, route managers, captains, etc.

It is my impression that nobody is especially interested in the reports. It is very rarely that somebody requests supplementary figures or questions the size of the entries. The whole procedure is a fixed routine without dialogue or comments. It would be nice if, once in a while, we could make a detailed analysis that would compare, e.g., the economy of the routes and the ferries. Our experience and knowledge as accounting officers are not used in a constructive way.

Events since the establishment of Scandlines Ltd.
– A Summary

1847: The first private railways are established in Denmark.
       Small private ferry companies handle crossings.

1860: The railway service on main routes is taken over by the state.
       In this connection a number of ferry routes are established.
1880: The postal services start ferry services on important routes.
1920: The first ferry with capacity to transport trains is put in on the main route.
1935: New train ferries transport entire express trains on the main route.
1955: Large car ferries with car decks on two levels are put in on the main route.
1970: Car ferry service expands rapidly.
       The largest net proceeds for the Railway Company are delivered.
       The Ferry Company continues to be a department under the National Railway Company and it is subject to the appropriation rules of the State.
1975: The National Railway Company obtains more liberal management including net appropriations and a more liberal staff policy.
       Ferry investments continue, however, to be controlled by government employment policy.
       Government's expansion of expenses and range of investments are managed according to plans. Plan 90 is an overall plan for the railways' position in the infrastructure of the country. The objective is to introduce modern target-oriented management and a customer-oriented management structure in the railways.
1983: Through modernization and budget reforms government encourages implementation of market mechanism, private corporate norms and other privatization efforts.
1984: At first, the modernization of both the railway and ferry services focuses on a new service and PR policy: 'Trains on time', 'The customer in focus', etc. The staff get new uniforms, the company gets a customer-related information policy, new logos and printing types.
       The organization is decentralized.
1987: The government decides to build a combined car and railway bridge on the key traffic route. The implication is a reduction of the company by at least half in 10 years (Plan 2000).
1988: The railway company launches an extensive wave of rationalizations. The objective is to decentralize economic responsibility to divisions, to make management visible, and to make the profit and loss economy transparent. Finally, it should be possible to measure the contribution of the individual activity to the total economy of the company. The aim is to transform the Ferry Company into a limited division/product line in the Railway Company.
1989: The shipping company division is established, and a former technical chief planner is appointed as divisional manager. This person was commonly regarded as both dynamic and powerful. The shipping company starts to develop its own market-oriented and decentralized management structure based on customer orientation, contract management, and quality development. Earnings and expenses are to be measured in relation to one another.
1990: The shipping company is forced to sell two super ferries in order to contribute to the joint economy. A makeshift solution where cargo carriers, in

haste, are converted into ferries creates great operational problems. The shipping company is exposed to public contempt as an inefficient organization with incompetent operational management.

1991: The economy of the railway company is strongly criticized by politicians, especially for its accounting practices and financial control. The director of the shipping company leaves his position in favour of a top position in the private sector, and a former financial manager at the railways takes on the responsibility for the shipping division. New co-operative agreements on international routes are established with foreign state-owned shipping companies. Each route and ferry must be an individual profit centre. The development starts from the bottom with establishing a ferry management liable for results (Troika management) together with route divisions assuming complete, local, functional responsibility (sales, operations, finances).

1992: The new management of the shipping company wishes more autonomy, preferably as a limited company. However, the railway management intends to hold on to the contributions from the shipping company as a help to the slender purse.

1994: The politicians wish to get a better hold of the public railway operations through private forms of management (outsourcing, contract management, company divisions, an independent board, etc.). The Chancellor of the Exchequer prefers a limited company. Top management in the Railway Company still opposes the shipping company becoming completely separated into an autonomous limited company. However, for a new Minister of Transport it becomes a leading issue. The personnel organizations are opposed to the idea of a limited company, and they threaten to resist it. Nevertheless, the politicians stick to the idea.

1995: Scandlines is established as an autonomous public limited company with a board consisting of private business people and the former director of the shipping company, who resigned in 1991, as chairman. The new chairman was close to the Minister of Transport. Although the divisional management had taken many good 'modern' management initiatives, it is completely replaced by a new management team recruited from the private shipping and ship building industry.

1996: DSB Rederi gets a new market-oriented name 'Scandlines' and a new, modern, market-oriented and totally co-ordinated matrix organization. A large number of functional managers are replaced. A new realistic plan for phasing out personnel is developed in connection with the fixed links taking over traffic. On the basis of the EU rules, a privately owned shipping company gets permission to use the Scandlines ferry berths in competition on an international route.

1997: The first stage of the new bridge replaces the old railway ferries, and - Scandlines is left with 1,500 redundant employees. The management succeeds in creating a smooth transition. Due to political pressure, Scandlines pays US$ 1.3 billion Kr. to the Treasury as payment for taking over the infrastructure (ferry berths, goodwill, etc.). Scandlines establishes new international ferry routes and commits itself to build a dynamic international market policy. Foreign shipping companies and routes are bought or engaged in co-operation. Modern high-speed ferries are bought on the free market. Technically advanced flex ferries, demanding only a few staff, are put in on the future main route. Market campaigns promote Scandlines as the future's most dynamic shipping company in northern Europe. The management recognizes that the strategic independence is limited, because the future main routes are managed in co-operation with the foreign state owned railway-shipping companies. A new financial control system has been implemented.

1998: Mid-1998 Scandlines has merged the Germany state owned company DFO. This company is now called Scandlines AG.

Endnote

[1] Exchange rate is per 4/1 1999 744,92 Danish kroner per 100 Euros.

STUDENT ASSIGNMENTS

1. Identify important aspects and requirements of effective management control. Pay special attention to controlling interrelated functions and activities and to the impact of the political and competitive environment in which the company has to operate.

2. What circumstances make effective control at Scandlines difficult?

3. Analyze situational factors promoting and impeding organizational change. What should Scandlines do in order to become a competitive player on the market-place?

—

PTT Post

Tom Groot
Peter Smidt

Introduction

In October 1996, PTT Post (the Dutch Mail Company, with sales of 6.9 billion Euros and 55,000 employees) acquired the Australian express parcel company TNT (sales of 1.7 billion Euros and 33,000 employees) at the price of 1.2 billion Euros. At that time, PTT Post was a daughter of KPN ('Royal PTT Netherlands', the Dutch post and telecom company). TNT was a listed company for on-time delivery of goods and for logistic services (companies' stocks and delivery services) mainly active in Australia, the Far East and in Europe. Before the acquisition, TNT and PTT Post were already co-operating in GD Express Worldwide, a joint company for *international* on-time delivery services in more than 200 countries. In the acquisition process (internally known as 'Operation Gold') GD Express is also integrated in the new organization TPG (TNT Post Group). TPG is currently one of the four largest companies in on-time delivery of documents, parcels and goods and logistic services in the world alongside UPS, Federal Express and DHL. The TPG organization is composed of the two former independent organizations: TNT and PTT Post (see Figure 14.1).

The name 'PTT Post' needs some explanation. The letters PTT stand for 'Post, Telegraphy and Telephony'. The abbreviation was used until 1989 when PTT was a governmental organization for postal services and telecommunication. In 1989, seven years before the acquisition of TNT, PTT was privatized and for that occasion renamed KPN ('Royal PTT Netherlands'). This privatized company was listed on the Amsterdam, New York, London and Frankfurt stock exchanges in 1994. On 28 June 1998 KPN was split into two organizations: KPN Telecom (for telecommunication services) and TPG (TNT Post Group, for global express, logistics and mail). The day after the separation of these two companies, TPG was introduced at the stock exchanges of Amsterdam, Frankfurt, London and New York as the first listed postal service company in the world.

The creation of TPG is PTT Post's response to the European Commission's intentions of introducing (international) competition in the state controlled national postal markets in the European Union in 2003. From 1989 onwards, PTT Post diversified its product offerings by adding courier, direct-marketing and logistic

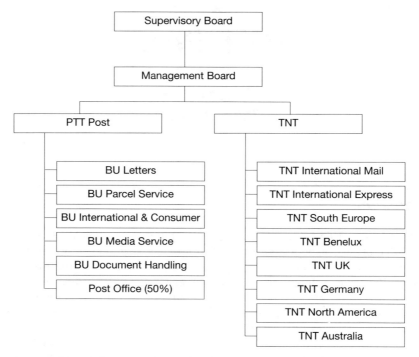

Figure 14.1 TPG organization as of 1997

services to the traditional mail delivery service. At the same time, geographical expansion was sought by co-operation with and acquisition of foreign logistic service companies.

The Dutch State still plays an important role in PTT Post as 44% shareholder of TPG. It also holds preference shares providing a majority vote in strategic decisions leading to changes in TPG's group structure. In the Netherlands PTT Post operates under the Dutch Postal Law, its current edition being valid until 1 April 2000. The Postal Law obliges PTT Post to provide postal services up to a weight of 10 kilograms to all Dutch citizens at uniform prices and under equal conditions (the so-called 'imposed services'). It establishes a monopoly position for PTT Post in handling letters up to 500 grams, in placing letter boxes along public streets and in issuing stamps containing the word 'Netherlands' and images of the king or queen (the so-called 'exclusive concession'). Since 1 August 1997 onwards the independent state agency OPTA ('Independent Post and Telecom Authority') inspects PTT Post's adherence to the Dutch postal law and to European regulation. It also monitors the Dutch postal and telecommunication market in its development from a monopoly to a liberalized, free market.

PTT Post delivers a daily average of 21 million postal items in the Netherlands. The price the company has set its customers for letters up to 20 grams is the lowest in the EU (except for Spain) and has not been changed since 1991. Yet, PTT Post is one of only a few postal services in the world able to generate a positive and growing net income of around 200 million Euros in 1994, 250 million Euros in 1995, and 300 million Euros in 1996. In 1999, TPG is present in 55 countries and its sales mount to 6.8 billion Euros. Yet it was only ten years earlier in 1989 when the former state agency PTT Post became an independent company.

This case describes a 20 years' period in which PTT Post changed from a state agency to an international commercial provider of a large array of mail, express and logistic services. Some important management accounting and management control issues will be more extensively analyzed and discussed. This case consists of three parts, each of which can be discussed separately. They need, however, to be read in consecutive order. Part A relates to PTT Post as a government bureaucracy, covering the years 1978–1988. Part B discusses PTT Post as a commercial provider of logistic services providing an overview of PTT Post's developments from 1988 until 1998. Part C concludes this case and is mainly concerned with an *ex post* assessment of the effectiveness of PTT Post's measures and change processes.

Part A: PTT Post as a government bureaucracy

Until 1989, the year of privatization, PTT Post, being a division of PTT (PTT Post and Telecom), was a state-owned company, managed by the *Ministry of Transport and Public Works*. At the same time PTT had a special position, because its accounting was governed by Company Law rather than by the Government Accountability Act. As a consequence, in its financial accounts PTT used accrual accounting instead of cash accounting. This allowed depreciation and accumulation of capital.

In the 1970s PTT was governed by a Director-General (DG) and six Chief Directors (HDs). The DG and HD are top-level civil servants in the Ministry of Transport and Public Works. The Director-General and the six Chief Directors formed the Board of Directors of PTT. This board made all strategic decisions concerning the mail, telephone and telegraph services. Direct political supervision of the board rested with the Minister of Transport and Public Works. Each of the Chief Directors headed a PTT department. Three departments were responsible for *operational tasks*: Mail, Telecom, and the Savings, Loans & Giro Bank. The Savings, Loans & Giro Bank was split off in 1984 to become a separate independent company. It then changed its name into *Postbank*. Three departments held functional responsibilities: Finance, Personnel and Operations.

The 1979 PTT organization is presented in Figure 14.2.

The Mail Department (which we would currently label *PTT Post*) had distributed the operational tasks over twelve districts. These districts more or less coincided with the Dutch 'Provinces'. The twelve districts are shown in the map of the Netherlands in Figure 14.3.

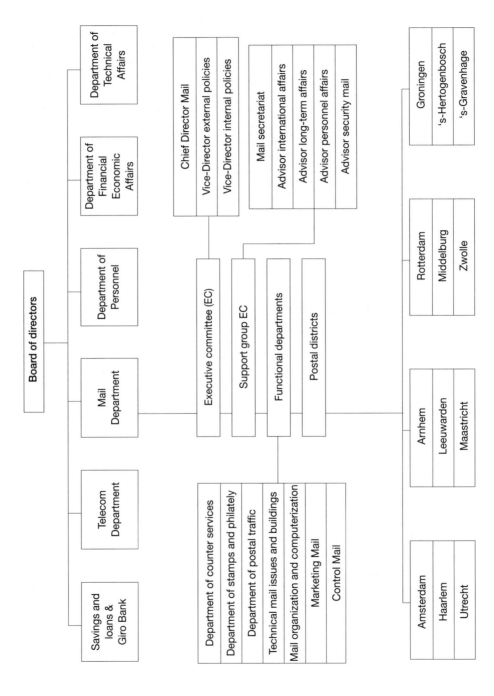

Figure 14.2 Organization structure of PTT in 1979

Figure 14.3 The postal districts in 1979

Each postal district was managed by a district director. This director was responsible for all operational activities in the Major Post Offices, the Pre-sort Centres, the Minor Post Offices, the Branch Offices (post offices in shops) and the Agencies (shops' post offices providing only a limited set of products and services) within his area. Generally, the district director held the office of general manager of a Major Post Office as well. The district director is supported by three vice-directors. The vice-director 'Personnel' took care of personnel affairs, the vice-director 'Operations' was responsible for the operational management of the post offices and pre-sort centres. The vice-director 'Inspection and Information' was

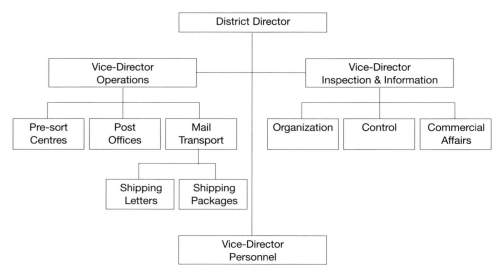

Figure 14.4   Organization structure of a postal district

responsible for workflow planning, finance and organization. The organization structure of a typical district is shown in Figure 14.4.

In the next two sections a short overview will be provided of the process of mail distribution and of the way budgets were set and financial accountability was arranged.

The logistics of collecting, sorting and delivering mail

Figure 14.5 shows the logistical sequence of processing mail. Basically, this process has not changed significantly since the 1970s.

The first step in the logistics of processing mail is the *collection* of postal items. This process consists of two elements; emptying post boxes and collection of the post items which have been presented at the post offices. Next, the mail is *transported* to a Major Post Office, where it is readily delivered for further processing. In the 1960s and 1970s each district had between 12 and 28 Major Post Offices. Each Major Post Office *sorted* the accumulated post items by Major Post Office, and kept the mail designated for its own distribution area. The postal items to be distributed elsewhere were transported to 48 Major Post Offices with shipping functions. After another round of sorting they were distributed to the full total of 270 Major Post Offices.

As soon as the mail packages reached the Major Post Offices they were *pre-sorted* by 'walk'. A 'walk' represents a single round covered by a single postman in delivering mail. Each postman receives his 'walk' package and sorts this package

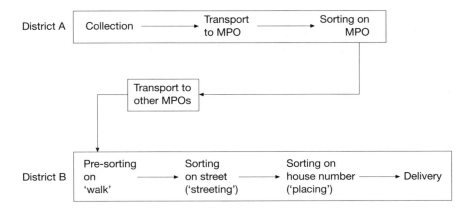

Legend:
MPO   = Major Post Office (48 with shipping function)
District A = the district in which postal items are presented
District B = the district in which postal items are distributed

Note:
When a postal item is distributed in the same district as the one in which it was mailed, then the immediate activity transport to other MPOs disappears from this overview and the activities of District B are performed by District A itself.

Figure 14.5   The logistics of mail collection, sorting and delivery

according to the sequence of streets passed by; in PTT Post jargon this is called '*streeting*'. After streeting the postman sorts his/her mail package in house number order (this is called 'placing'). After this final sorting step the postman goes out and actually *delivers* the mail.

Planning and budgeting at PTT

Annually the Board of Directors of PTT, based on the advice of the district managers, approved the *Policy Outlines*. In Dutch this document was called '*Beleidsindicaties*,' which was shortened to '*Belinda's*'. In this policy memorandum within the setting of the overall PTT Post and Telecom budget the priorities of PTT Post were established. The department of Financial-economic Affairs (FEZ) was involved in the preparation of the 'Belinda's' and in the preparation of PTT Post's budgets.

Before 1987 these budgets contained mainly non-financial items such as the number of personnel employed (stated in full-time equivalents) which in PTT Post jargon was called 'tasks'. Additionally, allowances were made for numbers of cars, and a special cash budget was allotted for small outlays only. The budgets did not include district revenues. Actual revenues from sales of stamps, rents of franking machines and other agreements were collected and administrated separately by the department of FEZ. The Public Housing Service, another government agency, managed maintenance and rent of buildings, although the department of Financial-economic Affairs took care of the accounts.

The main element of the budget was the number of full-time equivalent personnel by category, represented in the 'Workforce Table'. Throughout the 1970s PTT had built up a refined set of standards to determine the volume of personnel (the 'tasks') needed to process a given volume of post items (the 'traffic'). The standards were developed by a section called 'Personnel volumes, Labor studies, and Buildings' and included ratios such as the number of post items sorted in one hour, the average number of post items delivered from a single distribution outlet, and the average speed of postmen. Time and motion studies recorded the average time needed for each collection, sorting and delivery activity. Additionally, the number of walks, the average length of walks, and the average number of addresses in a walk were carefully registered. This system made a distinction between 'traffic-dependent' and 'traffic-independent' activities. For instance, delivery by postmen consists of two parts: a main route, which the postman has to travel irrespective of the volume of postal items to deliver. The time needed to follow this route is considered traffic-independent; its costs are therefore fixed. The postman's activities 'streeting', 'placing' and walking to frontdoors and back again to the main route is considered traffic-dependent; its costs are therefore variable. This approach permits PTT to calculate relatively accurately the number of employees needed at a given level of 'traffic'. Every three years, the set of standards was updated to incorporate changes in work methods and in walks (for instance because of new street plans and new houses). There were no standards for expenditures concerning buildings and equipment or for quality of service.

Based upon the budget for the postal district the district director prepared budgets for the Major Post Offices and the smaller offices under his responsibility. The district directors had budget responsibility for all the budgets in their region. District managers had full authorization for expenditures up to 1,500 Euros. For expenditures exceeding 1,500 Euros the district director needed the approval of the FEZ Department in The Hague. A similar procedure existed for personnel expenses; the district manager was authorized to hire deliverymen up to the number of budgeted tasks. Appointments for higher ranks than deliverymen had to be submitted to the Department of Personnel.

In this period districts directors were mainly evaluated on their personal performance in formulating new policies, on executing existing policies, and on quality of service. In the evaluation of budget realizations the reports on actual expenditures on personnel were carefully scrutinized and evaluated. The department of Financial-economic Affairs (FEZ) monitored the use of personnel through monthly labour information sheets, the so-called 'Workforce Table' (in Dutch 'sterktestaat') which is shown in Table 14.1. This table was prepared and analysed weekly. The item 'workforce' represents the assignment of 'tasks' to the particular district or Major Post Office. This volume was determined by the outcomes of their calculation model for an estimated level of traffic. As this latter figure was set only once every year, a facility was needed to allow an earlier upward correction if traffic increased. The temporary deployment of additional personnel could be reported under the heading 'indispensable additional work'. Surplus tasks, which for instance occurred when traffic decreased or because of a more efficient planning of 'walks', were recorded in the item 'labour surplus'.

Discussions generally focused on the justification of expenditures. The Workforce Table generally sparked debates on the necessity of increases in the standard number of tasks. Given the large and ever increasing workloads many districts strove continually for a larger workforce. A larger workforce meant an increase in the size of the district as well. It also helped the career of the District Manager: the larger the workforce, the larger the salary he earned and the better his career opportunities became.

In 1970 PTT Post started to measure the mail service's quality. It was measured by sending postal items to deliverymen and management. The system periodically registered both the times between mailing a post item and its arrival, and the percentage of trial letters which arrived at the right address. From 1975 on, the trial letters were sent to private residences as well. In 1985 PTT Post outsourced quality measurement activities to an external agency (Intomart) to secure objectivity. This agency sends out 3,000 letters daily to measure quality of performance.

Financial results

In the 1970s PTT Post suffered considerable losses up to 128 million Euros in 1979. These losses mainly affected the Director-General, as costs and revenues were only matched at the highest organizational level. These deficits were the subject of discussion in parliament. The debates were dominated by three themes: (1) the continued poor financial performance of PTT Post, (2) the low quality of service, and (3) the social function of mail delivery in the Netherlands. This third element was the main reason that in general the deficits of PTT Post and Telecom were accepted for the time being. The fact that the significant profits of Telecom compensated the losses of Mail may have played a role in this forbearance.

Defective financial control

In the second half of the 1970s the financial performance of PTT Post deteriorated and it became apparent that there was no effective financial control. The postal districts had no incentive to improve financial performance, as the district directors were only subjectively evaluated by the chief directors (HDs) on the number of tasks, their contribution to PTT Post's strategy and some quality measures. Financial performance was not measured nor rewarded. In reaction to the deficits PTT Post management decided on a general reduction of the number of tasks. At

Table 14.1 The Workforce Table ('sterktestaat')

	Code	Category	Volume[a]
A	Labour capacity		
	A1	Labour capacity for normal tasks	80
	A2	Labour capacity for part-time tasks	10
	A3	Indispensable additional work	2
	A4	Subtotal (A1–A3)	92
-/-	A5	Tasks not carried out	1
	A6	Total workload (A4 – A5)	91
	A7	Primary in-company training	12
	A8	Education and Training	10
	A9	Holidays	25
	A10	Labour-time reductions cf. Labour agreements	8
	A11	Illness	2
	A12		
	A13	Non-productive time (miscellaneous)	2
	A14	Labour surplus	3
	A15	Overtime	1
	A16	Rounding-off losses	1
	A17	Subtotal (A7–A16)	64
-/-	A18	Rounding-off profits	1
	A19	Total additional labour capacity (A17 – A18)	63
	A20	General Total labour capacity (A6 + A19)	154
B	Composition of Labour force applied		
	B1	Full-time employees	120
	B2	Part-time employees	18
	B3	Temporary employees	8
	B4	Employees from employment agencies	10
	B5	Employees contracted on Saturdays	4
	B6A	Overtime	3
	B6B	Overtime for additional non-contracted work	1
	B7A	Service from other units within region	12
	B7B	Service from other units within BU Letters	6
	B8	Service from other units outside BU Letters	2
	B9	Subtotal (B1–B8)	184
-/-	B10	Non-available personnel	8
-/-	B11	Restitution	2
-/-	B12A	Service to other units within region	11
-/-	B12B	Service to other units within BU Letters	7
-/-	B13	Service to other units outside BU Letters	2
	B14	Subtotal (B10–B13)	30
	B15	Total personnel applied (B9 – B14)	154

[a] in fte = full-time equivalents
The numbers in this table are disguised

Footnotes for Table 14.1 continued

A1:   *Labour capacity for normal tasks*: number of fte for standard work under normal circumstances

A2:   *Labour capacity for part-time tasks*: number of fte for part-time work under normal circumstances

A3:   *Indispensable additional work*: necessary additional work which is (not yet) included in standard work package

A5:   *Tasks not carried out*: work which is not executed, for instance because of less traffic or employee shortage

A7:   *Primary in-company training*: employee training necessary for execution of work

A8:   *Education and Training*: all additional training

A9:   *Holidays*: absence because of holidays

A10:   *Labour-time reductions cf. labour agreements*: only centrally agreed (across-the-board) labour time reductions can be registered here

A11:   *Illness*: total fte absence because of illness (1 year max.)

A13:   *Non-productive time (miscellaneous)*: all non-productive fte which could not be classified under another heading

A14:   *Labour surplus*: workforce that is available and present which is not committed to tasks A1, A2 or A3

A15:   *Overtime*: more fte for standard contracted tasks

A16+18: *Rounding-off losses and profits*: rounding-off differences between A20 and B15

B1:   *Full-time employees*: fixed and temporary contracts (min. half year to 2 years) of full-time employees in fte

B2:   *Part-time employees*: fixed an temporary part-time contracted employees in fte

B3:   *Temporary employees*: temporary contracts up to a half year

B4:   *Employees from employment agencies*: employees from employment agencies (excluding consultants and outsourced activities)

B5:   *Employees contracted on Saturdays*: special PTT Post contracts to process peakload on Saturday

B6A: *Overtime*: additional time needed for standard tasks

B6B: *Overtime for additional non-contracted work*: additional time for additional, non-scheduled tasks

B7/12A: *Service from/to other units within region*: fte used to generate/receive services to/from other units within the same region

B7/12B: *Service from/to other units within BU Letters*: fte used to generate/receive services to/from other units from other regions within BU Letters

B8/13: *Service from/to other units outside BU Letters*: fte used to generate/receive services to/from other units from other regions outside BU Letters

B10:   *Non-available personnel*: because of unfitness for work, long-term illness and unpaid holidays

B11:   *Restitution*: of hours time-off because of non-contracted work

the operational level this led to budget games: managers became reluctant to communicate efficiency gains, rendering financial control ineffective. This attitude was aggravated by a large gap between the parties involved in the process of financial control of PTT Post, notably the financial staff of the department of Financial-economic Affairs (FEZ), and the managers in charge of 'operations in the districts'. One of the persons involved in the period recently expressed this as follows:

> I had the impression that there was a feeling of 'we' and 'them', that is 'we' of operations and 'them' from headquarters. A saying from the time was: 'No FEZ pig in the Mail garden'. They simply were mutual enemies. Those FEZ guys could not be trusted; you had to avoid giving them information, because that could be used against you. On the other hand there was a strong feeling at FEZ that PTT Post was a worthless unit. It was held to be ineffective, costs were not controlled, and everything could be done

much cheaper. That's what they used to maintain, and we stated that it wasn't true. Of course that way little progress was made. This atmosphere influenced the nature of the budgeting process as well. If you wanted something it was a game to realize it. The search for extra funding opportunities played a large role: how and from whom can I get additional money for my unit?

Discovery of the customer

During the 1970s PTT Post management came to the conclusion that the market for postal deliveries required an active approach. In the early 1970s the first marketing employees were appointed. Also, the insight took hold that of the total volume of postal deliveries less than 10% concerned mail in which both parties involved were private persons. The remainder consisted of business to business mail and mail involving businesses and private persons. However, in the political appraisal of the performance of PTT Post the interests of private customers played a major role. After all, it is this group which dominates the electorate. Nevertheless, there was a growing awareness that the competitive situation which PTT Post had to face did not agree with this situation.

Quality of service

At the time PTT Post frequently hit the papers in stories about delayed deliveries and deliveries to the wrong address. These reports were frequently debated in parliament. They contributed to an image of a bureaucratic organization, which was unable to adequately meet the needs and requirements of its customers. A dramatic event took place in 1983: all civil servants went on strike, and so did PTT employees. PTT Post clients did not accept this and some big clients decided to have other companies, like Van Gend & Loos, distribute their business mail and direct mail items.

Technological developments

The developments in information technology and process technology offered opportunities for improvement of sorting and distribution processes. The first major innovation became operational in 1978 when the postal code was introduced. This introduction was part of a strategic plan, which had been formulated ten years earlier. The code consists of four numbers and two letters. Combined with the house number of the addressee, this system allows the unique identification of every single building in the Netherlands. As a consequence it is theoretically possible to sort postal items in a single run by sorting on house number. This is called sorting on the 'last significant bit'. The availability of postal codes allows the automation of several parts of the process of sorting mail. The introduction of the postal code allowed the start of a discussion on the concentration of sorting processes at a few sites or even at a single site for the whole country.

Some drastic changes

It became clear to PTT that drastic changes were needed. We will give an overview of some of the most important changes since the 1970s.

Redesign of logistic processes

The introduction of the postal code in combination with new, highly automated sorting machines, created the potential for substantial concentration of sorting activities. This opened up opportunities for reducing costs through economies of scale.

Up to 1978, 48 major post offices had a shipping function: they took care of the exchange of post items between districts. In the 48 distribution areas (the so-called 'exits') 270 major post offices and distribution centres were in operation. In 1978, PTT Post created 160 'pre-sort centres' and 12 'shipping hubs' (in Dutch: *expeditieknooppunten* or *EKPs*). In the 'pre-sort centres' local mail was separated from mail to the 12 shipping hubs (EKPs). Each shipping hub took care of most sorting activities and of transporting mail to other shipping hubs and to the post offices in its area.

In the new 1978 organization structure it was inevitable that each district had its EKP, both because of the organizational form of self-sufficient districts where each district was responsible for the full range of functions and activities, and because of the prestige of the influential district directors. Each director claimed his own shipping hub, although it was technically feasible to have a single shipping hub serve the whole country.

Tightening standards

The availability of the elaborate and detailed set of standards and the routine nature of many activities offered the potential for cutting costs by tightening standards. These standards were included in *norm sheets*. The norm sheets contain the total number of mail items to be processed and calculations of time needed to collect, sort, transport and deliver mail items. The result of these calculations is the number of tasks (in full-time equivalent employees) needed by each district. From 1982, PTT Post was in a process of gradually tightening standards (like number of mail items per full-time employee) for the 17,000 routes in the Netherlands. The aim was (1) to put more emphasis on efficiency and (2) to motivate operational units to constantly introduce technological and organizational improvements. However, there are clear limits to tightening standards. It turned out to be difficult to maintain all relevant data up to date for each of the 17,000 routes. Operational data were on average updated once in every three years. Moreover, only tightening standards generated a feeling of contrasting interests between the management level and operational level in PTT Post. Operational units were not motivated to disclose to management all efficiency measures they had taken or could take because of fear of budget cuts.

Illustrative in this respect is the tenth norm sheet that was issued in 1992. In this year, the labour unions no longer accepted tighter budget standards. As a manager put it: 'We seem to have come to an end in setting higher production standards. People think the organization is doing better, so why should they work harder if the productivity gains are captured by the organization? People think this is not fair any more. We therefore should put an end on discussions about norm-sheets. But what should be put in place instead?' The labour unions decided to bring this norm sheet to court.

Abolishment of direct state control

During the 1970s and 1980s, politicians were considering the privatization of PTT Post and Telecom in order to introduce more competition into the Dutch postal and telecommunication market and to reduce PTT's immense bureaucracy. In 1987, the Minister's Director-General Mr Cor Wit received government permission to make the first step towards privatization by putting an end to the direct State control of PTT. Mr Wit transferred the department's responsibilities to PTT and by doing so, he also ended the functional division of control. In response, PTT decided to create two separate *operating companies*: 'PTT Post' and 'PTT Telecom'. Each was responsible for all business activities related to its 'market'.

Decentralizing responsibilities to operational units

At the time only the Director-General (DG) and six Chief Directors (HDs) of PTT Post were responsible for profitability. As a consequence, the meagre financial results had no impact at lower organizational levels. This problem was increased by the fragmentation of responsibilities in the organization, and the fact that managers had expense budgets based on historic performance. As a consequence, first, managers only had an eye for their performance in relation to the standards and the Workforce Table. Second, managers could and did justify their results by the fact that they did meet their cost budgets. Indeed they did, but these historically based budgets added up to overall losses when confronted with revenues.

Mr Van Doorn, one of the senior managers at that time and responsible for most of PTT Post's reforms, commented as follows:

Decentralizing responsibilities to lower management levels and, later on, privatization of PTT Post was a good thing to do, because it made PTT Post responsible for its own conduct. No one could escape from his responsibilities any more. And what's more, good people don't want to escape: they want to get responsibility and when their performance is good, they want to be recognized and rewarded for it.

In 1986 and in line with this development, a consultancy agency proposed, in what is known as 'the Green Booklet', to decentralize financial responsibilities to operational units by introducing 'management contracts'. The green booklet proposed three alternative options for controlling operational units:

1. Control of costs only
2. Separate control of costs and revenues
3. Control of profits (costs minus revenues).

Pricing policy

At face value, for a monopolist, the easiest solution to insufficient profitability is raising prices. However, for PTT Post this was not a viable option because the necessary political backing was absent. As even the Department of Financial-economic Affairs believed that PTT Post could operate much more efficiently, any attempt to change this situation could be expected to fail. As a consequence, policy makers at PTT Post rejected this option in advance.

A new CEO

At this point of time (in 1988), Mr Ad Scheepbouwer was appointed as PTT Post's new CEO. He came from a large commercial logistics firm and had no previous experience in PTT Post. His initial appreciation of PTT Post is instructive:

> I found an organization with a very technical flavor: all operations are technically analyzable. I also encountered a very loyal workforce: most people work at PTT Post for many years. The organization was making losses and it was functionally organized: one production segment, one finance segment, one commercial segment. Each one was responsible for only one aspect of PTT Post's performance. When I talked to my managers, each one felt sorry for the poor performance of PTT Post. But at the same moment each one was assuring that his or her department was doing well in light of (a selection of) some operational measures. The only one who was fully responsible for the aggregated result was me, and I had just been recently appointed! I concluded I had one very big problem: lack of transparency. I really needed to know who were making losses and who were successful.

A former member of a headquarters unit at that time remarks: 'At that time, the notion slowly took root that things had to change. I was a member of a study group which focused on the management structure of the postal districts, and we came up with a number of recommendations. Everybody agreed, but nothing happened.

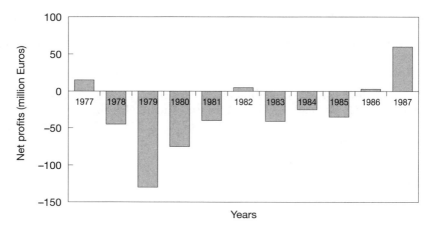

Figure 14.6 PTT Post's net profits in the period 1977 to 1987

The district directors had too much influence. At that moment we all felt: "it can all be done much better".' This suggests that the new CEO could capitalize on an existing feeling of a need for change.

By that time, PTT Post had generated financial results as shown in Figure 14.6.

The new CEO saw as his first priority a need to ensure that the company would not incur any more losses. At the moment he was appointed, he knew PTT Post's financial results until the year 1987. As can be appreciated from Figure 14.6, the financial reports mostly showed considerable losses.

STUDENT ASSIGNMENTS PART A

1. Describe the main problems which PTT Post faced around 1980. Discuss whether these problems have a common element, whether they are related and if so in what way.

2. What was PTT Post's strategy at the time?

3. Explain some of the budget games using the Workforce Table (Table 14.1) and the norm sheet.

4. Look at the three options for decentralizing control in PTT Post mentioned in the 'green booklet'. What option would you choose? Why?

5. When he entered the company, the new CEO needed 'transparency'. What does he mean by 'transparency'? How would you solve his 'transparency problem'?

6. What is the role of accounting information in the discussions provoked by the new CEO?

Part B: Privatization of PTT Post

One of the first challenges Mr Scheepbouwer faced was PTT Post's privatization, which took effect in 1989. The name PTT was changed to KPN NV ('Royal PTT Netherlands') and the Dutch State became its only shareholder. The privatization process gave a decisive push to PTT Post management to become even more focused on customer satisfaction and on financial results. Privatization gave PTT Post more autonomy from political decision making in parliament. Eventually, in 1994 KPN decided to go public and was listed at the Amsterdam, Frankfurt and New York stock exchanges. Several years before privatization, PTT Post was preparing for its new commercial role and took the following decisions.

Organizational restructuring

In 1988 PTT Post decided to reorganize the 12 districts, 160 pre-sort centres and 270 main post offices into five regions and 164 'responsibility units'. Each responsibility unit is responsible for several post offices and agencies, totaling to around 600 offices. This reorganization had several objectives. The most frequently cited reason for this reorganization was political: the power accumulated by the 12 district managers hindered top management's restructuring efforts. For instance: the creation of 12 shipping hubs was done because of the wish of each district manager to have in his region at least one shipping hub. At that time the creation of a limited number of shipping hubs was not only technically feasible but also economically desirable. A second objective was to create fewer organizational units, improving top and middle management's 'span of control'.

Decentralization according to 'the Green Booklet'

PTT Post had to put the Green Booklet's general principles into practice. It was decided to separately control the costs and revenues of operational units (according to the Green Booklet's second option). Much debate was devoted to the issue of what management style should be adopted in controlling operational units. Differences of opinion existed about control tightness. Two main streams can be identified in this debate. Some were in favour of a *loose and arm's length control style* focusing on a limited number of important issues. Others favoured a *tight control style* focusing on a broad spectrum of control issues. A manager defended the first position using the following arguments:

> Time and motion studies, irrespective of the level of detail, will never be able to provide sufficient detail to our planning. Every postman operates in a different situation: there is more wind on an island than in Amsterdam. There is no such thing as an 'average postman's day.' Besides, what happens when the postman receives less mail

than was planned for? He goes home! What happens as he receives more mail than planned? He applies for overtime work! In both situations PTT Post has to pay, which does not make the system very efficient.

Another manager defended the broadly focused, tight control style as follows:

> We cannot afford much autonomy in PTT Post, because collection, sorting and distribution activities are tightly controlled logistic processes. Once an area manager tried to deliver mail to a large customer quicker and asked the customer to use a wrong postal code so the system would put his mail aside. Contrary to expectations, the system withheld the mail and made it impossible to treat this customer differently. Everyone has become dependent on the centrally designed and operated logistic system.

Introduction of management contracts

After two years of experimentation, management contracts were implemented in the five regions and 164 responsibility units in 1988. The workforce as it appeared on the Workforce Table was now translated into costs. This facilitated comparisons across responsibility units and gave local management more control possibilities. The most important evaluation criteria were the following:

Business performance responsibility units:
1. Total productivity (traffic divided by A20 (refer to Table 14.3))
2. Size of the workforce (A20)
3. Percentage mail delivered on time and in the right box
4. Absence of personnel

Business performance sorting centres:
1. Quality of sorting process
2. Number of new business clients

Individual manager's performance:
1. Participation in national projects
2. Individual development and training
3. Customer service
4. Attraction of new customers
5. Relationship with personnel

This allowed managers of responsibility units to (within certain limits) change the composition of their workforce. The introduction of financial information did, however, not mean that district managers could freely exchange funds between salary costs and material expenses. Managers were rewarded based on the realization of management contracts. In practice, this meant that incentives changed from 'growth in A20' to adherence to 'reduction targets for A20'.

Obtaining financial transparency

Management contracts gave information on the financial situation of responsibility units but didn't provide insight into the financial results generated by *products*, like letters, parcel service, international mail, direct marketing mail, non-addressed advertising mail, express mail and logistic services. They didn't provide information on *markets* either, such as the consumer market and business market. PTT Post defined product–market combinations and calculated costs per combination, applying a cost price model (*KPV model*) based on process time per activity (deducted from time and motion studies) and related costs. The model made a distinction between traffic-dependent costs and traffic-independent costs. Traffic-dependent costs vary when the volume of post items change. Traffic-independent costs do not vary according to traffic and are therefore 'fixed' costs in the short term. For instance: the main routes postmen follow while delivering mail do not change when the volume of postal items varies: they are traffic-independent. The short tracks from the main route to house doors, however, are traffic-dependent: the more items the more visits to house doors will be made. Time and motion studies contain detailed information about the 17,000 'walks' postmen follow every day. The KPV model gave clues as to which product–market combinations were generating losses and which were generating profits. Priority was for each product–market combination to become profitable.

A new strategic plan 'Mail 2000'

In 1993, the strategic plan 'Mail 2000' was published and this plan called for a significant increase of efficiency and a higher quality of service. The plan proposed to take the following actions:

1. A higher proportion of mail will be sorted automatically. At that time, around 40% of the mail was sorted automatically. This had to become 98% by the year 2000.
2. The number of shipping hubs was further reduced from the existing twelve to six by 1998. This led to investments in machinery and buildings of around 650 million Euros.
3. The organization is reorganized by cutting out the management level of the five regions and rearranging the 164 responsibility units into 27 areas. This allowed KPN to cancel 1,300 jobs of mainly staff personnel. The new structure was implemented in 1995.
4. The activities *distribution* (which contains collecting and distributing mail) on the one hand and *sorting and transport* become two separated departments within the business unit (BU) Letters, each one reporting to a separate director. Both directors are members of the management team of PTT Post's BU Letters. This distinction facilitated improving distribution's *customer service* and sorting & transport's *operating efficiency*.

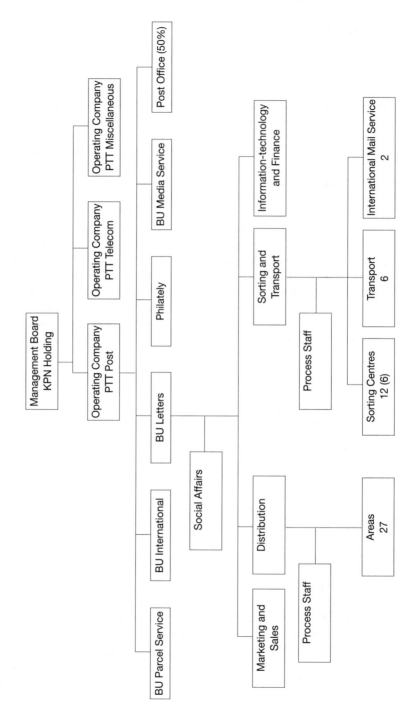

Figure 14.7 PTT Post business unit structure

Table 14.2 Sorting centres and areas served

Region	Sorting centre	Number of areas served
North	Zwolle	6
North-west	Amsterdam	5
West	Leidschendam	3
Centre	Nieuwegein	4
South-West	Rotterdam	4
South-East	's-Hertogenbosch	5
	Total	27
Transport Organization	Leerdam	Serves the whole country

In 1995, while this plan was being implemented, PTT decided to make the organization structure more transparent by introducing a business unit structure. Each business unit became responsible for specific product-market combinations (see Figure 14.7), e.g. parcel service, international mail, letters, philately and media services. The business unit Letters is by far the biggest and in financial terms most important unit: it is responsible for 90% of total sales of PTT Post. The introduction of business units opened up a new opportunity to accommodate the workforce: several hundred staff positions were eliminated. In this new structure, distribution is separated from sorting and transport. Sorting was done in initially 12 sorting centres, and from 1998 onwards in only six new large-scale, highly automated sorting centres and one sorting centre for registered mail. Transportation between areas was taken care of by six regional transportation organizations: these units operated the large trucks. Distribution was organized in 27 areas, containing a total of 350 local units. In 1993 the post offices were placed in an independent organization (a 50–50 joint venture with ING Postbank) and therefore were no longer consolidated as PTT Post's units. In 1997 the 12 sorting centres were reduced to six and transport was concentrated in one national organization (see Table 14.2). Table 14.2 lists the regions, their sorting centres and the numbers of areas they contain as of 1998.

The areas consist of 10 to 30 locations where mail collection, transport and distribution takes place. In each area a new department has been introduced, called 'customer service'. Here service is provided to commercial customers generating sales of 230 thousand Euros maximum (large clients are served by a corporate unit) and after-sales service is offered to all customers who have complaints. The introduction of customer service departments shows PTT Post's commitment to enhance customer services and support. On the same organizational level we also find a 'service centre' in which all auxiliary services are concentrated, from personnel affairs to finance, bookkeeping, organization and quality management (see Figure 14.8). These units provide support only for the execution of operational tasks and not for establishing new policies. That is concentrated in staff departments at the corporate level of PTT Post.

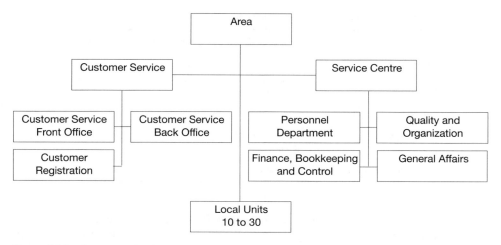

Figure 14.8 Area organization structure

More and more, the sorting centres have become key in operational planning and co-ordination. The regional distribution is shown in Figure 14.9.

Improving quality of performance

From 1992 onwards PTT Post improved its business controls in order to acquire ISO certificate 9002 in 1994 and 9001 in 1995. This makes PTT Post the first mail company in the world to have its operations certified. At the start of the business unit structure, PTT Post decided to follow the EFQM ('European Foundation for Quality Management') approach. One of the main supporters of the EFQM model, Mr Van Doorn who at that time had become Chairman of BU Letter's Management Board, gave as main reason for adopting EFQM:

> We needed a coherent management tool for systemizing and controlling our quality development efforts. We had the experience that stimulating improvements in one quality factor frequently led to simultaneous quality deterioration in other quality factors not included in the system. EFQM puts all relevant quality factors in a coherent framework.

One of the additional goals was to win the yearly prestigious Dutch quality award for the *Instituut Nederlandse Kwaliteit*: Post managed to win this prize in 1997.

EFQM management contracts

One of the driving forces behind quality improvement was the decision to integrate management contracts and the EFQM approach. From 1996 onwards, when the

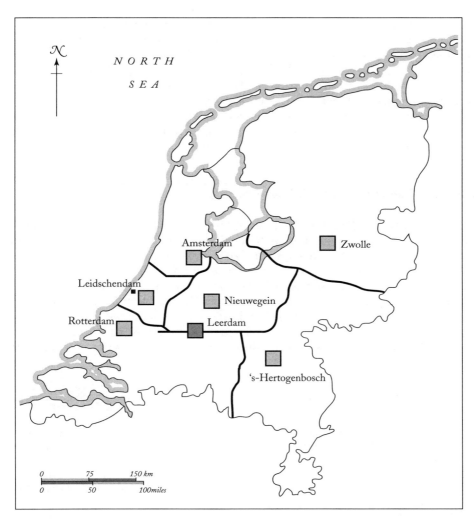

Figure 14.9 The new region structure, sorting centres and transport organization

area structure was implemented, the management contracts were specified in terms of the EFQM model. Similar contracts exist for EKP managers and simpler contracts for the 350 local managers. If we look at area managers' contracts, only four of the nine dimensions appear to be used. Some items deserve more attention:

- Delivery time relates to the percentage of letters that reach their destination within 24 hours.
- Delivery quality is the percentage of letters mailed that arrive at the right destination (irrespective of time needed).

- Interviews and surveys measure employee and customer satisfaction.
- Sales relate to income from franking machine sales and from contracts with small customers (less than 230,000 Euros).
- Operating result: this is not a common difference between profits and costs, since it is not possible to allocate all profits (sales of stamps) to every unit's contribution to performance. Operating result here is the difference between standard and actual costs. In calculating operating results, standard costs were adjusted for changes in traffic (a flexible budgeting approach). In 1998 the item 'operating result' changed to 'production per 1000 guilders (450 Euros)'.

Assigning financial responsibilities and improving financial control

From 1990 onwards, PTT Post built an elaborate information system for financial control of business units and areas (operational units), known as the *Executive Information System* (EIS). This system uses detailed data on postal item volumes and related costs (traffic-dependent as well as traffic-independent cost items). It uses a DuPont chart variance analysis which makes a distinction between controllable and uncontrollable variances (refer to Figure 14.10 for an explanation). The system can be applied to 'sales' and 'production' units (see also Figure 14.7 and Figure 14.8). In combination with detailed cost models (KPV/KIB) EIS is also capable of tracing the sales contribution and production results of each of the

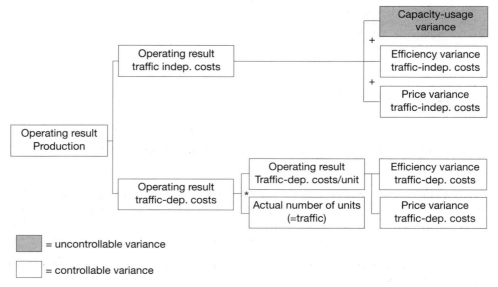

Figure 14.10 Analysis and benchmarking of Sorting, Distribution and Transport units' operating results

postal products, like individual letters, bundled packages to be delivered within 24 or 48 hours, special distribution for small and medium-sized business, special deliveries in 24 or 48 hours, and additional services. EIS permits the definition of different financial responsibilities of PTT Post's units (refer to Figure 14.7). For instance, the business unit Letter's 'Marketing & Sales' department becomes responsible for sales contribution margin and operating results for larger clients (sales of more than 230 thousand Euros per client). Sorting units are responsible for the operating results of sorting and transport. The distribution units (the areas) are responsible for the operating results of distribution, sales contribution margin and operating results for smaller business clients. Table 14.3 presents a financial report for the business unit Letters as a whole. Table 14.4 contains a financial report of a specific area within the business unit Letters (figures in both tables are heavily disguised).

Performance-based reward system

Each area manager, sorting centre manager and region manager can earn a significant bonus. The bonus consists of two parts: one is dependent upon BU performance and the other on individual performance as reflected in the management contract (and individual labour agreement). Each manager's performance on the contract items is yearly (subjectively) evaluated by his superior on a Likert type scale from 1 (poor) to 5 (excellent).

Co-ordinating the production chain

In order to co-ordinate across production units, so-called 'chain contracts' were introduced. These contracts were negotiated and monitored in six separate 'cluster meetings'; one for each sorting centre. In each cluster meeting, one representative of the transport organization, the manager of the sorting centre and managers of the areas (between 3 and 6) and the director *Distribution* and the director *Sorting and Transport* participate. The chain contracts are logistic contractual arrangements about the number of postal items and time of delivery between the area managers and the manager of the sorting centre in the region. A typical chain contract had the structure shown in Table 14.5.

As can be appreciated from Table 14.5, the contractual arrangements are independent of the number of postal items processed. The contracts between sorting centres, areas and the transport organization concern the time needed to deliver large chunks of mail from other sorting centres and mail between own sorting centre and areas.

Chain contracts do not include money, but are exclusively logistically oriented. A controller commented:

Table 14.3 Financial report, BU Letters (in € thousands)

		Budget	Actual	Difference	
1	External Sales	800	860	60	
2	Standard traffic-dependent costs	260	280	20	
3	Net marketing costs	8	8	0	
4	Contribution Margin Sales	532	572	40	
5	Standard traffic-independent costs	250	270	20	
6	Net overhead	18	20	2	
7	Operating Result Sales	264	282	18	
8	Internal sales to other Business Units	680	640	−40	
9	Standard traffic-dependent costs	380	400	20	
10	Standard traffic-independent costs	450	430	−20	
11	Overhead costs	60	70	10	
12	Total internal costs	890	900	10	
13	Operating Result Internal Transfers	−210	−260	−50	
14	Standard production costs				
15	Distribution	980	1,060	80	
16	Sorting	280	255	−25	
17	Transport	80	65	−15	
18	Total standard production costs	1,340	1,380	40	= (2) + (5) + (9) + (10)
19	Actual production costs				
20	Distribution	860	850	−10	
21	Sorting	210	260	50	
22	Transport	40	40	0	
23	Total actual production costs	1,110	1,150	40	
24	Operating Result Production				
25	Distribution	120	210	90	
26	Sorting	70	−5	−75	
27	Transport	40	25	−15	
28	Total Operating Result Production	230	230	0	= (18) − (23)

Consolidated results BU Letters

	Budget	Actual	Difference	
Operating Result Sales	264	282	18	(7)
Operating Result Internal Transfers	−210	−260	−50	(13)
Operating Result Production	230	230	0	(28)
Total Net Operating Costs	284	252	−32	
Withdrawals from reserves/provisions	40	40	0	
Gross operating profit	244	212	−32	
Additional Depreciations	−10	−10	0	
Net Interest	8	8	0	
Operating profit before taxes	242	210	−32	

Note: all figures are heavily disguised and do not represent the actual situation

Table 14.4 Financial report, area X (in € thousands, figures are disguised)

	Operating Result	Budget*	Actual	Difference	Explanation
	1 Operational personnel (in fte)	216	225	9	
+	2 Overhead personnel (in fte)	15	14	−1	
	3 Total personnel (in fte)	231	239	8	(3) = (1) + (2)
*	4 Average salary per fte	12	12	0	
	5 Salary costs	2,771	2,867	96	(5) = (3) * (4)
+	6 Material costs	928	1,092	164	
	7 Total operating costs	3,699	3,959	260	(7) = (5) + (6)
	8 Standard operating costs*	3,297	3,514	217	
	9 Operating results	402	445	43	(9) = (7) − (8)

* Operating results and costs based on actual volume (traffic)

	Operating Result	Budget*	Actual	Difference	Explanation
	Traffic-independent costs:				differences in costs because of:
	11 Capacity-usage variance	−2	1	3	actual − budgeted volumes
+	12 Efficiency variance	20	27	7	more (+) or less (-) production per st. input
+	13 Price variance	56	37	−19	budgeted − actual prices for inputs
	14 Operating result	74	65	−9	(14) = (11) + (12) + (13)
	Traffic-dependent costs:				
	15 Efficiency variance	−0.1	1.3	1.4	
+	16 Price variance	1.7	0.6	−1.1	
	17 Operating result per unit	1.6	1.9	0.3	(17) = (15) + (16)
*	18 Volume (mln. Pieces)	20.5	20	−0.5	
	19 Operating result	328	380	52	
	20 Total Operating Result	402	445	43	(20) = (14) + (19)

* Operating results and costs based on actual volume (traffic)

Table 14.5 Structure of a chain contract (figures are disguised)

Hour of the day	Percentage of postal items delivered at the sorting centre
Before 18.00 h	10
18.00–19.00 h	30
19.00–20.00 h	20
20.00–21.00 h	30
After 21.00 h	10
Total	100

Here we have a new problem. Because of the system of separate contracts, sorting center managers and area managers have an incentive to ask the transport organization to adapt to their needs as much as possible. Because of these pressures you will find half-loaded trucks driving around. Route scheduling is not always done in an economically optimal way.

STUDENT ASSIGNMENTS PART B

1. From Part A we know that PTT Post's strategy was *low cost production* and *high service quality*. What measures did PTT Post take in the 1980s and 1990s to attain these objectives? Make a distinction between measures of *organizational restructuring* and of *management control*.

2. Did PTT Post centralize or decentralize decision-making power to lower organizational levels?

3. Analyse the performance of business unit Letters and area X using Table 14.3 (Financial report, BU Letters) and Table 14.4 (Financial report, area X).

4. Comment on the EFQM-based contracts used by PTT Post's area managers. Do you think these contracts fit well into PTT Post's strategy?

5. How would you classify PTT Post's current management control system? What are its strengths and weaknesses?

6. Why did PTT Post split its organization into independent areas, sorting centres and transport organizations? What are the disadvantages of this system? How would you overcome these disadvantages?

Part C: PTT Post's financial performance

Reviewing PTT Post's financial results from 1977 onwards leads to the following overview of costs, revenues and profits (Figure 14.12 presents results indexed on 1977=100). This overview does not include TNT for reasons of a better year-by-year comparison.

Figure 14.12 and Figure 14.13 provide more detailed information about efficiency of operations (all data are also indexed on 1977=100).

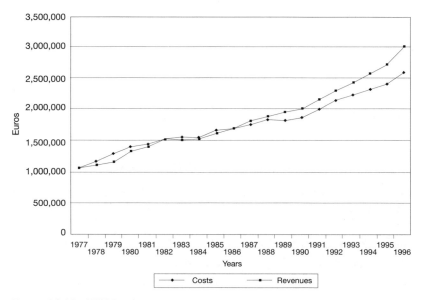

Figure 14.11 PTT Post's revenues and costs

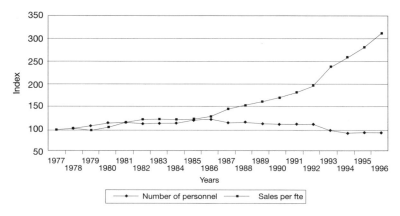

Figure 14.12 Number of personnel in fte, and sales per fte indexed on 1977 = 100

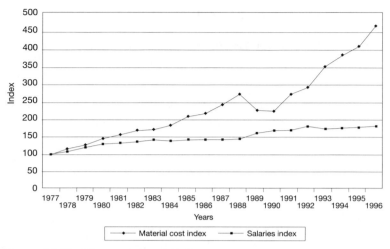

Figure 14.13 Changes in Royal Mail's cost structure

STUDENT ASSIGNMENTS PART C

1. Try to recapitulate the most important changes PTT Post introduced, using the labels 'motivators', 'catalysts', 'facilitators' and 'change event' (see Innes & Mitchell, 1990).

2. Interpret the results obtained by PTT Post. What measures are most effective?

3. What proof do you have for your answers to question 2?

—

Ondina, S.A. [1]

Salvador Carmona
Luis Fernández-Revuelta

Introduction

Ondina, S.A., a Spain-based manufacturer of cosmetics, was founded by Mr Dorado as a 'one man' company in 1948. Ondina's principal business consisted of the design, manufacture, and distribution of cosmetic products. Despite being a relatively small company, Ondina was vertically integrated and produced all critical components in-house. The number of different items manufactured by the company is fairly large, but broadly speaking they are all grouped under six major categories: deodorant, gel, shampoo, eau de cologne, perfume, and floral scent. The firm has steadily grown since its foundation and it is now one of the few domestic competitors of the multinational companies which operate in the Spanish market.

Background information

Mr Dorado set up a family-run workshop for the manufacture of soap and eau de cologne in 1932. Soon after the end of the Spanish Civil War (1939), Mr Dorado was granted one of the few permits to use industrial alcohol on a large scale. At that time, the blockade by Western nations of the dictatorship of General Franco prevented the operations of foreign entrants into the Spanish cosmetic market. This situation fostered a substantial increase in Mr Dorado's sales volume which brought about the establishment of Ondina, S.A. in 1948, a company wholly owned and managed by its founder.

Mr Dorado always had outstanding skills in ascertaining the dominant vogues in the cosmetic industry. After testing a product launched by competitors, he was able to make a precise estimation of its success chances as well as to produce a short list of its basic ingredients. He drew heavily on these skills to design the market strategy of the company, which annually offered two/three new products. All product formulas were kept secret by Mr Dorado, implying that he had to continuously provide the factory workshop with the exact composition of each individual batch to be produced. In 1963, Ondina launched its best selling product, a deodorant called Aurora. It enhanced the operations of the company by increasing dramatically both its sales volume and profitability indexes. This economic surplus reinforced Mr Dorado's ideas of keeping financial leverage close to zero, to guarantee the autonomy of the firm. In that respect, part of the surplus was invested in liquid assets (stock market) and highly profitable assets (real estate in the up and coming Spanish resorts). During the 1960s, the dictatorship of General Franco enacted some liberal reforms aiming both at gaining international recognition and attracting foreign investment. A consequence of these reforms was the enduring flow of foreign entrants into the Spanish cosmetic market. Ondina, however, was not yet affected by this situation; it operated in an expanding, protected market and its prices were lower than those offered by foreign competitors. In 1977, the first large supermarket chain started operations in Spain. These shopping malls spread all over Spain, and this in turn provoked a significant change in consumer behaviour: (i) cosmetic products could be freely tested by consumers; and (ii) product elements such as pack design became crucial in market strategy. Moreover, the liberalization of the Spanish economy that accompanied the promulgation of the Constitution of 1978 brought about an important drop in prices as import duties were lifted. Ondina, thus, faced severe competition from foreign competitors who offered high-quality products at lower prices.

After earning a Master's degree in chemistry, Mr Dorado's elder son, David, joined the Research and Development Department of Ondina and acted as deputy general manager. The steady decline in Ondina's market position, David argued, should be mostly attributed to a number of internal factors (e.g. centralization, vertical integration, inefficiency of the cost-plus system for price setting). As we will see below, David's proposals to flexibilize the Ondina structure were invariably dismissed by Mr Dorado. Thus, the relationship between Mr Dorado and David deteriorated both personally and professionally and peaked in March 1995. At that time, David and Mr Dorado quarrelled about the move of the fax machine away from the latter's office, where he controlled all transmissions as well as the related fax communication expenses. Mr Dorado bitterly opposed the idea. After the altercation, David left the firm.

This case focuses on the contextual events of David's proposal to change the cost accounting system of the company.

Industry and market

Cosmetic products are made from a combination of diverse raw materials which, as we will see below, undergo a relatively simple production process. Initially, the design process of these products did not draw on established and precise technologies but relied on the expertise of individual designers. The key success factor, thus, consisted of launching products whose fragrances anticipated, or at least followed, market vogues. This situation, however, dramatically changed in the 1970s as a consequence of the development of new technologies for the analysis and design of fragrances. Since then, cosmetic companies have found it relatively

Table 15.1   Evolution of the Spanish income per capita

Year	Income per capita (Euro, nominal figures)
1955	87.04
1960	132.17
1965	219.14
1970	456.88
1975	953.15
1980	2,681.62
1985	4,386.80
1990	8,438.89
1993	9,339.82

Source: Banco Bilbao-Vizcaya.

easy and cheap to design new fragrances or replicate those thriving on the market. By outsourcing raw materials purchasing, cosmetic companies could make substantial savings. Hence, the crucial success factor shifted from product design to packaging and advertising. Market research shows a sharp contrast in consumer behaviour between old and young people: seniors identify themselves with a concrete fragrance and consistently consume it; youngsters demonstrate low product fidelity, and are vulnerable to the effects of advertising campaigns.

At the outset of Ondina's operations, the Spanish cosmetic market was under-developed. A small number of firms struggled to establish reliable distribution channels to deliver their products to a low purchasing power market (see Table 15.1). Domestic firms started facing competition from foreign entrants in the late 1960s as a consequence of the timid liberalization of the Spanish economy. Foreign companies exporting to Spain, however, were charged high custom duties. Multinationals' subsidiaries operating in Spain suffered severe restrictions on the repatriation of dividends. This in turn made the prices of foreign entrants too high to compete in the Spanish market. The 1970s witnessed significant improvements in the country's road transportation and telecommunications networks as well as the liberalization of the economy. As far as the cosmetic industry was concerned, the critical event of the decade was the widespread implementation of new technologies for fragance analysis. In the 1980s, the cosmetic market slumped as a consequence of both the effects of the demographic stagnation of the second half of the 1960s and because the consumption of cosmetic products was already high. In this new environment, multinational companies underpriced domestic competitors, driving a good number of them out of the market. Simultaneously, multinationals undertook an ongoing process of acquisition of domestic firms which left just four large-sized Spanish-owned companies operating in the early 1990s. The market share of Spanish-owned cosmetic firms, hence, decreased from 95% in 1970 to 60% in 1980, and then to 30% in 1990. The cosmetic market of the 1990s was characterized by severe competition. Assuming a given level of quality, competition focused on price. In order to gain access to the increasing number of shopping malls, cosmetic companies had to make offers that might be accepted/rejected on just a tiny 2–3% price difference.

After the launch of Aurora, Ondina's market position remained fairly stable until the late 1980s. Its reputation rested on its good quality products because, in contrast, the firm's prices were higher than those offered by domestic competitors. In 1965, Mr Dorado thought that the time for the internationalization of Ondina had come. The company, thus, established a subsidiary factory in Paris both to add *glamour* among present and potential customers as well as to provide more efficient service to international markets. International sales, measured through the ratio of exports to total sales, increased to 6% of total turnover in 1968 and peaked at 12% in 1975. Since then, the figure has steadily diminished, stabilizing at around 2% of total sales. The Paris factory was consistently unprofitable and the decision to close it down was made ten years after it commenced to operate. During the late 1970s, the sales force adapted well to the need to service the large supermarket chains operating in Spain, and this in turn had salutary effects on Ondina's sales turnover (see Table 15.2; sales are shown in nominal, non-adjusted inflation figures). These results, obtained in an expanding market, overshadowed the increasing dominant position of multinationals, as noted above. In 1989, a multinational corporation made a generous offer to Mr Dorado to purchase Ondina, which he turned down. Since then, multinationals have, unsuccessfully, made further offers.

The mix of sales by category of products is shown in Table 15.3.

Table 15.2 Units and sales (1960–1994)

Year	Units	Sales (€ thousands)
1960	125,000	251.49
1965	550,000	748.50
1970	850,000	1,556.88
1975	1,500,000	2,125.74
1980	2,100,000	3,724.55
1985	3,500,000	4,940.11
1990	3,100,000	4,730.53
1994	3,000,000	4,311.37

Table 15.3 Sales mix evolution (1960–1995)

Product	1960	1970	1980	1990	1995
Deodorants (%)	75	67	60	50	45
Gel (%)	–	–	15	15	13
Shampoo (%)	–	–	10	10	6
Eau de Cologne (%)	15	10	7	5	5
Perfumes (%)	5	15	8	17	29
Floral scents (%)	3	3	–	3	2
Others (%)	2	5	–	–	–

Production

As mentioned above, Ondina manufactures six major categories of products: deodorant, gel, shampoo, eau de cologne, perfume, and floral scent. Once a sale offer is approved by Mr Dorado, he submits the composition of materials to the workshop because product formulas are kept secret. This process of calculation is crucial because the mix of materials is not always a linear function of production volume. Mr Dorado sometimes miscalculated the composition of materials, and this made the final product unreliable. The production process itself is, however, fairly simple and was developed in an old factory until 1988. The factory, however, lacked the capacity to cope with the increase in Ondina's sales and, thus, Mr Dorado decided to move the company's premises to a new, purpose-built building. The construction of the factory required an investment outlay of EUR 3.89 million.

The factory workshop consists of three plants: utilities, production and assembly (Figure 15.1). The utilities plant provides electricity for running the factory. The production plant comprises two mixing lines, where materials are either macerated (e.g. eau de cologne, perfume), or constantly mixed to obtain a perfect blend (e.g. soap), or, finally, heated for a long time (e.g. deodorant). Once the work-in-process of a given batch is ready, it is moved to the assembly line through aerial pipes. The

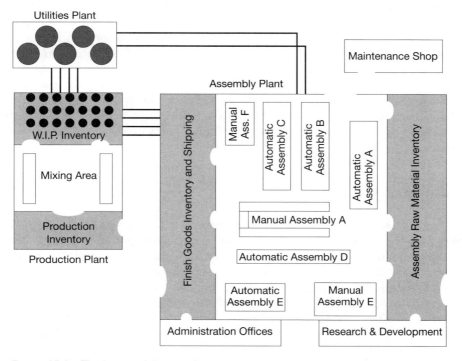

Figure 15.1   The layout of the new factory

assembly plant is formed by six lines of operations: A (deodorant), B (Gel), C (Shampoo), D (Eau de Cologne), E (Perfume), F (Floral Scent). Lines A, E, and F are labour intensive and machinery was moved from the old to the new factory. On the other hand, lines B, C and D fit better with the notion of high technology and their machinery was fully renovated after the move to the new factory. The assembly function consists of putting together the work-in-process from the production plant with other product elements such as bottles and labels. Quality is not 'built into the products' but is controlled once finished products complete the assembly process. Interestingly, however, quality control concerns the monitoring of the hygienic conditions of the products (e.g. product pH), but not 'conformity to specifications'. The latter check is not possible because product formulas are kept secret by Mr Dorado. Because of this, a common complaint of customers is: 'Fragance of this deodorant is not as usual'.

The assembly plant is surrounded by two warehouses; one for finished goods and the other for components to assemble. These warehouses are quite large and used to hold large amounts of inventory.

The move to the new factory and its concomitant effect on high-tech investment outlay brought about: (i) an important decrease in direct labour cost; (ii) an increase in production capacity; and (iii) an important increase in factory fixed costs. As the move to the new factory coincided with stagnation of the Spanish cosmetic market, Ondina underwent some social and economic problems due to its idle capacity. For the past several years, Ondina has been operating far below capacity and this prompted David to suggest to Mr Dorado the elimination of unprofitable products, their substitution by fewer new ones, and the establishment of a minimum level of sales volume as a requirement to make both old and new products. Although market research showed that consumers indeed valued Ondina's large variety of products, such a policy was deemed by David as too costly for the company. To back his ideas, in 1994 David asked Mr Dorado to hire an external advisor to under- take a report on Ondina's costs because he did not know much about Ondina's cost structure.

Costing and pricing

Mr Dorado was reluctant to use cost accounting data to make decisions. In the late 1960s, however, he was forced to implement a formal budgeting system to control international operations. Once exports stagnated, the system stopped working. Ondina's accounting systems had been purposely designed to communicate infor- mation to external parties (e.g. to the Spanish tax authorities), but the firm did not use reliable cost data. Product costs were calculated on the basis of raw materials consumption. Final cost was then affected by the nature of the product and market conditions (e.g. Ondina used to mark up deodorants 40–70% over material costs but used consistently higher mark-ups for perfumes, 70%). This procedure for cost calculation was established in the early 1960s and remained until the late 1980s

Table 15.4   Cost breakdown of 'Aurora' (old system) at 1995

Cost concept	€
Raw materials	0.22
Materials to assembly	0.46
Total material costs	0.68
Mark-up	50%
Final cost	1.02

(see Table 15.4, for the cost breakdown of Aurora, which is representative of a deodorant's cost structure). Problems with this system of cost setting emerged when Ondina's market share started to decline. Orders were supposed to be rejected if they made below the final cost figure. However, the acceptance decision depended to a large extent on Mr Dorado's changing decision model. For example, a large volume order of Aurora was rejected in May 1994 because it was priced at 0.03 Euro below total cost. In contrast, a lower volume order on that same item was accepted three weeks later in spite of a selling price of 0.08 Euro below final cost. Moreover, decisions on price setting and its related impact on acceptance/ rejection of orders were contingent on the period of the year in which the order was made. During the first quarter of the year, orders below final cost had high probabilities of rejection. As long as Mr Dorado needed to meet yearly sales volume targets, orders that underpriced final cost had high probabilities of acceptance, if made in the last quarter.

This cost calculation procedure shed some light on the decision to make some raw materials in-house. As noted above, it was not possible to evaluate the outsourcing of old products because Mr Dorado kept secret the formulas of these items. This situation slightly changed after David joined the R & D department. A crucial part of his job was to assess the technical and economic feasibility of potential products. Accordingly, he found compelling evidence for the possibility of saving 25–35% of raw material costs by outsourcing them. David was well aware of Mr Dorado's reluctance to share product formulas with other people. Therefore, he proposed that Mr Dorado outsource the raw materials of new products, if supported by a detailed cost analysis. Mr Dorado, however, dismissed the idea. He argued that product formulas were 'the treasury of the firm' and contended that David's calculations did not embrace 'the goodwill of Ondina'. In Mr Dorado's view, customers highly valued Ondina's capabilities to make all critical components in-house.

After a period of several months, David and the external advisor amassed detailed data on the cost structure of Ondina. Further analysis of these data shed light on both the need to eliminate unprofitable products and on obtaining cost savings in operating expenses, inventory, and space requirements. They prepared an alternative costing system which, in the main, intended to provide Mr Dorado with easy-to-understand cost information. If their plans worked, further and more sophisticated cost calculations would follow. The system consisted firstly of the identification of ten major cost categories:

- Production plant (cost of personnel).
- Production plant (raw materials).
- Assembly plant (direct labour).
- Assembly plant (components to assemble).
- Factory overhead.
- Indirect labour.
- Administration (cost of personnel plus utilities).
- Sales department (cost of personnel).
- Shipping.
- Advertising.
- Financial costs.

The outcomes of the new system focused on three central aspects: (i) the classification of products into categories of profitable and non-profitable; (ii) company areas amenable to bringing their costs down and, thus, making more competitive products; and (iii) the need to set lower mark-ups to keep pace with Ondina's price-cutting rivals. Table 15.5 shows the cost breakdown for Aurora under the new system.

These results, however, were publicly dismissed by Mr Dorado, whose outburst followed the presentation made by David and the extemal advisor about the features of the new cost accounting system. Mr Dorado argued that Ondina had an established reputation in the cosmetic industry which made it possible to compete with multinationals. He said that the company's reputation was based on his own knowledge of the cosmetic business, which allowed him to adapt the company's strategy to new environments. He blamed the sales force for submitting orders that

Table 15.5 Cost breakdown of 'Aurora' (alternative system) at 1995

Cost concept	€
Production plant (cost of personnel)	0.02
Production plant (raw materials)	0.14
Assembly plant (direct labour)	0.04
Assembly plant (components to assemble)	0.40
Factory overhead	0.04
Indirect labour	0.01
Administration (personnel plus utilities)	0.03
Sales department (cost of personnel)	0.07
Shipping	0.01
Advertising	0.08
Financial costs	0.01
Total cost	0.85

implied lower prices, and which in turn did not account for Ondina's goodwill. In short, he said that the company could not survive by slashing prices and was adamant in refusing implementation of the proposed system. By early 1998, the new cost accounting system is not still in use.

Endnote

[1] This case was prepared by professors Salvador Carmona and Luis Fernández-Revuelta of Universidad Carlos III de Madrid and Universidad de Almería, respectively. The case is based on actual evidence. However, firm's name, some of the figures, names and episodes have been disguised for confidentiality reasons.

STUDENT ASSIGNMENTS

1. Analyse the success factors of Ondina before and after the liberalization of the Spanish economy. Comment on the role of Mr Dorado.

2. How could Ondina remain as one of the few Spanish-owned companies operating in the cosmetic industry?

3. Why is Ondina's growth shown both in production units and sales volume (Table 15.2)?

4. Which was the rationale for pricing products on the basis of raw materials consumption plus mark-up? Compare the new cost system's weaknesses and strengths.

5. Which were the underlying reasons for Mr Dorado to turn down the proposal of a new cost accounting system?

List of contributors

Thomas Ahrens is a lecturer in Accounting at the London School of Economics. His research focuses on management accounting and organizational processes. His recent book *Contrasting Involvements: A Study of Management Accounting Practices in Britain and Germany* relates the role of calculative practices to their cultural context.

Urban Ask is a Product Director at Industrial & Financial Systems (IFS) R&D. He earned his PhD at the Gothenburg School of Economics, Sweden, and has been specializing in modern practices of managment accounting. He is currently responsible for the development of strategic performance management applications at IFS.

Antonio Barretta is lecturer of Business Administration at the University of Siena, Italy, in the Faculty of Economics. His field of research is management control and cost accounting in particular, both in the public and private sector.

Pierre-Laurent Bescos is a professor of Management Accounting at Edhec at Nice, France, and specializes in ABC/ABM, Target Costing and Information for Decision Making. He has written a number of articles and books on these fields. As well as being an associate of Creatis Consultants, he is also a member of several editorial review boards (*The International Journal of Accounting*, *Echanges* and *Revue Française de Gestion*).

Trond Bjørnenak is professor of Management Accounting at Agder University Collage in Norway, and specializes in management accounting and management control systems.

Per Nikolaj Bukh is an associate professor of Management Accounting at the University of Aarhus, Denmark. He specializes in performance measurement systems, knowledge management and intellectual capital reporting.

Salvador Carmona is a professor of Accounting at Carlos III University, Spain, and specializes in management accounting, accounting history as well as in the organizational and social aspects of accounting. He is a member of the editorial board of several international research journals.

Peter Clarke is a professor at the Department of Accountancy, National University of Ireland, Dublin. He is a past Chairman of the Irish Accounting and Finance Association in addition to being a former editor of the *Irish Accounting Review*. In addition to an interest in all aspects of accounting history, his research activity includes the development and diffusion of management accounting practices.

Luís Fernández-Revuelta Perez is professor of Accounting at the Faculty of Economics and Business Administration of the University of Almería, Spain.

Thomas M. Fischer is professor of Financial and Managerial Accounting at the Leipzig Graduate School of Management (HHL). His main research areas are Cost Management, Customer Control, Performance Measurement, and Value-Based Reporting. He is editor of two books and has written numerous articles in textbooks and business journals.

Markus Granlund (Ph.D.) is an assistant professor of Accounting at the Turku School of Economics and Business Administration, Finland. His research interests cover a wide range of technical and behavioural issues in management accounting.

Tom Groot is the Head of Department of Accounting and a professor in Management Accounting at the Vrije Universiteit, Amsterdam. He is also the Director of the Amsterdam Research Center in Accounting (ARCA).

Shao Huajing is an associate professor in the School of Management and Economics, Beijing University of Aeronautics and Astronautics,in the Peoples' Republic of China. In 1997–98 she was an academic visitor to the University of Edinburgh where she initiated her current research interests in activity-based costing and resistance to management accounting change.

Poul Israelsen is Professor of Accounting at University of Southern Denmark.His main research interest concerns the impact of ERP systems and contemporary production systems on management accounting.

Marko Järvenpää is a senior lecturer of Accounting at the Seinäjoki Business School and a researcher at the Turku School of Economics and Business Administration, Finland. He specializes in management accounting, especially in the fields of strategic management accounting, cost management, performance measurement and the development of the finance and control function.

Isabelle Lacombe works as a management consultant in France on ABC-ABM and shared services projects. Prior to this she worked at Hewlett-Packard, implementing ABC-ABM for the Business Unit 'Customer Support' in Europe. With a Ph. D. in Business, her thesis centred on the implementation of ABC-ABM in the service sector.

Kari Lukka is a professor of Accounting at the Turku School of Economics and Business Administration, Finland, and specializes in management accounting as well as in accounting theory and methodology. He also is the Editor of the *European Accounting Review*.

Preben Melander is a professor of Accounting at Copenhagen Business School where he specializes in behavioural accounting. His current research focuses on management accounting within the health service in Denmark. He is editor of the Danish journal *Accounting and Informatics.*

Falconer Mitchell is professor of Management Accounting at the University of Edinburgh, Scotland and is involved in researching various aspects of cost management and management accounting in Small and Medium Sized Enterprises. He is also vice-chairman of the Research Board of the Chartered Institute of Management Accountants.

Vesa Partanen is a senior research associate at the department of Accounting and Finance, Turku School of Economics and Business Administration, Finland. His research interest is in strategic management accounting, focusing on accounting change and organizational learning.

Angelo Riccaboni is a professor of Management Control at the University of Siena, Italy. His research interests are in management control systems, managerial incentives and accounting regulation. His most recent work focuses on management accounting change. He is involved in European research networks in accounting, such as CIRAF and Harmonia.

Hanno Roberts is a professor in Management Accounting and Control at the Norwegian School of Management. His areas of interest include intellectual capital, accounting and control in the knowledge-intensive firm, and the organizational aspects of management accounting systems. He is on the editorial boards of *Management Accounting Research* and the *Journal of Management Accounting Research.*

Peter Skærbæk is an associate professor, Ph.D. of Accounting at the Copenhagen Business School, Denmark and specializes in management accounting primarily within the public sector. Currently, he is conducting research on value-for-money auditing and annual reports within the public sector. He is also a member of the Editorial Management Committee of the *European Accounting Review.*

Peter Smidt heads the public governance research institute at Nijenrode University and works as senior consultant of Deloitte & Touche in the area of strategic financial information. His research areas are treasury and management accounting. He is the academic member of the Dutch Association of Corporate Treasurers committee on accounting for derivatives.

Tero-Seppo Tuomela is a senior research associate at the department of Accounting and Finance, Turku School of Economics and Business Administration, Finland. His research interest is in strategic management accounting, particularly in communicating and controlling customer focus through performance measurement.

Index